Julia D Carrothers

Kesa and Saijiro

Or, lights and shades of life in Japan

Julia D Carrothers

Kesa and Saijiro
Or, lights and shades of life in Japan

ISBN/EAN: 9783742830173

Manufactured in Europe, USA, Canada, Australia, Japa

Cover: Foto ©Andreas Hilbeck / pixelio.de

Manufactured and distributed by brebook publishing software (www.brebook.com)

Julia D Carrothers

Kesa and Saijiro

MT. FUJIYAMA AND AN INLAND VALLEY.—Frontispiece.

KESA AND SAIJIRO:

OR,

LIGHTS AND SHADES OF LIFE IN JAPAN.

BY

MRS. J. D. CARROTHERS.

AMERICAN TRACT SOCIETY,
150 NASSAU STREET, NEW YORK CITY.

CHAPTER I.
"Alas! Master, it is a daughter" — 7

CHAPTER II.
The Schoolmaster's Boy — 15

CHAPTER III.
New Japan — 22

CHAPTER IV.
A Midsummer Day — 34

CHAPTER V.
The Story of the Hairdresser — 41

CHAPTER VI.
Saijiro climbs the Mountain — 54

CHAPTER VII.
Tama's New Home — 62

CHAPTER VIII.
On the other side of the Hakones — 76

CHAPTER IX.
Rinjiro's Question — 92

CHAPTER X.
Seeing Buddha's Face — 105

CHAPTER XI.
A Midsummer Festival — 115

CONTENTS.

CHAPTER XII.
Winter in Yamamidzu 131

CHAPTER XIII.
Mitsu's Troubles 144

CHAPTER XIV.
Sunset on the Hakones 157

CHAPTER XV.
The Good Doctor 167

CHAPTER XVI.
The Storm in the Mountains 180

CHAPTER XVII.
From Yamamidzu to Tokio 188

CHAPTER XVIII.
The Chapel Service 206

CHAPTER XIX.
A Country Boy in Tokio 215

CHAPTER XX.
School Days 229

CHAPTER XXI.
Midwinter in Tokio 245

CHAPTER XXII.
Spring Blossoms 262

CHAPTER XXIII.
"Mushi" 277

CHAPTER XXIV.
Harukichi and Chiye 287

CHAPTER XXV.
The Dismantled Shrine 302

CHAPTER XXVI.
Missionaries on the Hakones   315

CHAPTER XXVII.
The Midnight Prayer........ 328

CHAPTER XXVIII.
The Little Visitor........ 343

CHAPTER XXIX.
Some Letters and a Wedding........ 356

CHAPTER XXX.
Kesa and her Father........ 370

CHAPTER XXXI.
A Winter Journey........ 376

CHAPTER XXXII.
The Home and the Prison........ 393

CHAPTER XXXIII.
Jinrikisha Rides........ 403

CHAPTER XXXIV.
A Sabbath in Hiroshima........ 411

CHAPTER XXXV.
A Beautiful Isle of the Sea........ 416

CHAPTER XXXVI.
Home Again........ 423

CHAPTER XXXVII.
Some Happy Days........ 428

CHAPTER XXXVIII.
Christian Homes and Christian Work........ 431

CHAPTER XXXIX.
Saijiro's Resolve........ 437

ILLUSTRATIONS.

MT. FUJIYAMA AND AN INLAND VALLEY..Frontispiece.	
YAMAMIDZU	15
TOKIO AND VICINITY—Map	22
YETARO'S SCHOOL	35
A JAPANESE COOPER	40
MEGUCHI, KESA, AND RINJIRO	46
YENOSKE AND THE PACK-HORSE	54
FEMALE MUSICIANS	70
JINRIKISHA TRAVELLERS	85
JAPANESE CARPENTERS	105
KESA AND MITSU	127
THE EIGHT-HEADED DRAGON	130
THE RABBIT AND THE CROCODILES	135
A JAPANESE TINSMITH	288
A JAPANESE MANSION	292
A JAPANESE BARBER	319
MOUNTAIN GIRLS	326
A JAPANESE SANDAL-MAKER	383

KESA AND SAIJIRO.

CHAPTER I.

"ALAS! MASTER, IT IS A DAUGHTER."

THE sun was just rising over Japan when the officer Fujisawa's fifth little daughter was born; and she was named Kesa, which means Morning.

Five girls in a Japanese family, and never a boy to inherit the father's name or to perpetuate the glory of his house! But Fujisawa was a man who accepted with patience "whatever the gods saw fit to send." So when the woman Meguchi, for years a faithful servant in the family, came to him with the words, "Master, it is a daughter; truly, a misfortune!" he simply said, "It is well," and turned away to hide whatever disappointment he may have felt.

Before he went to the custom-house that morning he spoke kindly to his wife and glanced at the little baby. Then he took in his arms the ailing three-year-old Hana and placed her in a sheltered nook of the garden, bidding some one look after her.

There were no rejoicings, no congratulations or sending of presents, as there would have been had a boy come into the household. The girl-baby was not worth any of these.

But Fujisawa was really fond of his children. And already the eldest was betrothed to the son of a valued friend, a rich merchant of Hakodate— a merchant, and yet of high-born family. There was no questioning as to whether the young people would care for one another when they were married. The match was simply a matter of business between the two fathers, and those most concerned were asked nothing about it.

The home of the little Fujisawas was near an old *yashiki*, or prince's dwelling, in the high part of Tokio called the Kudan. This place overlooks the bay and commands a beautiful view of the city, with its low buildings, its temples and groves. The horizon is bounded on all sides by mountains, the Hakones and the Nikko and Kadzusa ranges, while to the southwest rises Mt. Fuji, the sacred, "matchless" mountain, the pride and glory of the Japanese.

The house of Fujisawa was large and airy and was kept scrupulously clean. The family lived for the most part down stairs, the one long room of the upper story being a sort of smoking-room for Fujisawa and his friends. Especially did they enjoy this room during the long summer evenings, when the slides were drawn back, and those who were assembled there could look down over the lights of the city and up to the distant, silent stars.

The large parlor below was almost without furniture. The spotless white mats, the polished woodwork, the elegant vases with tastefully-arranged flowers, and the handsome scrolls were sufficient to show the high social standing of the family. Nor was there much furniture elsewhere in the house; only a few little tables and some mattresses, the latter now spread out to air in the morning sun.

The garden was the great delight of the Fujisawas and their visitors.

In the centre was a pond where hundreds of gold-fish sported, their backs now and again reflecting a ray of sunshine. Near the house a little stone bridge crossed the pond, and rocks were scattered picturesquely along its banks. At intervals, on the water's edge, were stone lanterns, in which lights were placed on festival occasions. And in the springtime there were beds of iris, purple and white.

All through the grounds were artificial hillocks covered with azaleas, and in one corner of the garden the graceful wistaria hung from a lattice in grape-like clusters. Grand old maples and cedars shadowed all, making a home for innumerable crows. But the chief ornaments of the garden, to Japanese eyes, were the cherry and peach blooms, which now, on this beautiful May morning, mingled their snowy white and pale pink in charming contrast. It was amid such surroundings that little Kesa came into the world.

The five girls were Tama, which means Precious Stone; Mitsu, Honey; Chiye, Wisdom; Hana, Flower; and now the baby Kesa. Tama was ten years old; Mitsu, seven; Chiye, five; and Hana, three.

There was no such variety of complexion and hair among them as is common in American families. They all had dark skins and black hair and eyes, and all had round, rosy cheeks, except Hana, who had always been delicate.

Their hair was dressed according to their ages, as is customary with Japanese girls; while the baby would soon have to submit to the usual process of shaving, which is rather severe on the poor little tender heads.

Every morning, except on the national holidays, the faithful Meguchi took Tama and Mitsu to the school near by, where they spent at least five hours in learning how to read and write and count a little. Their books were those which the Japanese think suitable for their girls, "The Woman's Great Learning," "The One Hundred Poems," and some of the sayings of Confucius. They had no grammar nor geography nor history to learn.

The girls were separated from the boys. The

scholars sat on the floor, held their brush-pens straight in their hands, dipped them in India ink, and covered the soft Japanese paper with queer black characters. Then the copy-books were hung up in the sun to dry. The children carried their noon lunches of cold rice, radishes, and fish to school in little wooden boxes which they called *bentos*.

The street down which the Fujisawas had to pass on their way to school was a quiet one. They went by the old *yashiki*. This is an inclosure with the *daimio's* or prince's house in the centre and the retainers' dwellings on the outside, looking from the street like a wall with windows, or rather lattices, for the Japanese had no glass.

Some of these inclosures are very beautiful, and since the princes have ceased to occupy them they have been put to various uses, such as Government schools, soldiers' barracks, residences for foreigners, etc.

In one of the outside houses of the *yashiki* lived Aka, a young woman whom the children knew. Aka often cried because the gods had not sent her a little child. She went almost every day to the temple and prayed, clapping her hands and calling on the gods to hear her. Tama and Mitsu felt sorry for her, her eyes were so red and her face was so sad. Besides, their mother often spoke of her as being so unfortunate, and said that her husband would soon send her home and get another wife, to whom perhaps the gods would grant a little son.

At one of the windows the children almost always saw an old lady, bent nearly double, whom they called "Baba" (grandmother). She always smiled and spoke pleasantly to them as they went by. There were also two girls who were taking lessons on the *samisen*, and Tama and Mitsu would listen to the music, the "tum-tum" of the Japanese guitar.

When school was out Meguchi would go for the little girls, and sometimes they all had permission to walk to a little hill from which they could see a short distance into the country on one side and in another direction could look at the white sails in the bay.

They always stopped at a tea-house to get a cup of tea and some sweetmeats, for which they gave a few copper coins. Chiye usually accompanied them on such occasions, and the three little girls looked so pretty and behaved so nicely, bowed so civilly and answered questions so politely, that strangers would often ask who they were. Then Meguchi would answer,

"Truly, thanks. These are the children of my master, the high officer Fujisawa."

And if any one asked her if he had a son, she would shake her head and say,

"Truly, a misfortune; no."

Then a shadow would fall for a moment over

the hearts of the older children. It was indeed an unfortunate thing that they were not boys. But their sadness lasted only for a moment, and they would soon be playing again as if Japanese girls were of just as much value as boys.

At six o'clock the children were expected to be at home to meet their father, who returned about that time from the custom-house.

When they entered the house they would go immediately to find their mother and say to her, "We have returned." And when the servant announced that the "master" had come, they would run to meet him, bowing down to the ground before him.

The evening meal of rice, tea, and fish followed the father's return, and soon after that the little ones would all be asleep on their stuffed *futons*, or mattresses, their heads resting on wooden pillows. Thus passed day after day in the Fujisawa household.

But now a diversion had come—in the new little sister, who, on this first morning of her life, lay by her mother's side fast asleep. She knew not yet the mother's face nor listened for her voice. She heeded not the sunshine nor cared for the flowers. But she was strong and large, and the mother looked fondly on the little head covered with long, soft black hair. Her garments were of silk, fashioned after the same pattern as those of the older members of the family.

Her tiny hands were almost lost in the wide sleeves. Her little feet were covered by the long robe.

The morning hours passed quietly by. Tama and Mitsu went off to school. Chiye and Hana played together in the garden. The baby slept on.

Afar off lay the Hakone Mountains, like a soft cloud-blank against the sky. On this very same morning a little child on those mountains wept bitterly because his mother gave no heed to his cries, having gone into that unknown land of the dead which Japanese and Americans alike have to enter.

YAMAMIDZU.

CHAPTER II.

THE SCHOOLMASTER'S BOY.

IN the heart of the Hakone Mountains, on the banks of one of those wild rivers which come rushing down their sides, dashing against rocks and leaping over precipices, is the little village, or rather hamlet, of Yamamidzu. It is truly in the shadow of the mountain, for the sun shines on it only a few hours in the middle of the day. The people, looking up, can see only a bit of sky directly overhead. On both sides tower the cliffs, thickly wooded and covered with a dense undergrowth of bushes.

The village itself consists of a cluster of ten or twelve houses on one side of the river. Among these are an inn, a temple, and a schoolhouse. The hamlet is out of the usual line of travel up the Hakones, and there is consequently but little use for the inn, which is old and dilapidated.

Just below Yamamidzu the foaming torrent makes a plunge over the rocks in a beautiful cascade. From its violence you would think that it was going to carry everything before it; but, to your surprise, you would find at the bottom a calm and rather shallow pool, whose waters flow underground until the river is apparently lost.

And so it looked on the day when little Kesa came to her father's beautiful home in the great "East Capital."

Young Yenoske, the son of the innkeeper, had a pack-horse, the only one in the village, and occasionally went down the mountain for supplies. This was almost the only communication which the villagers had with the outside world. But they loved the mountain and the river and were proud of their waterfall and the still pool, where the children bathed on the warm summer days.

At one end of the village a rude bridge crossed the torrent. It was a frail, dangerous structure, without a railing and with no supports. It swayed under the lightest tread, and any one who trod it carelessly was in danger of being suddenly plunged into the rapids below.

There was but one house on the side of the stream opposite the village, and this was a miscrable shanty. The thatched roof scarcely served to keep out the rain, the mats were old and worn, and the *futons* ragged and thin. In one room there was a chest of drawers, in another a little Japanese table on which lay the customary inkstone. Some books were piled up in a corner and papers were scattered around.

Seated on the floor near the table, his face buried in his hands, was a man about thirty years of age. He seemed feeble in body and disturbed in mind, and now and again moaned and rocked himself to and fro. The man was Yetaro, the village schoolmaster. Two years before he had come to Yamamidzu with his wife and infant son. Not one of the simple inhabitants of the village knew whence they came, and at first all looked upon them with distrust. Yetaro built a small house away from all the other houses of the village. It was in a wild, lonely place on the mountain-side and ever in the deepest shade.

The woman was frail and delicate. Some even said that she was possessed of the fox, according to a strange superstition which the people entertain concerning those who are in the slightest degree deranged. The young mother's sole pleasure was in her baby, whom she carried on her back long after the strong, healthy boy was too heavy a burden for one so weak and ailing. The father was a scholar, and gathered the village children into a school. But the pittance thus gained was scarcely enough to keep his family supplied with the barest necessaries of life. They were often hungry and cold and shivered in their scanty garments. But Saijiro, the baby, grew strong and ruddy and was happy with his mother, riding on her back or trotting by her side the livelong day. Of the silent father he saw little.

But now a great change had come. The gentle Kochi was no more. All the morning she had lain on her wretched bed breathing quietly, but taking no notice of the boy she loved so fondly. Every now and then he stopped his play to come and nestle close to her side. He would pass his hand over her face and lisp, "*Ka-chan, ka-chan!* I am very hungry, *ka-chan.* Wake up and give me some rice." But the mother did not answer him.

The village doctor sat by the sick woman's side, but had no power to help her. A priest came over from the village and mumbled his prayers, but Kochi did not seem to hear him. An old *baba*, the only person on whom Yetaro would call for help, from time to time administered nourishment. Yetaro sat for hours by the table, never looking up and not speaking a word.

At ten o'clock the end had come. The doctor went back to the village. Saijiro came in once more to speak to his mother, but no one paid any attention to him, and he went crying from the house. He was a sturdy little fellow of three years, with bright black eyes and round rosy cheeks. The officer Fujisawa would have given half his wealth and influence to possess him; and Aka's tears would have been dried could she have called him, even in his rags and dirt, her own.

Poor little Saijiro! He trotted away from the house down to a corner of the garden where there was an altar to the fox-god, Inari. He was hungry and lonely, and no one listened to his cries. Something was the matter with *ka-chan;* she heeded him not. So he lay sobbing under the shadow of the mountain, until his quick ear caught the sound of rapidly approaching footsteps. He looked up to see a boy of fifteen coming towards him. In an instant the child was on his feet, running with outstretched arms to meet his friend, who stooped to take him on his back.

"Why do you cry, Saiji?" asked the newcomer.

"I am hungry, Yenoske, and the honorable father is sad and the honorable mother gives me no rice. When will the mother wake up, Ye-chan, and cook the rice?"

"The honorable mother is dead and finished, Saiji, but Baba and I will take care of you and give you rice. See! I have brought you beans. We will go up on the mountain and gather flowers to lay on the mother's coffin."

The hungry child ravenously ate the sweetened beans. Then, with his hand clasped in Yenoske's, he bravely climbed the mountainside, looking for flowers and screaming with delight when he could point one out to his friend. Yenoske gathered them for him until they could carry no more. The snow had scarcely melted on the Hakones. There were still white patches here and there. But in sheltered places lovely flowers grew, and the trees were beautiful in their fresh green dress. Saijiro chatted merrily to Yenoske and was as happy as the birds twittering in the branches above him.

In the little house below lay the dead mother, and the father sat overwhelmed with grief.

Before Saijiro, and before the little Kesa in Tokio, stretched a long and untried path. Old Japan was passing away, and the new generation would find much to trouble and perplex them. But the baby slept on, and Saijiro knew nothing of pain or care. He felt safe with Yenoske and he loved the mountain. Its towering sides had grown as familiar to him as the faces of father and mother. When the mountain smiled with sunshine and held out flowers for him to gather, he rejoiced. When the mountain was sad and sent rain like his mother's tears down over the little house, he often wept in sympathy. When once upon a time he had seen it all white and glittering with snow, he had clapped his hands and danced for joy and called *ka-chan* to come and see it too.

It is not often that the eastern slope of the Hakones is covered with snow. The western exposures are much colder. On the eastern side are hot springs, which are a resort for invalids even in winter.

On this May day everything was lovely, and it was late in the afternoon when Yenoske and

Saijiro went back to the home where the dead mother lay.

Old Baba had prepared the body for burial. The priest had shaved poor Kochi's head; for the people believe that the departed become priests, and must enter the realm of the dead with shaven heads. Kochi was dressed in her wedding garments, and on the evening of the third day the square, box-like coffin in which the body was seated was carried to the temple. The priests chanted a solemn dirge over it. Then they bore it to the Buddhist cemetery and laid it in the ground.

The little son looked on and wondered what it all meant.

CHAPTER III.

NEW JAPAN.

In the summer of 1868, while Kesa was only a few weeks old, a great battle took place in Tokio, or Yedo, as the city was then called. It was fought at the beautiful temple inclosure Uyeno. The adherents of the Tycoon, who had been declared a usurper, met the Mikado's troops. The former were defeated, and the Tycoon soon retired from Yedo into private life in the old castle at Shidzuoka; while the Mikado removed his court from Kioto to Yedo, and changed that city's name to Tokio, which means the "eastern capital."

Tama, Mitsu, Chiye, and Hana heard from their house in the Kudan the noise of the battle, and were much frightened. But the baby Kesa knew no fear.

Do you ask how there came to be two rival rulers in Japan? Will you listen to a little story?

The history of Japan begins with a man called Jimmu, 660 years B. C. He was the sole emperor, and founded the sovereignty of the Mikados, who held their court at Kioto. Almost divine honors were paid to the Mikado, but in the course of a few centuries his real power was much re-

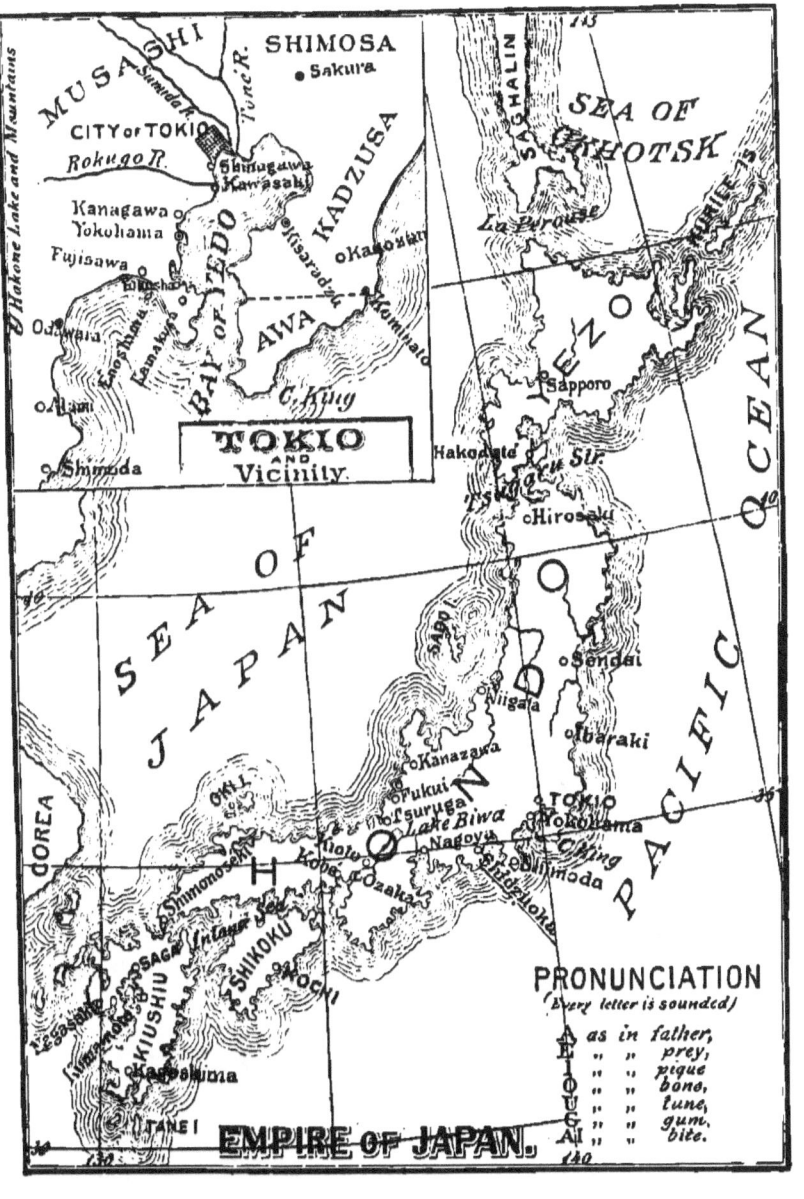

duced by the rise of a military supremacy, exercised alternately by two rival clans, who were frequently at war with one another. In 1180 the reigning Mikado was forced by Kiyomori, the chieftain of the clan then in power, to abdicate in favor of his son, a child of three years, while Kiyomori, the boy's maternal grandfather, himself became regent. After Kiyomori's death, a year later, Yoritomo, the leader of the rival clan, established his supremacy and took up his residence at Kamakura. In 1192 the then reigning Mikado appointed him Shogun, or military "commander-in-chief" of the empire—the office to which the title of "Tycoon" has been commonly but erroneously applied.

Thus the Mikado continued to be a sort of puppet, to whom great honors were paid, while the Shogun, or sometimes the Shogun's regent, was the real ruler of the empire and the leader of the armies.

Near the close of the sixteenth century a famous general named Hideyoshi acquired the chief military power, though he was never appointed to the office of Shogun. All Japanese children are acquainted with the stories of Yoritomo and Hideyoshi, the latter being better known as Taykosama, a title which means "my lord, the great lord." A few years after the death of Hideyoshi, which occurred in 1594, one of his generals, named Tokugawa Iyeyasu, was appointed Shogun by the Mikado and held his court at Yedo. That city continued to be the residence of the succeeding Shoguns, all of whom were of the Tokugawa dynasty, until the revolution of 1868 put an end to the office.

Early in the sixteenth century some Portuguese traders came to Japan. These traders were soon followed by Roman-catholic missionaries. They were Jesuits, and at their head was a man known through all the Christian world, Francis Xavier by name.

It is said that these first missionaries to Japan, though not free from the errors of the Church of Rome, were pious and self-denying men who labored faithfully among the Japanese. They gained many converts, and were loved by the people, whom they loved in return. But after Francis Xavier was dead, changes took place. Other representatives of the Romish Church came over, and they quarrelled among themselves.

What the Japanese thought of this we cannot tell. But at last the Portuguese formed a conspiracy against the Government, which was discovered, and they were driven out of the country. Then a terrible persecution of Japanese Christians took place. The converts were brave and patient, and many preferred a terrible death to giving up their faith.

The next people who had commercial relations with Japan were the Dutch. On the 24th of June, 1598, there sailed from Holland a Dutch ship with an English pilot on board. This pilot's name was William Adams. The crew had a terrible voyage. Adverse winds drove them hither and thither and sickness broke out among them. At last they were driven on the shores of Japan, where they were kindly received. But after waiting nearly two years for the decision of the Shogun concerning them, they were informed that they could not have their ship any more, and that they must make up their minds to spend the rest of their days "happily and peacefully in Japan."

The Dutchmen scattered themselves in different parts of the island, while Adams went to the Shogun's court at Yedo, where he became a favorite, had a fine salary, and rose to "high distinction." But he was very sad during his long sojourn in Japan. He had left a wife and children in England, and was never permitted to see them again. He tried several times to send letters, but whether they were ever received or not no one knows.

The Dutch and Portuguese were together in Japan for a time. At length, as we have learned, the Portuguese were expelled from the country. We learn from reliable sources that the Dutch assisted the Japanese in their persecution of the native Christians. This is a great blot on the record of the Dutch in Japan, although some writers try to excuse them. One of their own number says, "The Japanese both hated and despised us for what we had done."

In 1641 the Dutch were ordered to Nagasaki, and were confined in Deshima, a little island in the harbor. Here they submitted, for the sake of trade, to the most terrible humiliations. They were scarcely allowed to hold divine service on Sundays. They had "to leave off praying and singing in public and to avoid the sign of the cross." All of the Japanese officials connected with the Dutch factory were obliged to "trample upon the cross."

The Dutchmen were constantly watched. Occasionally they were allowed to take a walk into the country, but were always surrounded by spies. The principal men of the factory had to make journeys to Yedo to visit the Shogun. During these trips they gained some knowledge of the country. Deshima, although called an island, is in reality separated from the city of Nagasaki by a canal; it is scarcely more of an island than the Foreign Concession at Tokio. The scenery by which the Dutchmen were surrounded was very beautiful. High hills encircle the land-locked harbor and the verdure is almost tropical.

England and Russia made attempts to trade with Japan, but were unsuccessful. The law was fixed and unalterable. No foreigner, and no

Japanese who had been away from his own country, should ever step upon its shores again. And this law was in operation for two hundred years.

It was in the year 1852 that a squadron was fitted out by the United States Government for the purpose of visiting Japan and establishing commercial relations with that long shut-up country. The expedition was under the command of Com. Matthew S. Perry, and every American boy and girl ought to know about it.

The Mexican war had closed. California had become a part of the United States. The magnificent harbor of San Francisco was now ready for the commerce of the Orient. The Golden Gate was open to the trade of China and India. Naturally all eyes were turned towards Japan as a country on the great highway between the Occident and the Orient.

For a little more than two hundred years, from 1641 to 1852, Japan had been shut up. There had been no intercourse with any other nation except the limited trade carried on with the Dutch. No one had gone out of the country or come into it. Two hundred years! Think of what our country was only one hundred years ago, and perhaps you can form some idea of the stationary condition of Japan.

But on the 24th of November, of the year 1852, Com. Perry sailed from Norfolk, Virginia, on the steamship "Missouri," commissioned to arrange a treaty with Japan. He carried a letter from the President to the Emperor. His orders were to deliver the letter to the proper authorities and to demand an answer.

The story of the squadron's progress around the world would be well worth reading. They stopped at many ports and saw many wonderful things. On the morning of July 7, 1853, they first came in sight of Japan. Those of us who also have seen Japan for the first time on a summer morning know how those lovely shores must have looked to the ships' crews as they steamed slowly up the coast. At first the land was only dimly visible through the mist. Then as the sun rose higher and higher, dissipating the fogs, Japan stood revealed with her wooded hills, her green shores, her river flowing down to the sea, her little villages nestling under the cliffs and scattered along the water's edge.

We can imagine the consternation of the fishermen out in their junks when the steamers became visible, the hurrying and scurrying of people upon the shore. Then what ridiculous means they employed to keep the foreigners from seeing them, stretching cloths before the towns! They were curious, nevertheless. Men, women, and children climbed the hills to gaze at the strangers. Bells were rung, guns were fired, and beacon-fires were lighted along the shores. A general surprise and alarm prevailed throughout the empire.

So far as etiquette was concerned Com. Perry met the Japanese upon their own ground. He let them see that he was a commissioner from a ruler of dignity and power. After a great many vexatious delays the first interview with the Japanese authorities was granted, and the President's letter was delivered. An exchange of hospitalities having been made, the fleet left Japan with the understanding that the Commodore was to come again in the winter for the Emperor's answer.

Accordingly, in February of the next year he returned, and the treaty was concluded without war or bloodshed. Thus did Com. Perry succeed in opening the gates of Japan.

Other nations were not long in making similar treaties, and foreigners flocked into Japan. It was during this period that the title of "Tycoon" originated. It was really with the ministers of the Shogun at Yedo that these first treaties were made, under the impression on the part of the foreign Powers that he was the actual Emperor of Japan; and the ministers of the Shogun called him the *Taikun*, that is, "great ruler." It was not until 1868 that his true position became known and that the Mikado's ratification of the treaties made with the Shogun or "Tycoon" was obtained.

In 1868 a great revolution took place. This was just about the time when our story begins. Kesa was a mere infant and Saijiro a toddler of three years. The "Tycoon's" troops fought with the Mikado's troops. The former were defeated, and the "Tycoon" retired into private life. So there is now but one ruler in Japan. You see that while Kesa and Saijiro were yet small children momentous changes were taking place in the empire. God had, indeed, great things in store for them.

No shadow of anxiety, however, or forecast of trials to come, had power over the brightness of their baby lives. Little Kesa learned how to use her eyes, looking at first wonderingly at the sunbeams, the gay flowers, the pretty colored balls which are given to Japanese babies to play with.

Dressed gorgeously in silk and crape, she was taken to the temple and had her name recorded there as a member of the Fujisawa family. She learned how to stretch out her hands for things, how to cry when she did not get what she wanted, how to creep, to stand, to walk.

She had her first little sandals, then her wooden clogs; had some falls in learning how to use them; was taught how to step out of her shoes at the door and how to make a bow. She learned, also, to lisp in baby fashion the soft, sweet words of the Japanese language. Kesa was an active, healthy child, a great contrast to the peevish, weak little Hana. The tiny bell which she wore at her waist would be heard now in one corner of the garden, now in another, as she trotted happily from place to place. Often was the mother's heart relieved by the tinkle of that little bell when the child would be missed for a few moments.

One day when Kesa was about two years old the whole family, except Fujisawa himself, were going up to the temple. It was a Buddhist temple with the usual *toriye*, or bird-rest, in front. A flagged walk led up to the steps, and on each side of this walk were shops where the children could buy toys. Within the temple inclosure there was an image of a horse, and a tree in which a sacred snake was said to dwell.

The children gave some money to a man to have him free a number of caged birds. This is one of the acts of Buddhist worship. Within the temple were idols. Some of these were hideous and frightened the children; others had beautiful faces, on which they loved to look. Even little Kesa was taught her prayers, although she could not at all understand them, but she clapped and rubbed her hands, made her bows, and repeated the same words as the others.

This particular day was a festival. One of the gods was taken out in a gorgeous car. Those who were carrying him shouted and rocked the car violently, becoming much excited. There were many people in the street, and most of them had flowers. On the way the Fujisawas met Aka carrying a great wooden doll dressed in silk and crape. She looked very happy, and she told them why: she and her husband were going to adopt a beautiful boy, the son of a relative. In the meantime she consoled herself by dressing and caring for the doll. Soon the empty heart and home would be filled. No wonder Aka's face was bright with smiles. The children admired the doll and rejoiced with Aka. The young woman went on towards her home, and then something happened which the little Fujisawas remembered for many and many a day.

They had often heard of the foreigners who had made their way into the country, and they had listened to the story of those days when Com. Perry was at anchor in Yedo Bay, when beacon-fires were lighted, guns discharged, and bells tolled, as danger signals throughout the country. That was seventeen years before the time of which we are writing, and a number of foreigners had come to Japan since then. But the officer Fujisawa's wife and children, living in a secluded way near the outskirts of the city, had never seen any of these strange people of the Western Continent. They knew that Fujisawa himself had dealings with them at the custom-house, and that their sojourn in the city was a source of much perplexity to him and the cause of endless discussions in the little circle which assembled in the garden or in the upper room.

The children's secret curiosity to see the strangers was this afternoon to be gratified. As they were walking slowly along they heard the "Hai, hai!" of a runner, and immediately a pony-carriage passed, in which were a gentleman, a lady, and a little child. The group of sisters pressed closely to their mother and Meguchi, a trifle alarmed, yet interested in the lady and the fair, blue-eyed baby. The lady looked kindly at them and smiled on Kesa, who lifted her bright face but for an instant, then hid it in her mother's dress. It was but a flashing interchange of glances, and all passed on their different ways. But in the coming years they were to meet again and again.

CHAPTER IV.

A MIDSUMMER DAY.

The midsummer day was warm in Yamamidzu. It seemed as if every breath of air was shut out by the steep hillsides. The people sat in the street by the river and used their fans. The horse could not discover a cool place in which to stand, and found switching his tail to keep off the flies rather violent exercise. The dogs panted with heat, and went often to lap the cool water of the river.

At one end of the village, in the little schoolhouse, stood Yetaro, the master, reading in a loud tone some of the maxims of Confucius. The children liked to hear also of Confucius, or Kong-foo-tse, himself. He was born in the province of Loo, China, about 550 years before Christ. He was a wise and serious child, continually surprising his parents and grandparents by his remarks. Twice in his life, after deservedly occupying a high position, he was driven out of his native province. For twelve years he wandered about an exile, often hunted and harassed. The last five years of his life were happy and peaceful, passed in a pleasant valley, with friends around him. The literary work which he did has been

VETARO'S SCHOOL.

of great service to China, and his books are studied to this day in all of the schools. The teachings of Confucius in many respects are very good, but they do not recognize any Supreme Being. They inculcate reverence towards parents and ancestors. Obedience is taught, and everything is to be done "decently and in order;" but no remedy is provided for the power and curse of sin.

The Yamamidzu scholars, a few mountain girls and boys, strove to imitate Yetaro's reading, teacher and scholars screaming at the top of their voices. The stick which Yetaro held in his hand was more for the purpose of emphasizing his words than for the punishment of the pupils, who were docile and obedient enough and did their best to learn what was set before them. But do you think that on such days even a Japanese boy will not sometimes cast a glance out of the open slides and look with envy on the bees and flies and free little birds in the tree-tops? or that a vision of cool clear water does not flit across his mind's eye, and that he is not pleased when the hour for dismissal comes?

It was a poor little place, that schoolhouse. The roof was thatched and in some parts moss-grown, and it leaked when the heavy rains came pouring over the mountains. The matting was yellow with age and soiled and worn.

In a corner of the room Saijiro, now a little round-faced, rosy-cheeked boy of five years, clad in a simple white garment, his chubby brown hands clasping some lilies, lay asleep. What little wind there was just stirred the damp, dark locks that fell on his forehead. The little motherless boy had become the pet and pride of the villagers, who prophesied that he would be a scholar and fill his father's place in the school.

And now it was time to dismiss school for the day. Yetaro laid down his stick and gave the scholars permission to go. They made their bows and passed out, singing and shouting as they went down the street. But the big boy, Yenoske, remained. Going up to where the little one lay sleeping, and shaking him gently, he said,

"Up, up, Saiji! School is out. We are going home."

The child opened his almond-shaped eyes, rubbed them, stood up, and then, as if suddenly recovering his senses, leaped lightly on Yenoske's back. Thus he was carried rapidly through the village, and was soon on the frail bridge which crossed the river. Saijiro was used to it, and never trembled as the frail structure swayed to and fro under Yenoske's firm tread, while the torrent boiled and hissed below.

Yetaro followed them down the street, saw them safely over the bridge, and then turned in at the temple gate. He remained some time at his devotions, repeating one prayer over and over again. Yenoske knew his habits; so when he had reached the one house on the other side of the river he set Saijiro down on the little veranda and took his place beside him.

"I am going down the mountain to-morrow, Saiji," he said.

The child looked sorry, for these two were inseparable friends, and the little one was lonely with only his quiet father for a companion. "In how many days will you return, Yechan?" he asked.

"In three days," Yenoske answered. "And I will bring you something, Saiji—new shoes and candies. I will tell you, too, of everything I see. Some day, when you are big enough, you shall go with me, Saichan."

"Will it be very long before I am big enough, Yenoske?"

"Oh, a long time, Saiji. You must learn how to read and write and count."

"I shall soon learn, Yenoske. I am five years old."

Thus the two friends, big and little, talked until Yetaro was seen coming up the walk. Yenoske rose to make his bow, and Saijiro too saluted his father.

Politeness is so bred in the Japanese character that the poorest and humblest have manners that would grace an English drawing-room.

The villagers did not know exactly what to make of the *sensei*, or teacher. He was proud of his boy, but seemed to care little for his society, and left him to the tender mercy of others so far as pleasure and companionship were concerned. The Yamamidzu people said that the *sensei* was under a vow. When out of school he passed much of his time in the temple, prostrate before the idols or pacing up and down the stone walk. Many were his ablutions, his washings of head, hands, and feet. Many an hour did he spend in calling upon the gods. Sometimes he would dismiss school for a few weeks and go off to some shrine, walking until his feet were blistered and his bones ached, going over mountains, fording streams, in sunshine and storm, heeding neither flood nor tempest.

At such times Saijiro would be left to the care of a village "Baba," as pleasant and cheery an old body as the one in the *yashiki* near Fujisawa's house. The little one liked the change, for he could play with the village children, while "Baba" was tender and kind to the motherless boy. But his love for Yenoske was the strongest passion of his little heart, and Yenoske's devotion to him was unbounded.

Do the Japanese ever seem very strange to you and like the inhabitants of another world? Do you think they have not their chosen friends, their heart-loves, their joys and sorrows, their smiles and tears, just as you have? It seemed so to some of us at first, before we came to know them as well as we do now. We have long since learned that all the races of the human family are nearly related, and that the human heart is the same in all countries and ages.

The next dearest friend to little Saijiro was a dog, Ts'koi by name, which Yenoske had rescued from some cruel fate and given to him. Ts'koi was not by any means a handsome dog; he looked very much like a wolf; but he was faithful and fond of his little master.

But the *sensei* had come home; so Yenoske went back to the village to prepare for his trip to the great town at the foot of the mountain.

Yetaro made tea for himself and the boy, pouring it over some cold rice. Saijiro could use his chop-sticks as fast as any one, and soon emptied his bowl. The night came on. Saijiro lay down on his little *futon*, with Ts'koi beside him. Boy and dog were soon fast asleep. Yetaro lighted a tallow candle and bent over his Buddhist books, trying to find some light and comfort for his darkened, sin-burdened heart. The moon climbed high in the sky, peeping over the house and over all Yamamidzu. The river was golden under the yellow light.

The villagers sat outside their houses, some talking, some listening to the singing and playing of three blind musicians. The occasional cry of the Japanese nightingale, which hides in the thickest shades of the wood, was heard. The river rushed and roared. It was night on the Hakones. A little later, every one was asleep under the dark green mosquito nets, with the slides all shut. It would have been almost impossible to rouse any one, even if you had wished to do so.

It is hard to realize how poor these mountaineers are. No cows are on the mountain waiting to be milked; there are no full larders, no fields of waving grain. The people on the Hakones depend for their supplies mostly upon what can be brought on pack-horses from the towns at the foot of the mountain. They make cups, bowls, and other articles from the beautiful woods which they find around them, and give these in exchange for dry-goods and rice. The charcoal business is also carried on by the mountaineers.

As for their housekeeping, it is very simple. Rice is cooked when it is wanted, and *daikons*, large radishes, are pickled for family use. There is no furniture beside the cooking utensils and occasionally a table and a chest of drawers. A few fish are caught in the streams and a few vegetables are cultivated in almost perpendicular gardens.

Japan could not support its many millions of people if they did not live in the most economical manner and cultivate every inch of ground. Where they cannot use horses for ploughing, men do the work with their own hands.

A JAPANESE COOPER

CHAPTER V.

THE STORY OF THE HAIRDRESSER.

> "Stotsu, futalsu, mitsu, yotsu,
> Itsutsu, mutsu, nanatsu."

So sang in a weird minor key Fujisawa Mitsu, as she bounded her ball on the veranda and kept count of the strokes—one to eight.

The slides of the best room were open, and Mrs. Fujisawa, Tama, and Aka sat on the clean mats, each busied with some piece of needlework. Mrs. Fujisawa was putting together a dress which had been washed, Tama was embroidering a skirt, and Aka was sewing on a little garment for Rinjiro, her adopted boy. The poor doll lay neglected in a corner of Aka's room. She had no time to make doll's clothes now. She had plenty of work in these days, the happiest of her life.

On a little mattress near the ladies lay Hana, her eyes protected from the light by a blue cotton cloth laid lightly over them. This cloth had been dipped in holy water, water in which the image of the child Buddha had been washed. Both Hana and her mother confidently expected help from it. The little girl lay on her *futon*, quiet and patient, listening to the voices of other children at their play and to the murmur of wind through the tree-tops.

Chiye stood on the edge of the pond feeding the gold-fish with a thin wafer-like substance which they eagerly devoured. In one corner of the garden, near a little summer-house, sat Meguchi, sewing a seam and watching two of the children. One of these was Kesa, now almost two and a half years old, and the other was the merry-looking Rinjiro, six months older. They were loving playmates. Aka said jokingly that they should be betrothed now, and marry when they were old enough.

The children were not encumbered with much clothing. They wore simple white garments and had neither shoes nor stocking. They were rolling poor Daruma Sama backward and forward. Their delighted shouts reached Hana's ears and brought a smile to her pale face.

Daruma Sama was a Japanese saint. The story runs that, wishing to cross the sea on a leaf, he spent many years in prayer before he could accomplish the feat, so many years that he wore off his lower limbs. His image, therefore, has a large head and arms, while the rest of his body is a hemisphere that rolls about to the great delight of children.

It was August, and the garden was lovely with its late summer flowers. There were lilies there as white and pure as those Saijiro loved so dearly on his mountain. By the pond bloomed pale pink and blue hydrangeas. Early chrysanthemums looked up at the children with bright faces. Magnificent lotus-flowers reclined as languidly on their broad leaves as Oriental beauties on soft couches. Oto, the gardener, was painstaking and faithful, so that everything was carefully tended in his domain.

At last Mitsu's ball bounded away from her, rolling down towards the pond and Chiye. Mitsu slipped her feet into the straw sandals lying near her on the ground and went after the ball. But when she had picked it up she did not return to her play. She stood, instead, by Chiye, watching the feeding fish.

"Mitsu," said Chiye, as she threw her last wafer, "do you see that big fellow over there? the one that shines so and has the 'drop' on his forehead?"

"Yes," answered Mitsu.

"Well, I call him Shaka Sama"*—a Japanese name for Buddha. "He has rays coming out from him, and that mark in his forehead is like Shaka Sama's."

"Oh, Chiye!" said the shocked Mitsu, "you should not say that a fish is like Shaka Sama. We must not speak disrespectfully of the gods. Shaka Sama is so good and gentle. I love to

* Sama is a respectful title meaning "my lord" or "my lady."

look upon his face. It is so different from those terrible *onis*" (devils).

Chiye did not seem much impressed. But there is no telling what answer she might have made, for just then the opening and shutting of slides in the house and the murmur of voices announced the arrival of the hairdresser.

"There is Kei," said Chiye, listening to the sounds. "Let us go in."

Salutations were not yet over when the children entered the room where the new-comer was and went down upon the floor with the others.

"Truly, a long time," murmured Kei.

"For the favors of long ago we thank you," answered the children.

"Truly, thanks," said Kei. "How is your honorable father? and your honorable selves—are you well?"

A servant brought tea, which they all drank. Then Kei and Mrs. Fujisawa took a whiff from their pipes, knocking the ashes into the *hibachi*, or fire-box.

Now the hairdresser in Japan usually carries all gossip from one house to another. She is, in consequence, an interesting personage. She will tell how Miss Cho wore her mother's dress to the festival, how Miss Tama broke her wooden shoes and fell in the street, how Mrs. Kuginuki is always crying, and how the "go-between" has settled a marriage of this person and that. But Kei was not so fond of gossip as most of the hairdressers. She was a bright-looking woman with gray hair. She wore a dark gown and sash and carried a tobacco-pouch at her side. She talked merrily to the children while making preparations for her task. First an old mat was brought, upon which oil, combs, and a polished steel mirror were placed. Then Mrs. Fujisawa with a bow excused herself to her eldest daughter for being first and sat down. Kei unbound her thick long hair.

"Kei," said Mitsu, as she watched the process, "you promised some time to tell us about the fishing-village where you lived when you were a little girl."

"Truly, I did, O Mitsu," said the woman. "But it was a very poor place, a little place on one of the islands of the Inland Sea, near the town of Onomichi. There were only four or five houses—not like your honorable father's honorable mansion, but dirty and ill-smelling, fit for dogs. Still we loved to watch the water and the beautiful islands. *Dogu!* those islands are always green! We would sit on the shore looking for the boats and wondering how many fish the men would bring home. When they brought enough, the women had to carry them to Onomichi. This is a pretty place. The houses are large and clean, and there is a beautiful walk on a terrace where one can sit and see the water."

Here Meguchi interrupted the story by coming up to the veranda with sleepy little Kesa on her back and Rinjiro clinging to her skirt. Kei had to stop and admire the children.

"She has very large eyes," said the mother regretfully, referring to Kesa; for this was not in accordance with Japanese ideas of beauty; and Mrs. Fujisawa felt troubled, too, about her baby's round rosy cheeks.

Kesa, being sound asleep, was laid upon the floor, while Meguchi sat beside her to keep off the flies. Rinjiro crept to his mother's side, and Kei went on.

"It was a long walk to Onomichi. The women got very tired, carrying heavy baskets on their heads and heavy babies on their backs. Then, too, the women had to plant rice. Working with their feet in water and the sun beating down upon their heads gave them terrible headaches. *Dogu!*"—which means in Japanese, Alas!—"it was a hard life, O Mitsu. Yet often we did not have enough to satisfy hunger—only a little rice, some pieces of *daikon*, and some poor weak tea. Often the men got no fish. They came home tired and cross. They drank *saké*," (an intoxicating drink made of rice) "and slept heavily; but the women must go on working. The fishing nets were very heavy; we had to mend them and hang them up to dry.

MEGUCHI, KESA, AND RINJIRO

"One day when the father had brought some fish, the mother took me with the other girls to Onomichi. Honorable mother carried the baby on her back. We tramped all around the town, selling our fish, and at last started for home tired and hungry. The mother looked worn and sick. At last her strength failed. She put the baby upon the ground, sinking down herself. We were all little ones and did not know what to do. Some of the children cried, some fell asleep. By-and-by two men came along, and we begged them to help us. They carried poor honorable mother home. She never went to Onomichi again. *Dogu!* she died."

Kei wiped the tears from her eyes. The children looked sorry. Mitsu was waiting patiently for Kei to go on with her story.

"Nantaro was my darling. I loved him and gave him the best of everything. When the nights were cold I spread my own covering over him. He always had enough to eat, while I went hungry.

"One day the father brought a man to the house and said I must marry him. I hated the man, but I had to obey the father's command. He was rough and cross with me and beat Nantaro. I tried to run away. But Nantaro was too heavy for me to carry, so I had to go back. One day while the husband was out in his boat there came up a terrible storm. Rinto, the sea-god, was very angry. Waves dashed over the islands. I never heard of the husband any more.

"Then the honorable father was sick for a long time before he died. The beloved Nantaro turned out a bad boy. He grew unkind to me, running away at last altogether and for ever."

Poor Kei's tears streamed so fast that the children wept for sympathy, wiping their eyes on their sleeves. Presently the story was continued.

"*Dogu!* I cried night and day. I thought that the gods were angry with me for my sins, and I resolved to go on a pilgrimage."

"But, Kei," said little Chiye, "you had not done anything *very* wrong, had you?"

"*Dogu!* it seemed not, O Chiye; yet the gods were surely angry. I had heard of the holy place where, before foreigners came into the country and the war broke out, the Son of Heaven (the Mikado, lived. I wanted to worship at one of the temples there. I waited until a junk came to take me off the island. I went on board, with some clothes wrapped in a handkerchief, and sailed through the Inland Sea to Hiogo. I was sick and cold and miserable. The wind was bad, and we were a long time getting into the port. Please to wait a little, Mitsu," Kei interrupted her story to say, as Mitsu was about to take Tama's place. "I brought some pretty new hairpins for you and Chiye. Please to condescend to select, darlings."

The hairpins were sprigs of delicate crape flowers. Mitsu chose some cherry-blossoms, and Chiye tiny chrysanthemums. Then came tea, and for the elders a few whiffs from their pipes. At last, Mitsu being seated under Kei's skilful hands, the story went on.

"Hiogo is a beautiful town. Back of it there is a fine waterfall, where I went one day with another woman. We bathed in the deep pool and let the stream pour over our heads, and as we bathed we prayed that our sins might be washed away. Afterwards we prayed again at the temple. Then I started to walk to Kioto, carrying my bundle on the end of a stick. It rained. I was wet and weary. At last I came to a large city which I knew to be Osaka. I thought I would stay there a while and see if I could learn anything about my boy, my truant Nantaro. I lived with a woman close by a temple where there was a pagoda. Every day I tramped up and down the stone walk leading to the temple three hundred times, repeating the holy name of Buddha one thousand times."

Here Mrs. Fujisawa, who was a very religious woman, looked with wonder at Kei, covered her face with her hands, and said, "Truly, very good!"

Kei shook her head and went on.

"The stones were hard and my feet were sore. At last I could walk no more. The woman brought me some books to read; but I did not care for stories. I wanted to know the way of the gods, to know how I could please them, so that they would be good to me and make me happy. I studied with a priest, telling him of my troubles and my wish to please the gods. But what could he say? Only, '*Dogu!* I do not know how to help you. I cannot understand it very well myself.' At last I would go up to Kioto. A man had offered me a ride in his boat. I bade farewell to the woman and the priest.

"It was pleasant to sit in the boat, watching the trees on the bank and the light ripples in the water. Truly, Kioto is a wonderful place! The temples are larger and finer even than these in your honorable city. There are mountains all about, and in the mountains there are shrines where the devout go up to pray. But I, alas! could find no peace for my soul in Kioto, though I walked many and many a mile in the mountains, though I fasted and prayed. For all the while I was thinking of my boy and that perhaps I might find him. The gods would not hear me, because I sorrowed more for him than I did for my sins. Come, O Chiye."

Chiye had only to have her hair combed and the pretty hairpin stuck through a little knot on top of her head. While Kei was finishing her task the story too was finished.

"I tried not to think of Nantaro. I went on

many a pilgrimage. I put on the pilgrim's white garments and climbed the sacred Fuji to worship the great Buddha at the crater. Truly, it was a weary time; yet I got down to the foot of the mountain as sorrowful as ever. All the holy water of all the holy shrines could not wash away my sins. At last I came to Tokio. Here I joined some women-priests, shaved my head like theirs, and beat on a drum."

At this point, much to Mrs. Fujisawa's wonder, Kei threw back her head and laughed.

"The women were not holy. They talked of all sorts of things, wrong as well as silly, while they were beating their drums. Their eyes were everywhere. They never thought of the gods. So I gave it all up, learned how to dress hair, and got my little house."

"But did you never find Nantaro?" asked little Chiye.

"*Dogu*, no; my boy is lost. I would go all over Nippon to find him. I think that is the reason why the gods do not bless me. I would do as much to find Nantaro as I would to please them. Truly, *dogu!*"

Kei's tale was told, and after more tea and tobacco, more bows and compliments, she went away.

Soon after, Meguchi went with the five little sisters to the bath-house. There they splashed about in the great tank of hot water with their playmates. Apparently Kei's sad story was forgotten. But it had sunk deep into one little heart; Mitsu, after many years, would think of it often.

The soft evening light was falling over Tokio when the children came out of the bath-house and started for home. The canal beside which they had to pass was all golden in the sunshine. Boats laden with charcoal were being poled slowly along.

"Where does charcoal come from, Meguchi?" asked Chiye.

Meguchi pointed to the dark line of hills in the west. The baby Kesa raised her dark eyes to the heights where Saijiro lived. But she was only following the direction of Meguchi's finger. Her attention was immediately diverted to a man who passed them carrying some gayly decorated toys. She stretched her hands out eagerly.

"Who will buy my toys? Who will buy my toys?" cried the man.

Meguchi shook her head at him and said to the little one, "Condescend to wait for another time, darling."

Kesa asked for the toys no more. As for the charcoal, the children had all forgotten about it.

They were all at home to meet their father when he returned from the custom-house; but they had seldom seen him look so hard and stern. He said little at the evening meal, and soon after went with some brother officers to the upper room where they so often smoked and talked. A terrible thing had occurred in Tokio. There was great excitement throughout the city. The boiler of an English steamer had exploded, and many Japanese were among the wounded and the dead. The anti-foreign party, always ready for the slightest excuse to rebel against the presence of the strangers, were threatening severe measures. So Fujisawa and his friends sat far into the night discussing the unsettled state of things in the empire, and almost momentarily expecting a summons to the custom-house.

At the shrine in her chamber Mrs. Fujisawa knelt and prayed to her idol gods, vowing obedience to them if only her sick child might be cured.

CHAPTER VI.

SAIJIRO CLIMBS THE MOUNTAIN.

EARLY in the morning of the day on which Kei told her story to the children, Yenoske and the pack-horse stole quietly out of the village, went up to the main road and then down towards the great town at the foot of the mountain.

When Saijiro opened his eyes he remembered that Yenoske had gone and that it was a school holiday. His father's place by his side was vacant, and Saijiro knew that he should find him at his books. He sprang up, went out into the fresh air, and washed his face and hands at the spring which bubbled up near the shrine of the god Inari.

The day was as bright and beautiful on the Hakones as in Tokio. In the great capital the little Fujisawas had the beautiful, sparkling bay with its sail-boats to look at and the Hakones in the distance. In Yamamidzu, Saijiro had the river, and the mountain towering above him covered with trees and bushes and with lilies growing on almost inaccessible heights. The child stood for a moment when he had finished his toilet, and with water pouring from his dark hair

VENOSKE AND THE PACK-HORSE.

clasped his hands and bowed his head before the fox-god's shrine. He then went to find his father. Pushing back the slides, he saw him sitting at the writing-table, and went down on his knees, touching his forehead to the floor. Yetaro acknowledged the salutation and pointed to a bowl containing a little rice. Saijiro ate the rice and a small piece of radish.

"Is there no more, honorable father?" he asked, his hunger scarcely appeased.

Yetaro shook his head, but added, "Yenoske will bring some rice, my son."

Saijiro went quickly to a pile of Buddhist books which were in one corner of the room and began to look at the pictures. Some of these were representations of Buddhist hells. The god Yemma sat in state, trying the dead as they were brought to him. Saijiro was frightened as he looked at pictures of men thrown into caldrons of boiling oil. The terrible devils, some with one great glaring eye in the middle of their foreheads, did not tend to reassure him.

"Honorable father," said he at last, "where do all these devils live? and why do they throw the people into boiling oil?"

"It is *jigoku* (hell), Saichan," answered the father, "and the *onis* are punishing the wicked."

"But what is 'wicked'?"

"Saichan," answered Yetaro, "I will tell Yenoske to get you some books the next time he goes down the mountain. You cannot understand these."

Saijiro piled the books up in the corner and, followed by Ts'koi, went out into the garden. His favorite corner was just back of the house, where a hedge separated the schoolmaster's ground from the side of the mountain. The child had never attempted to go beyond the hedge, so the father felt no uneasiness about him. For a while he amused himself making a little garden, working industriously as he cleared away stones, dug, and planted. A big bee hummed around him. Some toads came out of their holes and looked at him, and ants worked near him, getting ready for the winter. There were birds in the trees above him, and occasionally a tiny lizard glided past him.

But bees, toads, ants, birds, and reptiles were safe at the hands of the little Buddhist boy; for the Buddhists say that when a man dies his soul enters into the body of some lower animal, and great fear is felt of crushing the frail tenement of some human soul. Saijiro's father was especially careful upon this point. The child was never allowed to kill or torture a fly. Often when he went to the temple with Yetaro, the latter would slip *cash* into his hands to enable him to pay for the release of some imprisoned bird; and the child, as he watched their happy flight into the sky, would feel that he had done something good, and had gained "merit with the gods."

Ts'koi lay down on the ground near Saijiro and watched him as he went backward and forward at his play. Ts'koi had coarse yellow hair and dull, inexpressive eyes. But he was devoted to his little master and to Yenoske. And well he might be, for they had discovered him one day on a rock in the middle of the rushing river, whining and yelping, evidently hurt and unable to help himself. Yenoske plunged at once into the torrent. Although rapid, the river was not very deep, and Yenoske succeeded in reaching the rock and bringing the dog to the shore and to his little friend. The dog's wounded leg was duly attended to by Baba, and he became Saijiro's inseparable companion.

At last Saijiro tired of garden-making. Far up on the mountain grew some white lilies. He could see them gleaming in the distance. If Yenoske had been there, he would have lost no time in going up to get them. Suddenly Saijiro concluded that he might possibly reach them himself. There was a hole in the hedge which he easily made larger. He crept through and stood for the first time on the other side. As a matter of course Ts'koi followed, and soon the two were on their way up the mountain.

The mountain-side was steeper here than the road up which Yenoske and the horse had gone in the early morning. But Yenoske and the horse had charcoal to carry, while Saijiro and Ts'koi were unencumbered. Saijiro had to take fast hold of the bushes and pull himself up by them. Stones, dislodged by his feet, went bounding down to the hedge, and the great trees seemed ever calling to him to come up higher. Poor Ts'koi was puzzled. He panted and puffed, but still kept on. At last the lilies were reached, and Saijiro, clinging to a bush, almost lost his balance as he plucked them from their stems.

And now he began to think of going back. But when he looked down, the dizzy height frightened him. Poor little boy! Tears gathered in his eyes and rolled down his rosy cheeks. The distance to the top of the peak did not look so great, and something still seemed to impel him upward. So on he climbed, every step rendering his return more difficult. At last, giving one desperate pull at a bush and drawing himself up, he stood on the summit. It was a beautiful place. Tall trees grew in an almost perfect circle around a grass-plot. Rocks, with soft mosses clinging to them, were scattered here and there; and in one spot was a tiny spring, whose ice-cold waters danced merrily over some bright pebbles.

But near the centre of the grass-plot was a fire, and around the fire bits of charred wood were lying. Saijiro stood for a moment watching the flames and wondering who could have made the fire in this lonely place. Suddenly there appeared from behind a clump of bushes a wild-looking man with long dishevelled hair and blackened face. In an instant the thought of demons and caldrons of boiling oil rushed into the child's mind. The harmless charcoal-burner appeared to him as some terrible being sent to punish him for running away. With a wild shriek he started down the other side of the mountain as fast as he could go, poor perplexed Ts'koi at his heels. The charcoal-burner tried in vain to make him understand that he would not harm him. The harder the man tried, the faster ran the terrified child. At last the charcoal-burner gave up the chase and sat down, wiping the perspiration from his face and uttering the expressive Japanese "*Dogu!*"

Saijiro and Ts'koi continued their flight down the mountain. The slope was gradual, the descent easy. They were both hot and breathless, both faint with hunger and thirst. Then Saijiro fell and lay exhausted on the ground, crying piteously. Presently he thought he heard children's voices, and getting up he went around some rocks, and to his great joy discovered several Yamamidzu boys bathing in a pond. The bathers ran up to the terrified child.

"What is it, Saiji? What have you done?"

"A very great thing has happened," gasped

Saijiro. "I have seen a terrible devil on the mountain."

This created something of a panic among the children. One or two wanted to go home.

"What was it like?" asked a boy of twelve or thirteen.

"*Dogu!*" answered Saijiro; "I don't know; only he ran after me, and had hair all over his face and a great shining eye in the middle of his forehead."

The boys were somewhat awed, but as moments passed and nothing appeared, they went on with their play. Saijiro pulled off his one little garment, jumped into the pond, and was soon as merry as the rest. They sailed boats, poled themselves about on logs, splashed, ducked their heads under the waterfall, and brought them out with water streaming from their black hair.

Saijiro forgot all about his father, Yenoske, and everything else, for the time. At last the boys concluded to go home. At the entrance of the village Saijiro met his father, who had been searching for hours with a new terror at his heart. He said little to the boy, however. Taking him by the hand, he led him to Baba's house and left him in the old woman's care. The demon of unrest had taken possession of him, and he was going on another long pilgrimage.

A cloud rested on the top of the mountain that night, and the next day the rain poured down heavily over Japan. It saturated the thatched roof of the little house where Saijiro and Baba passed the day and kept the little Fujisawas indoors. If they had gone outside they could not have seen the Hakones; these were covered with mist and rain. The teacher Yetaro, wrapped in his rain-coat, plodded along the great highway across the Hakones, scarcely heeding the storm.

Yenoske and the horse travelled all day up the steep, slippery mountain road. It was almost night when they reached the village. Saijiro heard them, and rushed out to meet them in the pouring rain.

CHAPTER VII.

TAMA'S NEW HOME.

THE year in Japan is marked by flowers. Early in the spring the cherry, peach, and plum trees blossom. A little later and the lovely camellia blooms, the iris and the wistaria make the gardens lovely. When summer comes on the hills are bright with azaleas, the lotus unfolds its grand flowers, hydrangeas bloom, and far up on the mountain-side fair white lilies bow to the breeze. In the early autumn come the chrysanthemums, the glory of Japan and her chosen emblem. In the winter we have the bright berry *nanten*, the single camellia, and the yellow jonquil. The seasons of these flowers as they come are celebrated by festivals, all the people doing honor to their beautiful favorites.

So three bright years came and went for little Kesa. Loving care was given her in her pleasant home. Her mother was tender and kind, her father proud and fond, her sisters usually good and gentle. There were tears for little Kesa, as there are for all children in this great round world of ours. Sometimes things would grieve and disappoint her, or her heart would be swollen with anger, when she would throw herself down and sob in a passionate outbreak. But as a general thing she was merry and happy, loving and loved. She was a handsome child, large and finely developed for her age, and she still kept the round, laughing eyes of her babyhood. She was living her baby life still, untrammelled by school duties, spending most of her time in the garden with Rinjiro or playing with a good-natured tailless cat.

Now had come a busy summer for the Fujisawas. The five years of Tama's betrothal were over, and soon she was to leave her father's house for her Hakodate home. How interested Kesa and all of them had been in the beautiful silks, satins, and crapes which the merchants had brought to the house! Fujisawa spared no money, and the ladies selected the richest materials for dresses and skirts and the most elegant brocades for sashes. The gay hairpins of the young girl were given up for long skewers of tortoiseshell and amber. Everything was ready, and in a short time the child-bride would look upon the face of her future husband.

A steamer had come into port at Yokohama on board of which were the young Mesoburo, the bridegroom-elect, his father, mother, and the go-between.

If you could have looked at the fifteen-year-old Tama as she sat in the upper room, you would have seen a slight, oval-faced girl, beautiful in Japanese eyes, dressed in the most fashionable style, and neatness itself in every detail of dress and adornment. Her hair was brought over the top of her head, rolled with exquisite crape, and confined by a large amber hairpin. Her eyebrows were shaved off, her face was powdered, her finger-nails stained and polished, her lips painted. No wonder kissing is unknown in Japan. Who would wish to kiss painted lips?

Her crape dress was of that soft gray shade which the Japanese love, and her crimson brocaded sash was the richest that could be purchased in the city.

Tama could read the "Great Learning" and repeat the "One Hundred Poems;" she was a good performer on the *samisen* and could sing a number of Japanese songs. At the tea-school she had learned how to make tea and how to present it gracefully to guests. She was skilled in sewing and embroidery, well instructed in all matters of Japanese etiquette. The principles of obedience to father, mother, father-in-law, and mother-in-law had been duly inculcated. Indeed Tama was not inclined to anything else. She and Mitsu were children after their mother's own heart, passive and gentle, rendering obedience as a matter of course and reverencing the gods.

But the rough, blunt little Chiye, whom Fujisawa called his boy, the mother did not understand quite so well; and Kesa, too, was inclined to question and rebel.

Fujisawa met his friends in Yokohama, and they went immediately to Tokio. In the afternoon the two young people who were to be so closely united met for the first time. There were no hand-claspings, no kisses, no caresses, no loving words. They bowed low and exchanged formal salutations.

"Truly, welcome to our humble abode," said Tama.

"Truly, I am well received and entertained," answered young Mesoburo.

But, as it happened, the young people were mutually pleased. Tama was considered a beauty by the Japanese, and Mesoburo was a fine-looking, courteous young man.

Kei's tears fell fast over Tama's dark hair as she arranged it next day for the bridal. "*Dogu!*" she said, "I have done this for you since you were a baby. How proud you were of your first little hairpins!"

Tama showed her the long pin of golden amber which her father had given her. Kei admired it exceedingly, but in her heart she wished she were sticking flowers and butterflies in her darling's hair.

Then came the process of teeth-blacking. This was to show Tama's devotion to her husband. She would never marry another, and no man should look on her to desire her for his wife.

"It is very becoming," said the mother and sisters when Tama's white teeth were covered with the ugly stuff.

Tama herself was more inclined to cry than to be pleased, but she said nothing.

They dressed her for the bridal. She wore a robe of white crape; her white sash was heavily embroidered with gold and silver threads.

Poor little child-bride going forth into an untried life, so young and unprepared! What were her thoughts as she contemplated leaving the beautiful home of her childhood and going off to the north with the stranger Mesoburo? Since she was ten years old she had heard it all talked about as a very fine thing and as a settled fact. It must be, and she accepted it. And the mother? Ah, mothers are mothers everywhere. Mrs. Fujisawa shed many a tear over her child's departure.

Early in the evening, when the lamps had just been lighted in the city and the new crescent moon was shining in the west, there came to Fujisawa's door four sedan-chairs, each carried by four coolies.

The ladies were all ready and waiting.

"The chairs have arrived," announced a servant.

Kei stood in one corner of the room weeping

as though her heart would break, and the women-servants were shedding tears.

Tama arose and quietly bade the servants good-by, putting a coin into the hand of each. They bowed to the ground before her. Meguchi's sobs were heard all through the house.

"Come, daughter!" called Fujisawa.

Tama, carefully attended by her mother and Aka, went out of the house and took her place in the second chair. Fujisawa occupied the first. After Tama came her four sisters, and after them some friends. In the rear of the procession were coolies carrying boxes containing Tama's wardrobe. The Fujisawa servants stood at the door watching the bridal train as far as they could see it, then turned and closed the slides. One of the five daughters had gone out from that home, and it was changed for ever.

People stopped to gaze as the party passed down the street. "It is a wedding," they said. "The daughter of the high officer Fujisawa is to be married and go far to the north."

At the gate of the house which Mesoburo had rented for the occasion, and to which he took his father and mother, that everything might be done in the best style, stood servants who prostrated themselves when the bearers stopped. Then they rose, opened the gates, assisted the bridal party to alight, and conducted them all into the great empty parlor.

"Welcome," said the father-in-law, saluting the bride; "and welcome to all. Truly, it is like poison to your soul to enter my humble residence. How are all the honorable members of your honorable family?"

In the meantime Tama and Mesoburo were down on the floor exchanging most formal and polite compliments. Would the bows and measured speeches never cease?

At last, however, all were upright, with the apparent intention of remaining so for some time. They took their places for the wedding ceremony. Tables were placed before the bride and groom on which were cups of *saké* and some sweetmeats. The go-between, the two fathers, and the two mothers sat near the happy pair, and the others arranged themselves so as to form a circle about them. Three cups of *saké* were taken with the usual pledges, and the two became husband and wife. It was a simple ceremony which did not take long. But after it came feasting, drinking, and smoking that lasted until a late hour.

"The bride is dressed very beautifully. How fine everything is!" "How handsome is the bridegroom!" "How happy are the father-in-law and mother-in-law to receive such a daughter into their house!" "What large boxes of clothes and wedding-presents!" "Great happiness! very great happiness!" Such were some of the comments of the guests. Then followed whole days of feasting and merriment. Fujisawa made a dinner, and to it came the young married people, the father-in-law, the mother-in-law, the go-between, Aka, and Baba, dressed in her best suit of gray and smiling all over. What a splendid entertainment it was! The Fujisawa mansion had been duly swept and garnished. The mats were new and spotless; the woodwork was polished until it shone like glass. A lacquered table was placed before each guest. Tall candlesticks supporting elegant wax candles were arranged at intervals, producing a beautiful effect.

At first there were only silver chopsticks on the tables and a small quantity of delicate rice candy. As the guests partook of this they made jokes and puns and congratulated the bride and groom. One said, "The snow of the north is like the whiteness of this confection." And another, "More beautiful than the faint gilding of the sunrise on a mountain-top is the pink of this rice-cake." And still another, "May the young people be as happily united as is the pink of this rice-cake with the white of that one."

Then, as though by magic, in came a great feast—soups in lacquered bowls: bean soups, thickened and sweetened; fish soups, with hard-boiled eggs floating about; rice in great bowls, heaped and white as snow. Each guest had a small rice-bowl which the attentive servants kept filled, this grain taking the place of bread. Then came immense platters of vegetables, and fish dyed all sorts of brilliant colors. There were lotus-roots and lily-roots and pieces of bamboo, crabs, lobsters, and eels, sweetmeats again, and *saké* and pipes.

The feast lasted two hours. All talked, laughed, and were merry. The father-in-law from the north told stories of the Ainos, the original inhabitants of Japan, how they wear beards, and how they catch seals in the waters around Yezo. Fujisawa told the Hakodate friends of changes in Tokio, of the foreigners there and what they were doing. The ladies simpered and giggled behind their fans. The children were glad, enjoying everything, yet well-behaved.

After the feast some slides were pulled back, and a band of female musicians appeared. Two had *samisens*, two beat drums, and one had a sort of tambourine which she struck. They gave an overture which would have sounded strange enough to our ears, but which the Japanese thought very beautiful.

The children knew the tambourine-girl. Her name was Cho, and she supported her aged father by her musical abilities.

Suddenly the musicians began a song—a dismal sort of chant it would have seemed to us—and from some corner came a dancing girl. She was dressed modestly, and all her movements were graceful.

FEMALE MUSICIANS.

"Beautiful upon the mountains is the waving of the branches of the pine-trees, O *yorokobi!*"—i. e., joyful—chanted the singers.

The dancer moved her fan in imitation of the trees swayed by the wind.

"Sweetly upon the blue, ethereal sky fleet the white clouds, O *yorokobi!*"

The dancer extended her arms and moved them to imitate the fleeting of the clouds.

"Fair upon the wooded heights bloom the lilies, nodding in the wind, O *yorokobi!*"

The dancer's hands were swept along the floor.

"Exquisite is the breath of the mountain zephyr upon the cheek of the tired traveller, O *yorokobi!*"

The girl raised her fan and blew gently upon it.

"Sad is the fate of the blind one who cannot look upon the beauties of nature, O *kawaiso!*"—sorrowful.

The dancer walked back and forth imitating the uncertain step of the blind.

"But happy, thrice happy, they who see these things and love them, O *yorokobi!*"

The girl walked as one bounding gracefully along.

"Strong and light of heart comes the lover over the mountain-path."

The girl assumed an expectant attitude.

"Fair is the maiden and pure who thus advances to meet him, O *yorokobi!*"

With timid, hesitating steps the dancer advanced.

"Happy the pair thus united;
"May they long live together;
"May their children be as the fruit of the orange, beautiful, golden, and many."

The dancer bowed and retired amid the cheers and thanks of the spectators.

It was late, and Fujisawa's grand feast in honor of his daughter's marriage was over.

The wedding occurred during the feast of chrysanthemums. All Tokio was gay with the sun-like flowers. The temple gardens were magnificent and all the people were going to see them. "We will go on the fifteenth day," said Fujisawa. "We will take the children and have a picnic."

Children and grown people bowed low at this announcement, and on the morning of the fifteenth they all assembled at the house to take jinrikishas for the gardens. It was a beautiful, golden October day, and the young folks were very happy. In the party were Aka, Rinjiro, and the *baba* from the *yashiki*. Meguchi, Kesa, and Rinjiro were in one jinrikisha. Kesa had on a crape dress and a little coat of rich embroidered silk. She wore nothing on her head.

Her face was powdered. Hanging from her belt was a bag in which she kept her amulet or charm. Rinjiro's dress was very much the same, except that the colors were graver and his sash narrower. The children could look down upon the city and the bay as the coolies drew the cart along the way.

"A great many sails, Meguchi!" said Rinjiro, as he looked down on the water.

"They are fishing-boats, Rinchan, going out to catch fish."

A whole fleet of boats was just going out of the Sunnida River towards the sea, and it was their white sails which had attracted Rinjiro.

But the coolies were pulling the jinrikishas farther inland. The bay was soon lost sight of. They went along a canal, past many a "go-down," or fire-proof house in which the Japanese store their goods. The streets were very quiet; only a few people passed them. They were going around the outskirts of the city to some large gardens on the west. Meguchi and the two little ones were in the very last jinrikisha. The older people were laughing and talking, occasionally calling from one jinrikisha to another. Hana was with her mother. Even she enjoyed the fresh air, the bright waters of the canal, the trees and flowers. The gardens were filled with people, all walking about and admiring the grand display of chrysanthemums.

"See, Kechan," said Meguchi, "there is Momotaro."

Momotaro, or Peach Boy, is a favorite with Japanese children. The story goes that he came out of a peach which an old woman found. She and her husband adopted the baby, and he became a great man. Kesa looked up, and there, sure enough, was Momotaro, made out of chrysanthemums, standing up with drawn sword, ready to attack the strong devils. Not far away was "Red Boy;" and in another corner was the mighty Shogun Yoritomo, with flaming robe and sword.

The children chatted away to Meguchi, who told them stories about these various personages. They ran hither and thither under the great trees, up and down the long avenues of chrysanthemums, with doves hopping about their feet and birds flying over their heads, always gentle, never quarrelsome or rough or rude. The older people walked about leisurely or sat to drink tea.

Oh, that display of chrysanthemums! There were bright yellow ones, massed together until they shone like the sun itself. There were pure white ones, so stainless that none could pass them without exclaiming. There were shades of purple and red and blue so many that the eyes of the gazer were dazzled. The Hakodate friends were charmed. "It is beautiful!" they said. "For the first time we have gazed upon such wonders."

The whole effect was heightened by the dresses of the people, in color like the flowers, and all this wonderful variety under a blue and cloudless sky. Happy little Kesa to grow up amid such scenes!

The next day Tama went away with Mesoburo and his father and mother. She wept at leaving her home, and her mother's heart was full of sorrow. Of all words of farewell there is none which has a sadder sound than the Japanese *saionara*, "if it must be so." Tama bowed low on the floor and spoke the farewell word to father, mother, and little sisters, and long years passed before Kesa saw her again.

The marriage did not turn out badly. Tama was well treated in her northern home, and did her best to be a dutiful daughter-in-law and wife. The house in Hakodate was pleasant. From the veranda Tama could look over to the shipping in the bay. Doubtless she thought often of her Tokio home and of the father, mother, and sisters so far away.

CHAPTER VIII.

ON THE OTHER SIDE OF THE HAKONES.

WHO will turn from the festivities and gayeties of the city to the silence and solitudes of the mountains? Who is willing, after mingling with those who fare sumptuously and dress richly, to tarry a while with the poor mountaineers who have scarcely food enough to satisfy their hunger?

Even the inn at Yamamidzu looked attractive in the bright October sunlight one day when Saijiro was about eight years old. In the courtyard a little group, not altogether unknown to us, had assembled. It consisted of a young man, a horse, a boy, and a dog. These were Yenoske and the pack-horse, Saijiro and Ts'koi.

The dog was lying quietly near the veranda in front of his little master, who was performing a variety of antics, now standing on his head, again on his feet, leaping, singing, and behaving altogether in a wild sort of way, which Ts'koi evidently regarded with distrust. Yenoske was sitting on the veranda with one foot under him and the other on the ground. Several pairs of *getas*, wooden shoes, and *zoris*, straw sandals, were beside him. Near him on the veranda were wooden dippers, plates, cups, spoons, boxes, and toys. Yenoske was counting all these things and packing them into two large hampers. He had turned merchant in a small way, and was going up to Hakone and down the other side of the mountain to peddle his goods in some of the large cities. The teacher had gone off to Tokio and had given Saijiro permission to accompany Yenoske. Ts'koi would go with them, and of course the horse was going too.

The rainstorms of September were over, and although the mornings and evenings were frosty, the weather was pleasant.

"Do you think we shall see foreigners?" asked Saijiro.

"Perhaps so," answered Yenoske. "We shall see some of the things they use. And we shall see the great Nagoya castle and the wonderful goldfish, the Hakone Lake, and such beautiful temples, Saiji, with *such* gods! You never saw anything so nice—grand golden images of Shaka Sama and his disciples. Our images here are ugly, old, and broken."

"I am going to carry Hotei Sama with me," answered the child, taking a little image from his sleeve.

Hotei Sama is the patron saint of children and has eyes in the back of his head—a very necessary arrangement for one who is supposed to observe all the actions of small people.

"Saijiro," said Yenoske, "we must go after

supper to the temple and make an offering and pray. It is not right to set out upon a journey without first praying to the gods."

Saijiro willingly assented. So after their evening meal the two friends, with Ts'koi at their heels, went down to the temple. Yenoske stood at the foot of the steps, rang the bell which was there, bowed his head, rubbed his hands, and repeated a few words of a Buddhist prayer. He then threw a few bits of coin into the money-box. Saijiro followed his example in every respect. There were a number of children playing about the steps. The temple grounds are like our parks. There babies are taken for an airing, there children romp, there all the gossips congregate.

It was almost dark when Yenoske and Saijiro returned to the inn. They found Yenoske's father and mother at supper, and sat down upon the floor beside them.

"Be very careful of the little one," said the mother, "and take great care of yourself."

"Worship at Inari's shrine whenever you see one, my son," said the father, "for the rice-god has not been good to us. There is a hard winter ahead. Baba will suffer with the cold. Her stuffed dress is worn out, she has no soft mat to sit upon, and there is no money."

Yenoske said little, but he purposed in his heart to bring Baba a padded dress and a mat. It is hard to keep warm in a Japanese house when the sun does not shine in the winter. The little *hibachis* do not heat the rooms very well, and old men and women suffer with cold. Baba's face looked pinched and wan; she had scarcely food enough to nourish her; but she laughed as much as ever and always had something pleasant to say.

With the first gleam of the morning Yenoske and his companion were on the road, travelling over a steep mountain path which led by a roundabout way to Hakone. Saijiro started off bravely and kept up with Yenoske, who went singing along. In one of the loveliest recesses of the mountain was a little tea-house, kept for the convenience of travellers who passed that way. A bright, fresh-looking girl and an old woman had charge of the place and dispensed tea and sweetmeats to chance guests.

"Come and rest; come and rest," they called to Yenoske.

He and Saijiro sat on a bench and had refreshments.

"Where are you going?" asked Yen, the girl.

"Up to Hakone and down to Nagoya," answered Yenoske.

"Oh, a long way," said the girl. "And the little master?"

"Thanks, he is going with me."

"A brave little man," said the old Baba.

It was a wild place, a sort of glen. Rocks rose behind the tea-house and on two sides of it. In front was a tiny waterfall like an end of ribbon fluttering on the side of the mountain. It was almost too late for flowers, but the changing October foliage made up for the lack of them.

"Truly, a nice place," said Yenoske.

"The honorable grandmother loves it," said the girl. "She has been here ever since she was as young as I am, and I expect to stay here until I am as old as she."

Then the grandma laughed and showed her toothless gums.

The Japanese are very fond of places like this and take great delight in the beauties of nature, so many persons stopped and chatted with Yen and the old lady. They had for refreshments beautiful peppermint cakes, as pure and white as any which are made in this country, some little cakes to eat with tea, hard-boiled eggs, and some of the famous bean candy. Everything was very neatly arranged, and Yen was a cheerful attendant.

The tea-house was on the road to the hot sulphur springs. Yenoske and Saijiro, after saying good-by to the girl and her grandmother, had not far to go before coming to a beautiful hotel. The wood about the house had been left in its natural state and was very odd and grotesque in its appearance, being gnarled, knotted, and twisted in all sorts of peculiar shapes. Here Saijiro for the first time in his life saw a chair, and he was allowed not only to examine it closely, but to sit in it. He saw sick people gathered at the springs, some of them covered with loathsome sores. The sulphur water is very hot and comes hissing and boiling out of the ground.

Saijiro was tired in the afternoon, so Yenoske put him on the horse; and thus they came in the early evening to the village of Hakone. Yenoske was well known there. He went immediately to the hotel where he was accustomed to stop. Arriving, they saw a blind shampooer, or rubber, just passing the door. His head was shaved. He carried a staff and blew a whistle. Behind him walked a coolie carrying a stick over one shoulder, on each end of which was a large bundle of paper.

A woman sat on the veranda washing her feet. One foot was in a little tub, and she was wiping the other with a blue towel. The landlady had some cloth in her hand, examining it, and another woman was just going up stairs. A maid-servant was kneeling near the landlady and looking on with much interest.

"Welcome, Yenoske," said the landlady as she saw him approaching.

Yenoske bowed low.

Just then the landlady spied poor little Saijiro asleep upon the horse. "And who is the young master?" she asked.

"Truly, thanks; that is the son of the Yamamidzu teacher. He is going with me down the mountain."

"He is welcome," said she. And when Saijiro was lifted from the horse she took charge of him, giving him a finer supper than he had ever had in all his life before, pressing him to eat, until for once the child was fully satisfied. Next she made him a bed in her own room. There he slept quietly until morning, never heeding the opening and closing of slides, the going and coming of travellers.

While Yenoske was sitting at the door after supper a party of travellers came up the street in sedan-chairs carried by coolies. As soon as the hotel people saw them they raised most deafening cries.

"Come in, come in; come in and rest. Condescend to partake of our humble refreshment."

"Honorable lady," said the coolies, addressing one of the party, "this is the best hotel in Hakone."

"So!" said the lady. "Then we will stop here."

From the chair alighted two persons, evidently mistress and servant. They went up to the other chair and saluted its occupant. The lady spoke.

"Honorable grandfather, we will rest here. How is your honorable health?"

"*Dogu!*" said the grandfather, "I am very cold."

"Then," said the lady, addressing the hotel servants, "will you give the respected old gentleman a seat by the kitchen fire-box and get ready quickly a cup of tea?"

Grandfather, shivering, was placed by the kitchen fire. The lady and her servant were shown up the broad, slippery staircase into the best room. The landlord came and went down before them on hands and knees.

"Truly, a beautiful day," said he.

"Truly, very beautiful," the lady answered.

"And how far have you travelled?"

"Thanks, from Tokio."

"The honorable grandfather, how old is he?"

"Truly, thanks. The respected parent is seventy-nine years."

"A great age. And what," said the landlord, "will you condescend to order?"

"We will take fish, eggs, and rice. The old gentleman will have soup."

The meal was soon served. Grandfather had a *futon* near the fire, and after taking a picture of a Buddhist god from his sleeve and mumbling a prayer, he went to sleep.

The next morning Yenoske and Saijiro saw these travellers get into their *kagos*, which the coolies lifted and carried away. The lady was

Kesa's aunt, on her way to her home in Nagoya, the great city beyond the Hakones.

Yenoske lingered in Hakone for a day, that Saijiro might see the lake there. The child had never seen so large a body of water. To go out in a real boat was a great pleasure. It was much better than pushing a log about the pond at Yamamidzu.

Hakone is indeed a beautiful place, famous in Japan for its sulphur springs and fine scenery. Sick and feeble people go from all over the country to bathe in its waters. Long promontories jut out into the lake. The little village lies prettily beside it. The wonder of it all is to find a large lake high among the mountains. There, too, side by side are hot and cold springs.

Saijiro had a happy day at Hakone. But next morning none of the kind landlady's persuasions could induce him to eat any breakfast. Even the old gate at Hakone, about which Yenoske had told such pretty stories, failed to interest him.

In ancient times, Yenoske said, nobles who went up to the court of the Shogun had to part with their wives and little children at the gate, because, for a time, the Government would not permit a noble's family to live in the capital.

But Saijiro would not look at the gate. Great trees waved their branches over him and the

JINRIKISHA TRAVELLERS

late wild-flowers smiled at him in vain. He walked listlessly along and at last began to cry.

Yenoske lifted him on the horse. Even that did not help matters. His head rolled about. He felt giddy and sick. He was in a high fever, and Yenoske's heart was very heavy.

At last Yenoske lifted the little boy down from the horse and laid him on the ground. He got some things from the pack and made a bed by the wayside. He wet his handkerchief at a little spring near by and laid it on Saijiro's head. The child tossed and moaned.

Some fine people passed by in *kagos*, never stopping to see what ailed a poor pack-horse driver and his little comrade. At last Yenoske walked down the road to see if he could find help. In a few moments, hearing voices and following the direction of these sounds, he came upon a group of three persons. A jinrikisha man was sitting in his cart; near him were two women, one sitting on the ground, the other leaning against a post. Yenoske hastened towards them, and they all bowed.

"*Dogu!*" said Yenoske, "I am very sad."

The man asked why.

"*Dogu!* I have my master's little son with me, and he is lying on the roadside very ill."

Then the man got up from his cart, and with the women accompanied Yenoske to the spot where Saijiro lay in a heavy sleep, Ts'koi by his side.

"*Dogu!*" said the *jinrikiya*, "truly, a fine child." And he added, "Bring him to our village, and we will get a doctor."

Saijiro was lifted into the jinrikisha, and they all went off the main road into a village. Here the hotel was a poor one, dirty and ill-kept. A fire blazed on some stones in the kitchen, and over the fire hung a kettle. An old woman sat near the fire, and beside her was a man smoking. Another man was repairing his straw sandals as he sat on the edge of the kitchen floor, which was raised from the ground. A traveller was just passing the hotel. He wore a broad-brimmed hat and carried a staff. Behind him walked a girl who evidently made some attempt at style.

"Come and rest, come and rest," said the landlady, when she saw Saijiro and Yenoske. Then accosting the *jinrikiya* she asked, "Who is this?"

The *jinrikiya* said, "I found them in the mountain, and the little one is very sick."

"Where is the doctor?" asked Yenoske, making his bows.

Saijiro was carried into the house, and the village doctor came. He had a case of medicines with him. He sat on the floor, looking very wise. Then he went through the process of cupping Saijiro, put medicated paper upon the child's temples, and gave him some powders. The next morning, to Yenoske's great joy, Saijiro was himself again, and the pair went on their way down the mountain.

At the foot of the mountain there is a large town called Mishima. A stream passes through it, cold and clear, running bright and rippling to join the river which is to carry it down to the sea. A lovely grove is there also, and in the grove a temple. It is always dark in the grove; the shade of the trees is very dense. Saijiro thought it a very solemn place as he and Yenoske approached the temple. For Yenoske had vowed that if Saijiro should get well he would repeat a certain prayer two hundred times. He was now going to fulfil his vow. He had some beans in his hand, bought from a man near the temple, and every time he said a prayer he dropped a bean into a box. "Amida Dai Butsu, Amida Dai Butsu," said Yenoske over and over, as he paced the stone walk leading up to the temple. When he had repeated these words two hundred times his vow was fulfilled, and he went to look for Saijiro. The horse was the only one of the trio he could find. The boy and dog were gone.

Yenoske, searching anxiously around, soon discovered that there was a great commotion in the town. Men, women, and children were rushing down the street, apparently in pursuit of some one. Several of the women had babies on their backs, and the poor babies' heads were rolling from side to side. Many of the children cried with fright, and one sturdy urchin lay screaming on the ground. Yenoske joined in the chase, not so much for the sake of seeing what was going on as for the purpose of finding Saijiro.

"What is it?" he asked of a breathless neighbor.

"A foreigner!" gasped the man.

Yenoske felt a sense of relief, but kept on. At last the foremost runner reached the hotel, and there those that were nearest to the foreigner saw him alight from a jinrikisha and take his seat on the kitchen floor, which, being slightly raised, gave him the privilege of putting his feet on the ground.

All the servants of the hotel shouted, "Come and rest. Come in, come in."

After a parley with the landlord, to which the crowd listened eagerly, the stranger was taken up stairs. The slides were drawn, and the multitude beheld him no more.

Now Yenoske spied Saijiro with several other urchins in the courtyard of the hotel. Immediately the little boy ran to tell Yenoske about the wonderful stranger.

"I have seen him! I have seen the foreigner! How white his skin is, how strange his hair, and what funny clothes he wears! I never saw anything like it before, Yenoske. Does he sit in a chair, and eat with a knife and fork like those we saw in the hotel?"

So Saijiro was much excited over the foreigner, and when, the next morning, he actually walked beside the jinrikisha for a short distance, and the gentleman looked at him and gave him a little book, he felt very happy, and stored all these things in his mind to tell old Baba.

The pleasant morning changed into a dull, rainy day. Yenoske wrapped Saijiro up in oiled paper, put a broad-brimmed hat on him, and placed him on the horse. Yenoske himself had on his straw rain-coat. The hampers containing wooden articles were also covered with paper. Every person they met was similarly provided for. Great umbrellas sheltered women and children, while their high wooden *getas* kept them out of the mud. Saijiro thought it fun to see these women running through the rain, holding umbrellas over their babies, securely fastened in their outside garments. The babies peeped over their mothers' shoulders with bright black eyes. He pitied the beggars who lay almost naked along the roadside. They asked Yenoske for money as he passed; but money was scarce enough, and he had little to spare. Meanwhile the foreigner was shut up tight in his jinrikisha and saw but little of the country.

So the day passed, with rain coming down drearily. Yenoske and Saijiro stopped a little while at noon for rest and food, and then went on to the place where they were to lodge for the night. Here a pleasant surprise awaited Saijiro: the foreign gentleman was to put up at the same hotel. The boy heard him utter a few Japanese words and could tell that he spoke kindly to the servants who waited on him.

The large city which they entered after several days' further travel was Nagoya. Saijiro had never seen so important a place before. He was never weary of looking at its castle and the immense gold-fish in the towers. He wondered at the great temple; its idols were far finer than those in the old temple at Yamamidzu. The shops and houses, too, were grand in his eyes. Then the people! The child had never known that there were so many in the world. He went to the theatre, saw the acrobats perform, and Yenoske also took him to see some wrestlers.

Yenoske disposed of his woodenware, the money for which he carefully hid in his dress. Yet he did not forget to procure a warm wadded gown for old Baba to wear and a cushion for her to sit upon. He also bought some clothing for his father and mother. "*Dogu!*" he said, "I wish I could get a garment for every person in the village, Saiji. I fear the people will suffer through the long cold winter."

Indeed, when after several weeks Yenoske and Saijiro returned to the village, snow had already fallen on the Hakones; winter had begun. Dreary enough it was in Yamamidzu through the cold season. Only occasionally, when the sun shone, did Baba get out of the house. Most of the time she sat on the floor beside the *hibachi*, often holding her poor cold hands over the coals. Many were the stories she told Yenoske and Saijiro about Old Japan, the Japan of her younger days, before foreigners came. For Baba, although interested in hearing about foreigners, believed in her heart that they were in some mysterious manner connected with the failure of the rice crop in Japan. She thought the gods were showing their displeasure against the Japanese by blighting the crop.

The teacher had returned, and the school went on during the winter. Saijiro was among the scholars. He showed his father the book which the gentleman had given him. It was in English, and the master could not read it. But there was in it a picture on which the master often gazed. A man hung on a cross, with a look of wonderful love in his eyes.

"Who is it, Yenoske?" he asked one day.

"*Dogu!*" said Yenoske, "I do not know very well, but I believe it is Jesus, one of the gods of the Christians."

The master's next question was uttered deep in his own heart only: "**Can he forgive sin? Can he forgive sin?**"

CHAPTER IX.

RINJIRO'S QUESTION.

KESA and Rinjiro had been working merrily all day, getting ready for the festivities of the New Year. Kesa was in her eighth year, a bright, active little maiden; and Rinjiro had developed into a manly boy. Both children went to school.

Chiye and Kesa, every morning as they went down the street, were sure to find Rinjiro waiting for them at the *yashiki* gate.

Servants took the oranges and berries which the children handed them and fastened them over the doors. There were pretty flowers, too, and ornaments of bamboo and straw, symbolical of long life and prosperity.

"I am eight years old," said Rinjiro. "I shall go to another school before long, Kechan."

Kesa looked sorry. How she would miss him!

But no shadow of any parting troubled her when the New Year came. She and Rinjiro, dressed in bright new clothes and the recipients of numberless toys, exchanged Japanese greetings of the season.

"A great happiness. Truly, the spring has come. A great happiness!"

Then away went Kesa to play ball with the girls, while Rinjiro ran with other boys to fly his new kite. But his head, as he tried to watch that gaudy paper butterfly mounting towards the sky, felt strangely heavy. By-and-by he went crying to his mother. He was burning with fever.

Poor Aka! Days passed, and the fever still burned. Her little boy tossed on his pallet. The hope in her heart grew fainter and fainter. She sat by his side weeping, her hair dishevelled. Yet she tried constantly to cool his head and soothe his wild ravings. She vowed an offering to the gods, the best of her earthly possessions, if her boy, her merry Rinjiro, were spared. She called and called upon the gods to spare him; but it was of no avail. The doctor cupped and blistered and administered his powders in vain. A dark, dreary day was just drawing to its close. Aka was sitting in her usual place, putting a wet cloth on the boy's hot head, when the slides of the room were pushed gently aside, and Kesa crept in softly and sat down beside her.

"Is Rinjiro better?" she asked.

"*Dogu!* no; Rinjiro is going to die, Kechan."

"But cannot the great god Bindzuru help him, Aka?"

Aka shook her head sorrowfully. "*Dogu!* I have prayed and prayed, and called upon the gods night and day, Kechan, but they will not hear."

Aka rocked backward and forward in her anguish. Kesa wept in sympathy; but Rinjiro lay unconscious of all this love and suffering. Then Meguchi came and took Kesa away. She was frightened when she found the child by Rinjiro's side, breathing that tainted air.

Darker and darker grew the room. One of the *yashiki* women brought a lantern. Baba came and offered Aka a cup of tea and some rice, but she refused everything. A priest arrived and mumbled some prayers over the sick child, but Aka would not listen to him. So passed the dark night. The river rolled on sullenly towards the sea. The wind blew. The waters of the bay were rough and wild. Few fishermen ventured out that night. The temple bells and drums, sounding solemnly through the still hours, were like mockery to Aka's heart. She knew that worshippers were calling on the gods who would not listen to her cries and before whom her tears were of no avail. Just at daybreak Rinjiro gazed into Aka's face with a conscious look in his eyes, the first for many days.

"Honorable mother, am I very sick?" he asked.

"*Dogu!* yes, my darling."

"But must I die, mother?"

"*Dogu!* I fear you must, my darling."

"Then, mother, why was I born?"

Oh! if Aka had only known that not far from her there were those who had been sent to explain the mystery of life and death. They might have told the dying little one how our Heavenly Father places us here to live our appointed time, be it long or short, and gives us this life in which to prepare for a better one. They might have knelt beside this dying bed and commended this soul to the Good Shepherd, who loves his lambs and gave his own life for them. But these teachers did not know of Rinjiro; and long afterwards kind hearts were pained to hear of the little boy who had died asking, "Mother, why was I born?"

The pretty kites which had been given to Rinjiro for the New Year lay all untouched in one corner of the room. The new dresses and shoes were all unworn. The active, eager child would never again be seen playing about the *yashiki* or waiting for Kesa at the gate. Rinjiro was dead. The little body, prepared for the grave, was placed in a sitting posture in the coffin. Books, playthings, and money were buried with him.

"He may need them in the other world," said Aka.

Kesa, with the other mourners, followed the little coffin to the temple. She felt very solemn. Rinjiro had gone away—where she did not know, and no one seemed to know.

The coffin was placed on the altar, amid lights and artificial flowers. Priests mumbled prayers over it. Then Rinjiro was laid to rest in the Buddhist cemetery and a new name was written on his tomb.

Aka expected now to go back to her parents, but for some reason her husband did not send her away. He adopted a young man to succeed him in his business, and he brought home another woman to be a wife to him. This woman twitted and teased Aka as of old Hagar taunted Sarah, Abraham's wife. Aka's tears fell like the rain and she had no peace.

After the funeral Kesa went and sat down by Hana's side. "Who will take care of Rinjiro now?" she asked of the weary, restless child, who was lying in her mother's room beside the *hibachi*.

"The honorable mother tells me of the good *hotoke* Jizo who takes care of little children when they go into paradise," said Hana.

"Aka prayed and prayed to the gods to make Rinjiro well, Hana. And you and the honorable mother ask them every day to make your eyes better. I'm not going to pray, sister. The gods never listen."

"Oh, Kesa," said Hana, "you don't know what you are talking about. The gods are angry, and I must pray a great many times before they will hear me. I have said Shaka Sama's name over five hundred times to-day. I counted the times on my beads. The holy Daruma spent nine years on his knees, and Shaka Sama's disciples had long patience before they became

Buddhas. And some of the *hotokes*, like the god Jizo, have been thousands of years on the way to perfection. The honorable mother quiets my pain by telling me of the holy life and deeds of Shaka Sama. I should like to be with the gods in paradise, Kechan."

"What would you do there?" asked Kesa. To this healthy, merry child death seemed a long way off and paradise vague enough.

Hana merely answered, "I am going to think all the time of the holy Buddha."

But Kesa's little heart found no satisfying answer to its deep questioning. Rinjiro had gone away. Why? Where? Would she ever see him again? One day late in February of that same year the slides of Aka's room were pushed softly back and Kesa's bright face appeared. Aka dearly loved the child, her Rinjiro's little playmate and his affianced bride.

"Aka," said she, "the honorable mother sends you these cherry-blossoms and wishes you to go with us to 'see flowers' to-morrow."

It was the season of the year when Japan is full of blossoms, the time when the peach and plum trees bloom, the time of festivity, merriment, song, and dance.

Poor Aka shook her head, but the little one still pleaded.

"Please, Aka, condescend to accompany us. Honorable mother sends her compliments. We are to go in a house-boat down the canals and up the river to Mukojima."

"Last year," answered Aka sadly, "Rinjiro was here. He walked beside us and held my hand. Now I cannot go without him. Thank the honorable mother and sisters, darling. *Dogu!* thanks, thanks."

So all the next day, while the Fujisawas were on the water or under the cherry trees at Mukojima, Aka sat in her room mourning for her lost boy.

Kesa was very happy seated on top of a house-boat with Chiye and her father beside her. They were not allowed to go out much, these carefully trained children of Fujisawa's, and were always interested in what they saw. Indeed any one might have enjoyed the scene that morning. There were so many boats on the narrow canals that collisions were frequent. Then the sailors with their long poles would push the boats apart, making a deafening noise the while. Sometimes the Fujisawas would pass a boat containing a party of their friends and would exchange pleasant greetings, mostly about the weather and sweet spring flowers.

"What a large boat!" suddenly said Chiye. "And what fine ladies are coming down the steps."

They were passing a *yashiki*, and the ladies were daughters of one of the old-time nobles.

They were dressed in handsome silks and crapes. Servants carried immense umbrellas over them. Behind them were other attendants who carried lunch-boxes and tea-caddies. They were evidently going to have a great feast somewhere. On swept the boat down the great tidal canals, so full of life that morning. The merry people were singing and dancing, with their heads keeping time to music, or telling jokes and stories.

Little Hana lay on her pallet in the boat looking out upon the water and holding in her hands a bunch of fair white blossoms. Mitsu sat beside her. Childhood for Mitsu was over, and there is no golden period of girlhood in Japan.

"Mitsu," said Hana, "Aka would not come to see flowers because Rinjiro is dead. Do you think the gods have flowers in paradise?"

"*Dogu!*" said Mitsu, on whose heart a dark shadow was falling, "I do not know. We cannot get into paradise for a long time; not for thousands of years, perhaps. And if we are wicked, we shall come back to the earth a worm or a dog or a poor bug."

Hana looked sorrowful.

"What are you saying to the child?" asked the mother almost angrily. She could not bear to see a cloud over her darling's face. So the conversation dropped.

By-and-by they entered Yedo Bay, and Fujisawa said, "There is the custom-house, and there are the houses where the honorable foreigners live."

The boats danced merrily over the bay. Chiye and Kesa, looking towards the south, could see the forts built when Com. Perry arrived off the coast. To the north was the river; to the east the fishermen's island, Skudajiwa; and to the west the great city, with the long dark line of the Hakones behind it, and back of them still Mt. Fuji.

As they passed the mission-houses they saw a lady with a little girl standing on the veranda watching the boats—the missionary's wife and her little daughter Marion. But they were not allowed time to see anything long. Up the river they went, under the bridges, over the bright laughing waters, beside the *daimios*', or nobles', homes, past trees bending over the water with crows cawing in their branches, now catching a glimpse of some great temple roof, now delighted with a great mass of flowers, as some cherry or peach swept its blossoms over the boat.

When they came to the landing the sailors fastened the boat to the shore and they all scrambled out. A beautiful road, sloping gradually from the water, led to the "cherry-tree walk." This is a lovely avenue with cherry-trees on one side and peach-trees on the other. Fujisawa led his family to some benches under the trees and ordered tea.

They took some, but it was bitter and they

did not like it very well. Then up came a man with flowers, sweet blossoms from the trees.

A few copper *cash* bought as many of the blossoms as they cared for. Kesa and Chiye, leaving the flowers, walked with Meguchi down the avenue. Kesa missed her little playmate Rinjiro, who was always so merry on festival days; and she and Chiye thought often of Aka. But, like all children, they were not sad long, and laughed with Meguchi, enjoying the gay scenes. At noon they went to an eel restaurant, where Fujisawa ordered eels broiled on skewers for them all, with the usual accompaniments of rice, radishes, and tea. It was a real feast for the children and they enjoyed it greatly.

Late in the afternoon they crept into the boat again, Chiye and Kesa getting inside with the others. The tide was with them and they returned rapidly. The oarsmen had nothing to do but to guide the boat. The moon was just rising when they reached their home.

"Truly, thanks," said the children to their father; "we have had a happy day."

Fujisawa went to smoke in the upper room. He was not altogether satisfied about his children. Deep in his heart he longed for something better than the old ways of Japan afforded them. But still he shrank from putting them under the direct influence of foreigners, especially the Christians. There was a school for girls in connection with the Government school. Why not send Chiye and Kesa to that?

Later in the spring an invitation to Aka to accompany Mrs. Fujisawa, Mitsu, and Kesa to Inoshima, Kamakura, and Dai Butsu was eagerly accepted. Aka was so glad to have an opportunity to worship before the great image of Buddha and offer flowers and fruits upon the altar there.

Kesa was happy at the prospect of a journey in the cars to the great foreign city Yokohama, and looked forward with anticipations of pleasure to the day of starting.

She was almost frightened, though, by the rapid motion of the cars, and at first clung to her mother's dress. Soon, however, growing braver, she enjoyed the view from the window. They passed rapidly through the fields and villages which lie between Tokio and Yokohama. They were soon in the latter city, for it is only an hour's ride. There they spent the day at a friend's house, so as to start early the next morning for Inoshima.

Kesa enjoyed a jinrikisha ride on the "Bluff," where so many of the foreigners reside. She thought the houses very grand and the little English children on donkeys very pretty, with their long fair hair under broad-brimmed hats. Her mother pointed out to her the consulates, postoffice, and fine shops. Kesa had never seen such grand things in all her life before.

The next day they took jinrikishas and went over the fields to Inoshima, a beautiful peninsula on the coast dedicated to the goddess Benten Sama. They stopped often during the day, so that it was evening before they crossed the sandy isthmus which connects the peninsula with the mainland. Inoshima was lovely in the light of the evening sun. "Truly beautiful!" "For the first time!" "Wonderful!" These were some of the exclamations of the Tokio ladies.

The sea broke along the shore, thundering on the rocks in some places and dancing in bright ripples up to the shore in other places. Some naked children, standing in the shadows of the rocks, were catching crabs.

The ladies left their jinrikishas at the foot of the one steep street of the village. They paid the coolies, received their thanks, and went to one of the hotels. After their supper of fish and rice they sat at the open window and looked out on the ocean. Very early in the morning, before sunrise, they were all on the beach, waiting to worship the sun when it came up out of the sea. As it appeared, mounting above the red and golden waters, they bowed their heads in adoration. A missionary looking from his slides saw the group upon the sands, the three women and the little child, and thought with sadness of their ignorance; but even then the thought was in his heart, "Would that such reverence and fervor always characterized the worship rendered to the Sun of Righteousness!"

What a grand ride Kesa and all of them had that morning along the shore to Dai Butsu! The waves dashed headlong over the land. Kesa shrank back whenever one came too near and was afraid of being swept away. But the coolies knew their business well and brought them up safely to the great bronze image. Kesa worshipped reverently with the others, all of them chanting, "Amida Dai Butsu, Amida Dai Butsu." They also placed flowers before the idol, which looked down upon them calm and dignified, as it had done upon worshippers for many long years.

A pretty ride through the rice-fields brought them to Kamakura, from Yoritomo's time to 1333 the Shoguns' capital, where they saw many relics of Yoritomo and visited his grave.

These were pleasant days for Mrs. Fujisawa, Mitsu, and Kesa. Aka was happier than she had been since Rinjiro's death. Hana heard all about it when they were at home again. The grand image had been her dream by night and day, and she longed to see it for herself.

JAPANESE CARPENTERS.

CHAPTER X.

SEEING BUDDHA'S FACE.

SPRING had come on the Hakones, too. The Fujisawa children could see that there was less snow on them as they looked at them from their garden.

There were several boys of Saijiro's size in Yamamidzu. Chintaro, the barber's boy, was an especial friend, with his rosy cheeks, sparkling eyes, and fun-loving nature. Mantaro, the carpenter's son, was noted for his acrobatic performances. His greatest delight was to propel a board down to the very edge of the cataract, jump from it into the raging river, and after battling with the strong current for a time, to the terror of spectators, suddenly reappear on the bank, dripping, and grinning from ear to ear. He was the best stilt-walker and kite-flyer in the village and excelled in all boyish games. Then there was Nanjiro, a delicate child of ten years, who always had a baby strapped on his back. Ginjiro and Mejiki lived in the largest house of the place and were good scholars.

The girls were Ken, Riki, Hisa, Tama, and Taka. Besides these there were some little children and three or four babies.

Near the temple lived a little blind boy, Kojiro by name. He spent most of his time in the temple among the grim old idols. He loved to hear the monotonous chanting of the priests, the sweet sound of the bell, and the cooing of the doves.

At noon one day, when the sun was shining over Yamamidzu, Saijiro sat with Kojiro on the temple steps. The child's sightless eyes were turned upward towards the sun.

"It is warm, Saijiro," he said, "and the air is sweet."

Saijiro answered, "Yes; the sun is shining, Ko, and that makes it warm."

"I think, Saichan, the sun must be like Shaka Sama's face and the warm air like his breath. You know the image of Shaka Sama behind the altar? I have seen the faces of all the other gods, Saiji, but I cannot reach his; and oh! I want so much to touch it."

"You shall, Ko," answered the eager Saijiro, ready to do anything for his friend. "I will help you. We will climb up and see Shaka Sama."

The two boys rose and went up the rickety temple steps. Kojiro did not need Saijiro's guidance into the building, for he knew every hole and crack of it. But before entering he stood for an instant, pulled the bell-rope which hung there, folded his hands, and bowed his head while he

SEEING BUDDHA'S FACE. 107

uttered a prayer. The two priests who usually officiated in the temple had gone to dinner, and the children had the place to themselves. Saijiro took hold of Ko's hand when the latter had finished his prayer and led him to the altar. Before it was a table, and on the table were offerings of rice and beans and pyramids made of carrots and turnips.

"Ko, be careful," said Saijiro, as he led his friend to the narrow, slippery steps up which they had to climb before reaching the great image.

Kojiro shivered a little. It was cold and dark in the temple. "Am I near Shaka Sama?" he asked. "I cannot feel any warmth, as I do from the sun."

But Saijiro held him firmly by the hand, and he patiently mounted the stairs. Then they had to make their way along a narrow ledge, around tall candles and artificial flowers. Kojiro trembled as for the first time he touched these things which were so sacred to him. At last the boys came up to the image of Buddha. It was seated on a lotus-flower, and looked down on them calm and majestic, as are all images of Buddha.

"Now, Ko," said Saijiro, "climb up on the lotus."

By placing their feet carefully upon the petals of the flower the boys managed to get up to the image itself. Then Saijiro was puzzled. The surface was smooth; there was nothing for his friend to take hold of. At last he succeeded in scrambling up the side and getting on the immense hand of the image. Now, holding by Buddha's sacred thumb, he stooped down and pulled Kojiro up. But still the blind boy could not reach the face.

"Get up on my shoulder, Ko."

Kojiro tried this, but it was not easily accomplished. There was nothing for him to stand on, nothing for him to hold on by. Kojiro felt almost as though he were doomed to disappointment. Should he never see Shaka Sama's face?

Saijiro examined the idol carefully. "There is a place on Shaka Sama's neck where the folds of his honorable robe are. I think I can lift you up."

This feat was not accomplished without difficulty, even danger. But at last Kojiro stood on the holy Buddha's neck. Then, lost to everything else, he passed his fingers over the sacred face that he had so long desired to touch. His thin little fingers traced and retraced the outlines. He felt the eyes, the nose, the forehead, the lips, the chin. Never had image a more devout worshipper.

"I see him! I see him!" he called to Saijiro, who stood waiting on the sacred thumb. "My hands have touched his face. I have seen Shaka

Sama! I know he is beautiful because he is so smooth."

"But we must go down, Ko," called Saijiro at last.

Poor little Ko! how was he to get down? Fearless as he generally was, everything was new here. He had nothing to cling to.

"I cannot come down, Saiji," he cried. "I shall fall."

Indeed, Saijiro himself began to be alarmed. "*Dogu!* what can we do?" he said.

Just then the old priest came in.

"I will call to the *bon-sama*," said Saijiro.

The priest, hearing voices, looked this way and that in the temple, but failed to discover the boys.

"Bon-sama! Bon-sama!" called Saijiro.

The voice sounded far off to the priest. He began to tremble. Always superstitious, the Japanese are ready to believe anything.

"Bon-sama! Bon-sama!" shouted Saijiro desperately from his height on Buddha's thumb.

The old priest lifted his eyes to the altar, and in the gloom and distance just discovered two moving figures on Shaka Sama's arms and neck. They were *onis* calling to him! With a cry he rushed from the temple, meeting on the step his younger, jollier brother.

"What has happened?" asked *bon-sama* number two.

"*Dogu! onis* in the temple!"

This somewhat staggered the younger priest; but some villagers coming along and being told the story, all agreed to enter the temple together. In the meantime the children, thoroughly frightened themselves, stood trembling and clinging to the idol. It was a relief to Saijiro to see the men enter, armed as they were with clubs and farming implements.

"Let us call together, Ko," he said, as the searchers peered cautiously into corners and up at the altar. So together they shouted.

"Who are you?" questioned the men.

"We are Saijiro and Kojiro," the boys answered, "and we came up to see the holy Shaka Sama's face and cannot get down."

The "*Dogus!*" and "Wonderfuls!" and "Strange things!" were not few among the assembled company.

A strong man went up to the idol, lifted Saijiro down to the altar, and then rescuing Kojiro carried him quite down to the temple door.

"What were you doing, Ko?" asked his father as he led him home.

"Honorable father, pardon," answered the child. "I wished to see Shaka Sama's face."

A day or two after the adventure in the temple, as Saijiro and Ts'koi were running up the village street, they met Baba with the large girl

Tama. Baba leaned heavily upon her stick, and Tama carried a bundle of clothes.

"Where are you going?" asked Baba of Saijiro, who made her a respectful salutation.

Saijiro knew well enough where Baba and Tama were going. They were making their way slowly down to the pool to wash their clothes. It was Sunday. The simple mountaineers knew that the Japanese Government had ordered the seventh day to be observed as a day of rest, instead of one day in six, as of old. They also knew that the year began much earlier than formerly and that the months were changed. The Government so ordered it, and the changes were easily effected. Saijiro, who was running about with no definite purpose, turned and went with Baba and Tama down the path along which the villagers frequently trod; for the women all had to go to the pool to do their washing. The river was too rapid and dangerous to allow of any liberties being taken with it.

It was a lovely day. Just enough of winter lingered in the air to make it fresh and bracing. The patch of sky overhead was of a deep blue. The mountain was beautiful in its fresh spring dress. Sweet little flowers bloomed by the roadside. There was even, at the end of the village, a single cherry-tree white with blossoms. The people thought it the most wonderful and beautiful thing they had. Fruit-trees were rare in that region, and the people on the mountain came to Yamamidzu to see this tree. If they could but have seen the cherry walk at Mukojima, where the Fujisawa children spent such pleasant hours!

But Saijiro was happy enough. He ran on ahead of Baba, carrying the bundle on his head. Tama had laughingly tossed it to him when they met, then taking Baba's hand to lead her carefully down the steep descent.

"*Dogu!*" said Baba, "the little flowers are very pretty, and how beautiful is the honorable cherry-tree."

"Saichan, Saichan!" called a little voice from above.

Saijiro looked up to see little blind Ko standing at the head of the path. He wore a white dress, his feet were bare, and his long hair, not yet cut as a priest's—for it was Ko's desire to be a priest—floated behind him on the breeze. Saijiro gave his bundle a toss which sent it rolling down to the pond; then running rapidly back towards Ko, he took him upon his back and was at the pond before the others, whom he had passed each time with a polite "Excuse me." He safely deposited Kojiro upon the ground and found a mossy seat for Baba beside him.

Tama rolled up her dress and waded out into the water with the clothes, which she beat between two stones. Saijiro lay down on the ground between Baba and Kojiro. It was a pretty scene. From the height above them down tumbled the waterfall. The pond was like a pearl set with emeralds, so pure was the water, so green the earth. All around grew pretty spring wild-flowers. The blossoms of the cherry-tree could be seen, a mass of white among the trees, as they looked up towards Yamamidzu.

"Baba," asked little Ko, "shall I ever see?"

"Ko sees many things, Baba," broke in Saijiro. "He sees more things than I can think of."

Tama was all this while busy washing her clothes and Baba's. She had ripped apart their dresses of blue cotton cloth and was beating the pieces on the rocks. She did it cheerfully, and sang in a low monotone a song of spring. It could not be called a merry tune. It sounded plaintive enough. But Baba and the children enjoyed it so much that at last they stopped their talk to listen. It was one of the songs of the *Hiakuninishiu*, or "One Hundred Poems," of which Japanese women are so fond.

"Oh, my love!" sang Tama. "I have lost him in this world. Shall I ever see him again? Shall I meet him in the next?"

"Riki is learning to play the *samisen*," Tama called out to Baba when she had ended her song. "Old Kinchi is teaching her."

"That is fine," answered Baba. "We shall have music in Yamamidzu now. Are your clothes all washed clean, Tama? It is growing late, and we must go home."

Tama led Baba, and Saijiro carried Ko up the steep path to the village. Leaving Ko at his home, Saijiro turned and crossed the bridge. Before reaching his house he heard his father's voice.

"The honorable father is at prayer," said Saijiro to himself.

Yetaro was prostrate before the idols in his bedchamber. Candles were burning on the altar and the smoke of incense filled the room.

"*Dogu!*" thought Saijiro, "I wish the honorable father could find the honorable foreigners' God—the one who hung upon the cross."

CHAPTER XI.

A MIDSUMMER FESTIVAL.

KESA and Chiye, under their mother's careful direction, were changing the water of the vases on the altar. Neither of these two girls had the reverence for the deities of Japan which the mother tried so hard to inculcate. Fujisawa himself was something of a skeptic; but he encouraged his wife and daughters to be regular in their attendance at the temples, believing that a Japanese woman should love and worship the gods.

"Kesa, be careful. Do condescend to take a little more pains, child," called the mother, as the contents of a vase were spilled upon the floor.

"Pardon me, honorable mother," said the child.

Meguchi hastened to wipe the water from the mat. "The honorable elder sisters would not have done so," she said.

"How beautiful!" said the servants when they saw Benten Sama's freshly decorated shrine. It looked like the altar in a Roman-catholic church, with artificial flowers, candles, and incense-boxes.

Benten Sama was a favorite goddess with the children. They loved to hear stories of her life on the beautiful island of Inoshima—of how she could change herself into a swan or a snake, and of how she appeared to people in trouble—a gracious goddess with long, flowing hair and beautiful robes. They had pictures of her standing, with the other "gods of luck," on top of the treasure-boat which is thought to come into the harbor at Tokio at the new year and bring presents and good cheer for all. Mrs. Fujisawa's Benten Sama looked very pretty, standing serenely in an elegant lacquered case, with flowers and candles before her.

Chiye and Kesa found the duties of idol-worship rather irksome. They could not see the use of placing flowers and eatables before images.

"They do not eat," said Chiye in confidence to Mitsu one night.

"No; but the gods in paradise see that we offer things to their images and they are pleased," answered Mitsu.

"Mitsu, the honorable foreigners don't have images of their gods," said Chiye.

"But some of them do," answered Mitsu. "I have myself seen the honorable strangers' images—a woman, like Benten Sama; and a child, like the holy infant Buddha; and men, like Shaka Sama's disciples."

"Well, Fusa goes to school, and she says they have no images. Oh, Mitsu, how I wish the honorable father would let me go to the school!

I have seen Fusa's books; they are about all the different countries in the world. We do n't learn anything except about Japan and the gods and heroes."

"What more does a Japanese girl want to know?" asked Mitsu.

Chiye Fujisawa seemed to have been born with a thirst for knowledge. Long before this she had mastered all that a Japanese girl ordinarily learns in school, and had begged to be allowed to study the Chinese classics. Fujisawa engaged a Chinese teacher for her, but even the classics failed to satisfy the eager girl.

Tama and Mitsu played beautifully on the *samisen*, but neither Chiye nor Kesa cared much for music. They loved to hear Mitsu's skilful touch on the instrument and to listen to her songs of old Japan, but had no fancy for playing or singing themselves.

"Where are you going?" asked Chiye of Kesa a few hours later, as she came into the room where Chiye was studying.

"I am going with Mitsu and Aka to carry flowers to Rinjiro's grave," answered the child.

Just then Mitsu appeared, all ready for a walk and carrying beautiful flowers.

She gave some of them to Kesa, and after a respectful *saionara* to their mother the two girls went to the *yashiki* for Aka, who joined them at the large gate. It was where Rinjiro had always met Kesa in the days when they went to school together.

Aka carried lilies. "How beautiful!" said Mitsu and Kesa as she showed them the pure white flowers. They were mountain lilies, and just then Saijiro had his hands full of them and was carrying them to Baba at Yamamidzu.

"Aka, if it had not been for what Kei said that day she told us her story, I believe I should have liked to be a nun," said Mitsu as they walked. "But I so well remember her words: 'The women are not holy.' She said that while they beat the drums and prayed their hearts were far away, and that they did all sorts of wrong and foolish things."

"*Dogu!*" said Aka, "I long to go on pilgrimage. Many women go. Why cannot we?"

They were going up the broad walk to the temple. Doves came and hopped about Kesa's feet.

"Why does Hachiman Sama, the god of war, have doves for his messengers?" asked Kesa. "He looks so fierce and is so ugly, I should n't think the doves would like him at all."

Near the grim idol Hachiman stood a white horse made of wood. He was Hachiman's servant, as the fox is fabled to be the servant of the god Inari.

Kesa stopped for a moment under a grand maple-tree. On one side of her was a terrible *oni* holding in one arm a "heavenly lamp." On the other side was the tree where the sacred snake was said to dwell. But neither Kesa nor any one else had ever seen the snake. While Aka and Mitsu went up to the temple, Kesa bought some rice from a man and fed the doves. They crowded around, cooing softly as the child threw the grain to them.

The cemetery was just behind the temple. Kesa followed Aka and Mitsu to a well-known grave. A little pair of wooden shoes hung on the tombstone, and near by were playthings. Aka threw away the faded flowers which were there and put fresh ones in their place, and then sat down and wept for the little Rinjiro who lay buried under the stone.

At last she said, "Kesa, you must come and help me make rice-cakes, sweep the rooms, and get Rinjiro's toys and clothes ready. Rinjiro is coming to be with us, and we must prepare."

"Will he really come?" asked Kesa.

"Yes, my darling, at the feast of the *Bon*."

"There is going to be a preaching; let us go and hear the sermon," said Mitsu as they went back towards the temple.

A number of people were making their way up to the steps. Many of them were very old. Hundreds of shoes were near the temple steps, for no one goes into the temples with shoes.

"Who will preach?" asked Aka of a man.

The man made a low bow and said, "The great *bon-sama* from Shibo preaches to-day of the holy Shaka Sama."

The people, about five hundred in number, sat on the temple floor, with their faces turned towards the altar. Aka, Mitsu, and Kesa sat near the door. An aged, venerable priest, with shaven head and yellow robes, occupied as chief speaker the place of honor, and around him were grouped priests of inferior rank.

The western sun sent long rays of light into the temple. They fell on the gilded images of the Buddhas and on the golden lotus-flowers. The priests began a low monotonous chant; and some boys, likewise with shaven heads, swung incense, the odor of which filled the temple.

The priests chanted the praise of Buddha, their holy Shaka Sama.

"Pure and holy and absorbed in heavenly contemplation was the great Amida. He left his father's palace and dwelt with the poor and lowly. Amida Dai Butsu! Amida Dai Butsu!"

Then the old priest rose, and stretching out his hands said,

"Listen, O people, to the doctrines of the holy and blessed Buddha.

"He was born in the far-off country India, a prince of high degree. He despised the delights of his father's house, and determined to become a priest to the most high and holy one, the Brahma of the Indians. But neither did he find peace in listening to the teachings of Brahma.

"He looked forth one day and beheld a man killing a poor dumb animal. He heard its cries and saw its precious life-blood spilled.

"Then his spirit was roused within him. He retired under a banyan-tree and spent days and nights in holy contemplation. He saw beautiful visions, knew all things, and became a god.

"He travelled far and wide over Tartary, Nankin, and Ceylon. Many were his disciples and gentle were his precepts. Read, O people, the story of the sixteen disciples of Buddha, who were 'flowers of heaven.' "

Here the people all bowed their heads. The great image of Buddha was resplendent in the sunshine.

"He founded hospitals for the sick. He gave in mercy to the poor. He became absorbed into the divine essence.

"Study the eight steps to perfection:
"I. Right belief.
"II. Right judgment.
"III. Right utterance.
"IV. Right motives.
"V. Right living.
"VI. Right occupation.
"VII. Right memory.
"VIII. Right meditation.

"The devout Buddhist, O people, must believe the correct thing, must apply his faith to his daily life, must speak the truth, must always have a perfect end and aim in view; his outward life must be without sin; he must faithfully do his duty; he must remember correctly his past conduct and keep his mind fixed on permanent truth.

"Listen, also, to the ten commandments:

"I. Do not kill.

"II. Do not steal.

"III. Do not commit adultery.

"IV. Do not lie.

"V. Do not become intoxicated.

"VI. Take no solid food after noon.

"VII. Do not visit dances nor concerts nor theatrical representations.

"VIII. Use no ornaments nor perfumery in dress.

"IX. Use no luxurious beds.

"X. Accept neither gold nor silver."

The people bowed and murmured assent to each of these precepts and commandments. Little Kesa heard it all, sitting by Aka's side that summer afternoon. The doctrines were good, but they brought no peace to Aka's soul, no hope of meeting her darling again.

But the crowd was dispersing, and in the summer twilight the three walked quietly home.

A few days later Kesa went to help Aka get ready for the great festival of the "*Bon.*" For "the spirits of the dead come back and spend three days of every year with their friends," say the people.

It is a solemn festival and comes in midsummer, when the sacred lotus is blooming in the ponds, emblem of the sanctity, seclusion, and restfulness of the Buddhas. Kesa and Aka made rice-cakes and placed them on the shrines erected to the memory of the dead. They unfolded Rinjiro's clothes, that he might find them ready for him. They laid out for the child-spirit the gaudy, unused toys.

"Oh, if we could see him! If he would only come and play with us and tell us what the gods do in paradise!" said Kesa, as she assisted in sweeping, dusting, and making everything ready. She and Aka talked a great deal about Rinjiro during the three days that the spirits were supposed to spend in the house.

"He would have been your husband, Kechan. The honorable father and I had promised that he should be your honorable husband and that you should be his honorable wife."

"But we should have played together for a long while," said Kesa, whose ideas of the relations of husband and wife were rather indefinite.

"Yes; you would have gone to school together and played together for a long while yet," answered Aka; and she sighed when she thought of all their lost happiness.

The Fujisawa mansion was also swept and cleaned and ready for the spirits. No child had left the house, but there were grandfathers and grandmothers, for two or three generations back, to come. Rice, flowers, and clothing were made ready for them. Drums were beaten incessantly, and the very air seemed filled with prayers of the living and spirits of the dead.

Kesa went with Aka on the evening of the third day of the feast to the bank of a canal. The tide was going out. They lighted little tapers, placed them carefully on the water, and they were carried out to the sea. Rinjiro's spirit was being lighted back to its shadowy home.

"Good-by, Rinjiro, until next year," said Kesa; and Aka's tears fell fast.

The streets were full of people, all carrying tapers or watching them as they were borne by the tide out to the ocean. Men were dancing in the streets the sacred *Bon* dance, chanting a solemn litany, waving their fans, and swaying their bodies to and fro. How weird it all was! Kesa held fast to Aka's hand as they walked rapidly through the streets to their own quiet homes.

A few days after this the summer vacation was over, and Kesa went back to school. She was not fond of books, as Chiye was. In a passive way she went through the school routine, giving little trouble, but paying little attention;

reading monotonously the dull Confucian books, and mechanically repeating their precepts. The teacher was getting old. He had taught the fathers and mothers of some of the children, keeping on in the same routine year after year.

A foreigner going into the school during a reading lesson would have seen the *sensei* walking about with a ruler in his hand and the pupils all sitting on the floor with books open before them. But such a noise! They all read together, emphasizing the small words, drawing in their breath, and making a peculiar inflection at the end of each sentence.

Kesa read out her lesson clearly; her voice could be heard above the others as they chanted the precepts of the "Woman's Great Learning."

"When children are able to take their food they should be taught the use of the right hand.

"When able to talk, the lads must be instructed to answer in a quick, bold tone, and the girls in a slow, gentle tone.

"A leathern girdle should be given to the lads, and a silken one to the girls.

"At the age of seven they should be taught to count and to name the cardinal points.

"At the age of seven boys and girls must not sit on the same mat nor eat at the same table.

"At eight, when going out or coming in, they must wait for their superiors, being taught to prefer others to themselves.

"At nine they must learn to number the days of the month.

"Girls, after they are ten years of age, must not leave their apartments.

"Placed under governesses, they must be taught to be mild, both in deportment and language. They must learn to spin, wind off thread, and to weave cloth and silken stuffs, and thus perform those duties which properly belong to women in providing clothes for their families. They may see to the preparations for the sacrifices, and arrange the vessels and the offerings of wines and vegetables."

In the "Book of Rites" are these precepts:

"Let children be always taught to speak the simple truth, to stand upright in their proper places, and to listen with respectful attention."

"Wives must serve their husbands' fathers and mothers as their own.

"At the first cock-crowing they must arise, wash their hands, rinse their mouths, comb their hair; they must fasten on their bags of perfumery, then go to the chamber of their father and mother and father-in-law and mother-in-law, and having entered, in a low and placid tone they must inquire whether their dress is too warm or too cold.

"In asking and presenting them what they wish to eat they must cheer them by their mild manner, and must wait until their father and mo-

KESA AND MITSU.

ther and father-in-law and mother-in-law have eaten, and then retire."

"Children must not occupy the principal place in the house nor seat themselves in the middle seat nor walk in the middle of the way nor stand in the middle of the door. They must not ascend high places nor approach steep precipices, nor may they indulge in slander or ridicule."

Poor little Kesa! These maxims are all good enough in their way, but she might have studied them all the bright days of her childhood and never have known anything of the beautiful world in which she lived—of its trees and plants and flowers, of its animals, and of its races of men and their history. No wonder that Chiye was dissatisfied.

Kesa wrote Chinese characters in her copybooks, and Mitsu taught her the "One Hundred Poems." Mitsu was also her teacher in sewing, embroidery, and paper-flower making. But Kesa was not a very apt scholar in these things and often tried her teacher's patience.

Neither did she like her *samisen* lessons. The teacher went to the house twice a week, and the little girl would sit patiently beside her and try to imitate her as she struck the strings of the instrument with her ivory stick and sang her songs of love and beauty. But Kesa was no musician and *samisen*-playing had no attraction for her.

"Come, Kesa, it is time for your sewing," said Mitsu one day as the child stood idly by the lotus pond. "For shame!" she added, as Kesa turned petulantly away. She was not fond of sewing.

"But I have a pretty story, a new one, for you," said the gentle Mitsu; and Kesa went slowly towards the house. "The mother waits with her work, Kesa, and Hana is anxious to hear the story."

Kesa quickened her pace and went into the room where her mother and sisters were sitting. Mitsu put Kesa's embroidery into her hands with many directions as to how the work should be done. Then she began her story.

"Once upon a time, just when the world was made—"

"Who made it?" asked Kesa.

"The gods, of course, little sister. But let me go on with the story. Well, the whole world belonged to a fairy who had three children, two sons and a daughter. Now the fairy was about to die—"

"I did n't know that fairies ever died," interrupted Hana.

"Well, this one died or went away from the world, and he left the moon to one boy and the sea to another and the sun to his daughter. The boy who had the moon was very much pleased, and he has it yet."

"But he takes it away sometimes, sister," said little Kesa.

"Yes; but he always brings it back again. Well, the boy who had the sea did not like his part. He hated to be cold and wet all the time. The girl had the sun, and one day when she was spinning with her maidens the sea-boy rushed in and overturned the spinning-wheels and frightened them all so that the sun-girl ran and hid herself in a cave. Then the world was all dark, because the light of the sun really came from her beautiful eyes.

"So the fairies went and begged her to come out, but she would not. At last they went and danced before her door. Then Ama opened just a little crack and peeped out.

"'See, here is a fairy more beautiful than you are,' said the dancers, holding a mirror before her face. Ama was very curious to know who the fairy was, so she came out of the cave, and then the rest of the fairies closed the door.

"Ama promised to go back to the sun if the wicked Susano were banished. So Susano went down to the earth, and as he was walking sorrowfully along he saw an old man and woman crying over a beautiful young girl. Susano asked what the matter was, and they told him that every year a terrible eight-headed dragon came and devoured one of their daughters and that this was the last one of eight. They told him, too, that the dragon was to come again that very day and that they would lose their last daughter if no one was found to rescue her.

"Susano told them to dry their tears, for he could easily destroy the dragon. Then he showed them how to brew some beer, and they made a fence with eight gates and placed a vat of beer at each gate.

"Pretty soon the dragon came trailing along. He was so large that he covered eight hills and eight valleys. When he smelled the beer he went up to it and drank so much that he became intoxicated. Then Susano went to him and cut off all his heads. When the dragon was quite dead Susano stepped up to his tail and began to cut that in pieces. His sword struck something very hard, which proved to be the most beautiful sword that had ever been seen. So Susano took it out and the Emperor of Japan has it.

"Then Susano married the beautiful girl, and they lived in a fine palace and were happy ever after."

Kesa and Hana thought this a fine story; but Chiye said it was very foolish and she did not believe it ever happened at all.

THE EIGHT-HEADED DRAGON.

CHAPTER XII.

WINTER IN YAMAMIDZU.

WHILE Kesa was studying the "Woman's Great Learning" in Tokio, Saijiro on the mountain was likewise gaining a knowledge of Confucius and Mencius, and their counsels to boys.

"At ten," says the book, "lads must be sent abroad to tutors and remain day and night, studying the arts of writing and arithmetic, wearing plain apparel, always learning to demean themselves in a manner becoming their age, and, both in receiving instruction and in practice, acting in sincerity of purpose."

"At thirteen they must attend to music and poetry."

"When the father calls, his son must answer promptly and without delay; he must drop whatever work he has in hand, or if he is eating and has food in his mouth, he must spit it out and run quickly. If the son who has aged parents goes away from the house, it must not be now to this place and then to that, nor must he delay his return beyond the proper time nor retain an undisturbed countenance when his parents are afflicted by sickness."

"It is the duty of every son in winter to warm

and in summer to cool his parents' beds; in the evening to wish them rest, and in the morning to inquire after their health; when going out to announce it to his parents, and on returning to go into their presence. His walks abroad must always be through the same places; he must have some settled business."

"While the tutor gives instruction the pupil must learn, and with gentleness, deference, and self-abasement receive implicitly every word his master utters. When he sees virtuous people he must follow them. When he hears good maxims he must conform to them. In a gentle and submissive manner he must perform the duties which he owes to his parents and brothers, and must never behave proudly, presuming on his own abilities.

"He must cherish no wicked designs, but always act uprightly. Whether at home or abroad, he must have a fixed residence and associate with the benevolent. He must carefully regulate his personal deportment and control the feelings of his heart. He must, both when rising and at rest, keep his clothes in order. Every morning he must learn something new and rehearse the same every evening, doing all with the most respectful and watchful attention."

"Of the three thousand crimes included under the five kinds of punishment, there is none greater than disobedience to parents."

Saijiro had also to learn the "One Thousand Character Classic," which consists of maxims and precepts. One thousand characters are used in this book, no two of which are alike. The maxims are poetical in the original, and the children repeated them in a sing-song style, drawing in their breath and prolonging some of the words.

Saijiro studied faithfully and was a good boy in school. But he loved play too, and many a merry game did he have with the village children.

There came a happy New Year's Day for the Yamamidzu people. It was warm and sunny, and even Baba could sit outside on her cushion and watch the games. The whole village joined in the sports. Yenoske had been down to the town and had brought up a supply of provisions. The women had pounded the rice into a fine powder and had made *mochi*, hard cakes, from it. They had candy and plenty of rice and *daikons*. The girls had bright sashes, balls, and battledores and shuttlecocks. The boys had new belts and gorgeous kites. The village hairdresser and barber had done their best. The bath-house had been well patronized and everything was bright and fresh for the New Year.

Congratulations were heard on all sides. Yamamidzu was bright and beautiful, and the people forgot that there were such things in the world as hunger, cold, and weariness. Kojiro was happy, too, on this bright New Year, and laughed and clapped his hands with the rest of the children.

The boys and men flew kites, and the girls and women played battledore and shuttlecock. The girls counted and sang merrily as the pretty feathers were tossed to and fro.

Some wandering minstrels had stopped in the village to make music for the people. A blind woman sat on a mat in the middle of the street, and while she sang and played her daughter, a girl of thirteen, danced. She gained great applause, and all the Yamamidzu people said she did well. The woman sang of the new year, and of the opening of the peach and plum blossoms.

Later in the day a story-teller recited some tales of ancient Japan and of the glories of Taykosama. Then the children gathered around him and clamored for a story.

"Ah," said the man, "I will tell you the story of the eighty-first brother." Then the children all dropped their toys and listened. The man sat on a mat and held a fan, with which he rapped on a small table.

"Once upon a time there were eighty-one brothers. They were all jealous of each other, and all wanted to rule the same kingdom and to marry the same princess. The princess lived in the province of Inaba, and all the brothers started off to find her. All of the eighty brothers joined in hating the eighty-first brother, and they treated

THE RABBIT AND THE CROCODILES.

him shamefully and made him carry the heavy luggage."

Here the man held up before the children a picture which represented the eighty-one brothers travelling among the mountains, the eighty-first brother carrying the pack.

"By-and-by the brothers came across a poor hare lying in the road and crying. His hair was all plucked out and he looked very miserable. The brothers told him to go and bathe in the sea and then lie down on a mountain and let the wind blow over him. But the poor hare was then in still greater distress; the wind blowing over his cracked skin put him in terrible pain. While he lay crying there the eighty-first brother came along. He asked the hare how he got in such a plight. Then the hare told him that he was on an island and wanted to get over on the mainland. So he called to a crocodile, and they made a bargain. They were to count how many crocodiles there were in the sea and how many hares there were on the land. So the crocodiles ranged themselves in a long row to be counted and the hare crossed over on their backs."

Here the story-teller showed the children another funny picture. All the crocodiles were in a long row, and the hare was running across.

"But," continued the man, "the silly hare, just as he had gained the land, laughed aloud and told the crocodiles his scheme; and the last crocodile seized him and plucked off all his hair.

"The hare further told the eighty-first brother that he had followed the advice of the eighty brothers and had bathed in the sea. Then the eighty-first brother told him to bathe in the river and take a good roll in the bushes. Having done this the hare was quite cured, and he befriended the eighty-first brother, so that he married the beautiful princess."

"A very great thank-you," said the children, and they clapped their hands and went away.

About noon two visitors entered Yamamidzu. They were Yen and the old grandmother from the mountain tea-house. Yen's face was powdered, and she wore a silk sash and finer hairpins than the village girls had ever seen before. She was a real belle among them, and was greeted with many exclamations of surprise and delight. But she led the old grandmother carefully by the hand and was mindful of her comfort in every respect.

"Truly, welcome," said the villagers, crowding around them. "It is a long walk for the grandmother. And how is the honorable old lady?"

"Thanks! Baba is very well, and she is very happy to come," answered Yen.

Then the grandmother was seated on the mat beside the Yamamidzu Baba, and the two Babas laughed and chatted and smoked their pipes. Yen joined the merry group of girls, and soon her laugh was heard above the others. Saijiro and Ts'koi were here and there among the people, and even the schoolmaster Yetaro tried to be cheerful.

Yenoske was invaluable to the little boys. He helped with the kite-flying and shouted with the children if some kite made a particularly high flight into the blue sky.

But the bright hours wore away and the cold winter night came on. The people had to go into their houses, but the story-telling, playing, and singing were kept up until a late hour.

It was the last time that the Yamamidzu Baba went out. The next day an unusually severe storm set in. The wind swept through the mountain gorge and carried the snow in great drifts through the village street. Baba's strength seemed suddenly to fail, and she lay on her *futon*, scarcely caring to move. She could still tell her stories, however, and Saijiro and Yenoske often begged for them. Her thoughts went back to the old days when her children were small and her strong young husband went up and down the great mountain Fuji.

"*Dogu!* I was not one of the holy ones who went up to the summit, although honorable husband spent two months every summer up there," said Baba one night when Yenoske and Saijiro sat beside her.

"At the very top, Baba? And what did he do there?" asked Saijiro.

"Every year," answered Baba, "during the sixth and seventh months the mountain was 'open,' and pilgrims came from all over the country to worship at the crater. *Dogu!* it *was* a sight when the pilgrims came in their white dresses, carrying their staves. Hundreds and hundreds passed by the house every summer. At the top was a village where the pilgrims could rest, and honorable husband had charge of one of the houses and fed the holy travellers, taking a few pence from each for rice, tea, and sweet *saké*.

"I was very lonely when the husband went up the mountain. I would go with him as far as I dared. There were beautiful flowers at the base of Fuji—lilies, poppies, and other beautiful plants. But farther up there was nothing but ashes. Our feet would sink in them, and we could scarcely walk. Then honorable husband would send me back with the baby, and I would work in the garden and keep the house clean.

"Often the top of the mountain would be hidden from me by the clouds, and then again it would stand out clear and white against the sky. There was always snow on it. I was glad to see the top, and often looked up to where the honorable husband was.

"But, *dogu!* one day he went up to spend the two months on the mountain, and never came back again. Some said he fell down the crater; others that he had been murdered. Search was made for him, but he was never found."

"What did you do then, Baba," asked Yenoske.

"Honorable father-in-law was a servant of a *samurai*,* and I went to live with him. The house was in a lonely place, and we had to work very hard. Our master the *daimio* was severe, too, and we were heavily taxed; we scarcely knew what was our own. At last some of the farmers determined that they would not stand it any longer, and they rose in a body and killed some of the officers. It was a long time before the strife ceased, and we were all very unhappy. But at last peace was declared between the *daimio*

---

* Under the Shoguns the feudal system prevailed in Japan, the *daimios*, or territorial nobles, owning tracts of land within whose limits their will was law. The whole population was then divided into four classes: the *samurai*, or military families, from whom the retainers of the *daimios* were recruited, and who had the right to wear two swords, as a sign of gentle birth, the farmers, the artisans, and the merchants or traders. Since the revolution of 1868 the feudal system has been abolished; the *daimios* have surrendered their lands, castles, and retainers to the Government, and the people of Japan are now divided into the three classes of nobles, gentry, and commoners, the last including the peasantry, artisans, and traders.

and his servants, and we were all ordered to Yedo.

"The *daimio's* household was very large; and then there were the two-sworded men and their retainers and wives and children. *Dogu!* it was a great train. We moved very slowly. The *daimio* rode in a beautiful closed *norimono*" (a large litter, carried by several bearers), "and all the people prostrated themselves before him as he passed. Hotels and tea-houses were made ready for his accommodation; but we, who were in the train, often got no rest day or night.

"Dead bodies of thieves and murderers were exposed along the road, that men might see that justice had been done. Sometimes the whole train was stopped by a man throwing himself in the road before us and presenting a petition to the *daimio*.

"At last we reached the great city and were comfortably settled in our *yashiki*. The *daimio* had feasts, mock-battles, and theatricals, and there was much visiting. The *samurai* were idle and drank much *saké*. The women had nothing to do and quarrelled among themselves.

"One day all Yedo was excited. The soldiers were called out, temple bells were rung, and fires were lighted. Some strange ships were in the bay. They were from America, and all they wanted was to deliver a letter to the great Emperor. When this was done they went away. Soon after there was a terrible earthquake. There was no difference between the land and the sea. The earth trembled and seemed to rise in great waves beneath our feet. Houses were shaken down and people were killed.

"Some years after that there was a great battle in Yedo. I don't know just what the fighting was all about, but our prince's establishment was broken up, and my son, Yenoske's father, came to Yamamidzu, and I followed him."

All this was not told without many interruptions. Baba had to be rubbed and warmed, and cups of tea were given her.

"Baba, you are very old; shall you die soon?" asked Saijiro.

"*Dogu!* I suppose I shall," answered the old woman.

"But you haven't been wicked enough to be put into burning oil, have you, Baba?" said the child, who still retained vivid impressions of the Buddhist hells.

Poor Baba could not answer this question. Soon after telling her story she grew almost unconscious, only rousing now and then to take a little nourishment.

The stormy weather continued. Small-pox broke out in the village, and some of the babies died. One day there was an unusual stir in the town. In the midst of a driving storm some men arrived carrying a car in which was an image of the god of the sick. From village to village in the mountains, wherever there was sickness or distress, this idol had been carried. The Yamamidzu priests met it and services were held. But the sickness did not cease. Provisions grew scarce. Yenoske worked hard at his carving, and at last started down the mountain with his woodenware, in order to get some food. Saijiro went with him to the end of the village street. Yenoske had on high wooden shoes, which kept him out of the wet snow, but his clothing was scanty and his feet and hands were red with cold. There were few travellers on the road. Two women going up to Hakone carried umbrellas which were weighed down by the snow that had fallen on them.

At a large tea-house a girl leaned against an open slide looking over the white landscape. She recognized Yenoske, and asked him to sit down and have a cup of tea. "How are the people of Yamamidzu?" she inquired.

"*Dogu!* they have small-pox there, and there is much distress. Baba is dying, and we have little food," answered Yenoske.

"Truly, misfortunes!" said the girl.

Yenoske did not linger longer to talk, but hurried down to Odawara, got his rice, and went back to the village.

The school was carried on during the winter, but Yetaro was sick and coughed a great deal.

One day he went in to see old Baba. She opened her eyes and said, "*Sensei*, your boy is a good boy."

The teacher sighed and said, "Baba, you are going to die, and I shall soon follow you. Where are we going?"

But Baba went back into her stupor again and made no reply. Thus she slept her life away. One golden April evening a coffin was carried up to the temple. All the Yamamidzu people followed it; and when the funeral services were over the slow procession went up the mountain to the cemetery where poor Kochi lay, and Baba's body was laid to rest.

CHAPTER XIII.

MITSU'S TROUBLES.

"*Dogu!* honorable father, *dogu, dogu!* please do not make me marry the man."

Fujisawa Mitsu was pleading with her father. A brother officer had sent a go-between to ask Mitsu in marriage for his son. Some business relations made the match a particularly desirable one for Fujisawa, and he insisted on his daughter's acceptance of the offered husband.

Mitsu had seen the young Akichi, knew his father's family, and dreaded going to live with him.

"*Dogu!* Mitsu, you are sixteen years old; it is time for you to be married. And as to happiness, some women are happy and some are not, and that is all there is about it. I expect to be obeyed, and you need say no more." Fujisawa closed the slides behind him and went away.

Mitsu's tears were falling fast. The gentle mother felt sorry for her suffering child, but dared not interfere. Fujisawa was liberal in many ways, and for the most part kind to his wife and children, but he expected implicit obedience from them, and would suffer no remonstrances when once he had made up his mind as to what they should do. So he went off to the custom-house leaving Mitsu crying and Mrs. Fujisawa trying in vain to comfort her.

At last little Kesa slipped in and sat down by her sister's side. "Why are you crying, honorable sister?" said she.

"*Dogu*, I must be married!" answered Mitsu.

"But is that *very* bad, honorable sister?" asked Kesa, who remembered well Tama's happy marriage, with its feastings, rejoicings, and congratulations. "You'll have beautiful things— silk dresses, amber hairpins, and beautiful sashes. Oh, Mitsu, I should like to get married! But now I shall never marry. Rinjiro was to have been my honorable husband, and now he is dead."

"Oh, Kesa," said Mitsu, smiling in spite of her tears at the child's earnest way of taking her early widowhood, "there are other husbands left, and you will find one, and a good one too, darling. But, Kechan, I do not want any fine clothes. It is Akichi, and we hate him; and his home is so dirty and noisy."

So Mitsu sobbed on, while Kesa sat by her side not knowing what to do and with a sorrowful, puzzled look in her dark eyes.

"The gods bless you, my daughter," said Mrs. Fujisawa, who always turned to her idols for comfort in trouble.

Then she went to Hana, and Kesa got ready for school. Mitsu went out of the house, down the quiet street to Aka. They had grown to be loving friends of late. Something drew them together in a strong sympathy; and Aka forgot her own troubles as she listened to Mitsu's story, and shed tears which were not for Rinjiro.

Fujisawa gave Mitsu beautiful dresses and an amber hairpin, but there was no interest felt in the preparations such as there had been for Tama. Fujisawa was stern and gloomy, Mrs. Fujisawa quiet and sympathetic, and Mitsu tearful and sullen by turns. Kesa felt that a shadow rested over her home, and often sought Mitsu and sat beside her. The sisters said little, but Mitsu found comfort in Kesa's presence. She was a blundering little thing, not very quick to learn, not always obedient; but her heart was full of love and her sympathies were deep and strong.

Old Kei shed tears when she arranged Mitsu's hair for the wedding, but they were not like those which had fallen for Tama.

It was a dull March evening when Mitsu was taken to Akichi's home as his bride. The house was a gloomy place near the east wall of the castle. In the spring the grass on the slope which stretches from the wall to the moat is green and beautiful; but it was dry and brown when Mitsu went to her new home, and everything looked dreary. The house was noisy and disorderly, very different from Fujisawa's refined, beautiful home. The father-in-law had a number of women in the house beside his lawful wife. Some had children and some had none; and the women disputed, quarrelled, and drank *sake.*

No loving welcome was given to Mitsu. A room was assigned her with no outlook except at one corner, where she could catch a glimpse of the castle wall, with the trees above it and a gleam of shining water at the foot of the slope.

The only one of the family at all congenial to Mitsu was a young girl named Hota, who had been sold as a kind of slave to an old man in the family. She told Mitsu of her love for the young Jukichi and of his love for her. She showed Mitsu a fan on which her lover had written verses composed by himself. They likened the pale Japanese girl to branches of plum-trees, rich peach-blooms, and snow on the mountain Fuji. The other women of the household hated Mitsu and Hota, were jealous of their mutual friendship, and gave them no peace.

There came a spring morning which Mitsu long remembered. It was when the blossoms were all beautiful upon the trees—the blossoms to which Jukichi had compared his love. Hota was not to be found in the house. Late in the day some fishermen discovered her body floating in the bay. She held in her hand the pretty fan, and in the folds of her dress were trinkets given her by her lover. She had thus ended her miserable life. So Mitsu's only friend left her, and the days passed heavily and wearily.

One cold, wintry day almost a year after Mitsu's wedding an old woman and a young girl were walking down one of the side streets of Tokio, going towards the castle. Their heads were muffled in their *dzukins*, or winter hoods, so that only their eyes could be seen. Those of the old woman were bright, though her form was bent; and the sparkling face of the girl could not be entirely hidden even by the covering that she wore.

They were Fujisawa Chiye and Meguchi. Both of them carried small objects that looked like sticks, but which were in reality something very highly prized by the Japanese—plum branches that would bloom out when put in water.

"Meguchi," asked Chiye suddenly, "do you think that Mitsu will have a vase to put the plum-blossoms in?"

"*Dogu!*" answered Meguchi, "poor Mitsu! I fear not."

"Then let us stop and buy a pretty bamboo vase for her," said Chiye.

The little shop where such things were kept for sale was near them. They turned aside, and, sitting down on the floor of the shop, asked the shop-keeper to show them some vases. There were a good many styles—some simply a hollow piece of bamboo, and some cut into quite elaborate patterns; some were painted, and some had Chinese characters written on them.

"Here is one with a pretty poem from the *Hiakuninishiu* on it," said Chiye. "Mitsu loves the *Hiakuninishiu*."

After a little bargaining the vase was bought, and Chiye and Meguchi went on, going all the while towards the castle.

There was a beautiful display of tea-cups, tea pots, and little dishes in the shops. This was the street for china.

Then they turned into the paper street, where all the merchants sold paper. These merchants sat by the *hibachis*, with their pipes, and called to the passers-by to examine their fine stock of paper. But Meguchi and Chiye kept on, and at last reached the house where Mitsu lived. They stood outside and called, "It is very cold."

An answer was heard from within, and a sour-visaged woman opened the door. She saluted them and bade them enter. The room was dark and gloomy. No pride was taken in keeping mats clean and woodwork polished, as in the Fujisawa mansion. There were no bright coals in the *hibachi*, and Meguchi shivered, while Chiye looked at things with contempt.

"Poor Mitsu, to have such a place to live in!" she thought.

Then she said aloud, "Where is Mitsu?"

There were several women in the room. One of them was ripping a dress, preparatory to washing it. She nodded in the direction of some slides, behind which Mitsu was supposed to be. Chiye and Meguchi, following this direction, went up to the slides, drew one of them open, and discovered Mitsu sitting on the floor in a dejected posture. She looked pleased to see Chiye and Meguchi.

The latter glanced hastily around the room. "Where is the little baby?" she said.

"*Dogu*," said Mitsu, her eyes filling with tears, "he is dead and finished. He died day before yesterday, and they took him away and buried him somewhere. Such a nice little boy, too!"

Meguchi sat down beside her and began to rub her—a Japanese way of giving consolation.

"*Dogu*," said Mitsu, "it is hard. The husband was very cruel, and he has not looked at me since. He drinks much *saké*, and is often angry. Oh, Meguchi, where is the mother? I wish I could go home."

Meguchi longed in her heart to take her home, but dared not. Chiye unwrapped the bamboo vase and showed it to Mitsu, with the plum branches. "They will come out in a few days," she said. "They are the first we have had, and we bought a vase with a poem written on it."

Mitsu found words to thank her young sister,

although her heart was so heavy. It is wonderful how fond the Japanese are of the plum-blossom. They are very poetical, and the unfolding of the buds has a deep significance to them. Possibly the blossoms may have reminded Mitsu of the little budding life of her baby.

"*Dogu!*" said Meguchi, "it was a darling little one. It is very sad, O Mitsu. But there is trouble at home. Aka weeps night and day. Her tears fall like the rain. Hana is very weak and sick, and the mother never leaves her. Her eyes are bad, and the doctor does her no good. A letter has come from Tama. She is always happy. Her little boy is well and strong, and the father-in-law and mother-in-law are very kind. Truly, Tama is fortunate."

Poor Mitsu! the tears gathered in her eyes; but just then a rough voice called her name, and she hurried away to perform some services for her mother-in-law, whom she was bound to obey, and who seized every opportunity of annoying her. Mitsu grieved and pined in this uncongenial home until she was a mere shadow of her former self. She longed to die, yet had no hope that death would bring her anything better.

The afternoon was turning bitterly cold. Meguchi and Chiye hurried home to get out of the cutting wind. The storm grew wilder and wilder. The storm-slides were all closed; yet the wind rattled them and pierced through the crevices.

.

Many an old woman and little child that night trembled for fear that their house might fall on them.

At midnight there came the dreaded cry, "Fire! fire!" All the bells in the city set up a terrible clanging, and all the people were roused.

Fujisawa, opening a slide in the upper room, saw a fierce red glare in the direction of the castle. He had listened apparently unmoved to the story that Meguchi and Chiye had to tell. The marriage was his work; he alone was to blame; and he was unwilling to acknowledge all its evil even to himself. But when he saw the wild light of the conflagration he thought of his child's danger, and hastily slipping on a warm garment, and calling Oto to follow with a lantern, he went out into the cold of the winter night.

Oh, how the wind blew, and how rapidly the flames spread! He had but a short distance to go before getting into the midst of the turmoil. People were running with mats, slides and household furniture, and big bundles of bedding and clothing. Beggars and coolies, merchants and soldiers, rich and poor, high and low, mingled in one mass of anxious, hurrying humanity. Parents and servants carried children on their backs. Sons carried their aged parents. There was no thought of anything save escape from the flames.

Strange to say, most of the people carried lanterns, although the light from the fire was sufficient for all purposes. The fire-gods were carried around and the firemen were all out. Oh, the wildness and confusion of one of these great fires in Tokio! It takes such a little while to burn down thousands of the frail wooden houses. Many of them have fire-proof structures, or go-downs, attached to them, where the people can store their goods until the fire is out, and during the progress of a fire men carry mud around, with which they plaster up all the cracks in the go-downs. This English word, which seems a misnomer as applied to the only buildings that do *not* "go down" before a fire, is a corruption of the Malay *gadong*, warehouse.

Fujisawa and his servant were advancing against the crowd, and had difficulty in making their way. At last, by going through the back streets, they reached the house where Chiye and Meguchi had seen Mitsu in the afternoon. It was still standing, but the people were preparing to leave. Fujisawa muffled his head, and in the confusion no one noticed him. He found himself surrounded by a group of frightened, screaming women, who in a great panic were trying to gather up some of their possessions; but he saw no Mitsu. He went through the outer room, and, going up to the slide, softly spoke her name. Tremblingly she opened the door, revealing to her father a pale, frightened girl.

"Mitsu," said the father, "come with me."

"Shall I take the clothing, father?" she asked.

"Bring some things, and come quickly."

Hastily she selected the articles that she most prized and made them up into a bundle. Fujisawa took her by the arm, and they slipped out of the house.

The wind had increased, and the confusion was terrible. The hot flames rolled on. Birds left their lodging-places in the trees and flew about terrified and screaming. Horses made a stampede, and dogs and cats joined in the wild flight. The temple bells were tolled and the drums were beaten. Fujisawa, still holding on to Mitsu, had to run with the others. Poor Mitsu soon felt her strength giving way and sank down at his side.

The servant came and offered Fujisawa the lantern, saying, "I can carry her on my back."

So Mitsu was lifted on to Oto's back, and on they went. No one else had paid any attention to the fainting girl. Every one was occupied with his own affairs. The tops of the palace trees were all on fire. Thickly the sparks flew, and children shrieked as the burning cinders fell about them. At last Fujisawa came near his own residence; Mitsu had recovered somewhat and was able to walk; the fire and crowd were left behind; and thus, at midnight, Fujisawa Mitsu was brought home.

The morning dawned on a scene of desolation.

The burned district covered a great portion of the central part of the city. Thousands were left homeless. But they went immediately to work, and before evening temporary shelter had been erected for many families.

Fujisawa Mitsu lay for days sick and helpless on her pallet, tended by old Meguchi, and Chiye and Kesa had to go to school by themselves.

It was the third day of the month, and Chiye and Kesa, with Fusa and Cho, two girls from the *yashiki*, had been enjoying the "feast of dolls." The dolls which had been in the Fujisawa family from time unknown were brought out and arranged in the usual order. The emperor and empress occupied the highest places, and the inferior dolls were placed below them. The girls had mild, sweet *saké* and candies. Chiye, as the eldest, did the honors. She had pretty spring hairpins in her hair; they were of crape, fashioned into flowers and butterflies. When the girls were tired of the dolls, they took their battledores and shuttlecocks and played in the garden. In this new springtime the garden was as lovely as ever. Never had iris or wistaria bloomed more beautifully; the grass never was smoother, the sun never was brighter, and the girls never were happier. With faces powdered, lips touched with *beni*, pretty dresses and bright sashes, they tossed the shuttlecocks gracefully and skilfully.

"The wind-god is good," said Fusa, Chiye's

friend; and they all sang that little song which Japanese children have sung for so many generations, praying that the wind might not blow too hard during the game of battledore and shuttlecock.

Mitsu and Hana watched them from the house. Poor Hana never could play with the children, but she accepted her sufferings patiently.

Kesa had permission to go with Meguchi to see the young visitors home. They bowed very politely to Mrs. Fujisawa when they went away and said that they had had a pleasant time.

As the girls went down the street they saw a flower-seller with pretty spring flowers on his stand, and stopped to look at the blossoms.

"Will you not condescend to buy some, my little ladies?" said the man.

Kesa asked to be allowed to carry Aka a flower, and Meguchi consented.

"But what is this?" they all asked, as they spied something new to them.

"*Dogu*, that is a foreign flower—the thorn-rose," said the man. The children looked longingly at it, but had not money enough to buy it, so they got a bunch of camellias and gave them to Aka, who smiled on Kesa, while her eyes filled with tears.

CHAPTER XIV.

SUNSET ON THE HAKONES.

WHILE Kesa was playing with the girls in Tokio, Saijiro was having a merry time with the boys on the Hakones.

It was a holiday, and the children had spent the whole afternoon in the temple inclosure. They played leap-frog, hide-and-seek, catching-the-devil, and fox-and-goose. Kojiro had clapped his hands and cheered as loudly as any of the boys, and even the old priest laughed as he watched the plays.

These mountain boys were fond of play, and Saijiro was one of the strongest, brightest, and merriest of them all. But he was also fonder of study than most of them, and his air indicated a superiority of birth and breeding which the villagers did not fail to recognize; to all, as to Yenoske, he was the "little master."

It was growing late, and the sun had already gone down behind the mountains. Yenoske had joined the group of boys who, tired of play, were resting on the temple steps.

"Let us tell stories," said Kojiro.

The boys agreed, and called upon Yenoske for the first.

"*Dogu*, what story do I know?" said Yenoske, rubbing his head.

But the boys insisted, and Yenoske began:

"Once upon a time there was a very wicked prince. He lived in the province of Hizen. He had a great castle and a great many retainers. These all carried swords and fought for the prince. Near the castle lived an old man who reverenced the fox-god and every morning offered sacrifices on his altar. The prince ridiculed the old man and his wife and would not worship the fox-god. Then the fox-god sent terrible dreams to the prince. Every night on *oni*, ten feet high, with only one eye, and wrapped in white, came to his bedside. The prince would shiver and shake in his bed and at last grew so thin and pale that every one noticed it.

"One day he went to the old man and began to talk with him.

"'Why do you take so much pains to worship the fox-god?' he said. 'You are poor; the crops are not good; your wife is sick.'

"Then the old man said, 'Why do you look so thin and pale? I know the fox-god is visiting you with his vengeance.'

"Then the prince grew paler still and wanted to kill the old man. But he went back to his house, and every night the demon grew larger and larger, and his one eye more and more terrible. At last the prince had a war with a neighboring prince. He was defeated and cut himself open. And every one said it was because he ridiculed the fox-god and the poor old man who prayed to him."

"Thanks, very great thanks, Yenoske," said the boys, who had listened with eyes and mouths wide open to this story of the demon.

"Now, Chintaro, it is your turn."

"I like Momotaro," said Chintaro, throwing himself down on the grass.

"He likes Momotaro because he was fat like himself," said the boys.

"I like him because he was good to his adopted parents," said the indignant Chintaro.

"Well, go on with your story," persisted the crowd.

So Chintaro told the well-known tale. "One day an old woman went down to the stream to wash. A great peach rolled down and the old woman took it home to her husband. 'Husband, here is a peach for you,' said she as she entered the house.

"'*Dogu*, what a large peach!' said the old man, who was feeble and lay on his couch.

"The old woman cut it into two pieces, and out rolled a baby. The baby grew to be a fine large boy and made his adopted parents very happy. But he read in a book of a demon who had great treasures beyond the sea. His parents were old and poor, and Momotaro wanted to get the treasure and make the old man and woman comfortable. So he bowed a *saionara* to them and went off. He had gone but a short distance when up came a dog, a bird, and an ape, who offered to help him. So they all got into a boat and went to the demon's home. The door was of wood, very heavy, and strongly bolted. But Momotaro and his three brave companions beat open the door, killed the demon, and got the treasures. So they all came home in a big sail-boat, with coral, gold, and clothes; and the old woman and the old man were comfortable and happy ever afterwards."

Chintaro turned a few somersaults and went on. "I like to hear about the thunder-god. My! would n't I like to help him beat his drum! And yesterday we read in school about the big turtle who carries the world on his back, and when he shakes himself we have an earthquake."

Then little Nanjiro was called upon for his story.

Giving two or three jumps for the benefit of the baby hanging on his back, he began: "Once there was a very bad girl. She cried when her hair was combed, and a little black demon went and sat on her head. She was angry because she had to sew, and demons pulled her work to pieces. She did n't want to go to school, and black demons pinched her legs. At last the demons pulled her out from her father's house and she had to go and live in a dark, bad place.

"There was another girl who was very good. She was patient while her hair was being dressed, and beautiful white fairies came and gave her lovely hairpins. She was diligent in school, and the fairies made beautiful flowers grow along her pathway. She worked long and diligently at her sewing, and the fairies gave her beautiful clothes, and at last she got a fine husband and a beautiful boy."

"Who cares to hear about girls?" said Chintaro contemptuously. "Mantaro, tell us about the old man who made the trees blossom."

So Mantaro told the story that the Japanese love so well, of the good old man who sprinkled ashes on the trees. The trees burst into beautiful blossoms, and the prince of the country, who was resting in the shade, came and rewarded the old man.

Then a bad old man tried to do the same thing, but he only succeeded in sprinkling ashes in the eyes of the prince and made him very angry.

Then Saijiro was called upon for his tale.

"Well," said he, "I will tell about a book I am reading with the honorable father. Once upon a time there was a man who wanted to travel. So he visited a great many kingdoms. One was the kingdom of Babyland. In it there lived a great number of very small people who had no teeth and no hair and who had to be carried about. And they spoke a strange language. It was 'goo-goo' and 'da-da' and 'mama.'"

"*Dogu!* Taijiki belongs to that country," said the boys, as they laughed heartily. Taijiki was Nanjiro's baby.

"Then," continued Saijiro, "he went into the kingdom of Avarice, where the people would not do anything unless they were paid. He had to go on some sort of a flying-machine, and got caught in a tree. He begged the people to take him down, but they only came and looked at him and said, 'Honorable sir, if you have money and can pay us, we will bring a ladder and help you down.'

"There is a picture of a man in a tree, with all the people looking at him. At last he took some money out of his sleeve, showed it to the people, and they let him come down.

"Then he went into the kingdom of Lying. He found a schoolhouse, and on it was a notice that the honorable teacher would teach lying on a certain day. The man went there on the appointed day, but there was no teacher. Only there was another notice, telling the scholars to come the next day. Every day he went, and every day there was the same notice posted up. At last he got very angry, found the man, and asked what he meant.

"'Honorable sir, do not be so angry,' said the

man; 'I advertised to teach lying, and that is the way I do it.'"

The boys thought Saijiro's stories very fine. They had never heard any of them before.

"Now Mejiki," they said, when they had discussed the various kingdoms.

Mejiki thought a moment, and said, "I have a new book which honorable father brought from Tokio. It was sent by my honorable uncle. In it is.a new story. Once there was an old man who had a terrible lump on the side of his face. One evening he went out to take a walk, and while he was walking the sun went down, and he lost his way. He did n't know what to do, and at last hid in the hollow of a tree. While he was there he heard a noise as of many people singing and talking. The old man peeped out of the tree and saw some imps coming down the road. At first he was much frightened.

"The imps stopped near the tree and made a fire. Then they began to dance. The old man was so pleased that at last he got out from the tree and began to dance too. The imps cheered and said, 'Old man, you dance well. We will take off your lump.' Then they took the old man's lump off, and he, very much pleased, went home without it.

"Now he had a neighbor who had a lump on his face. When he saw the cured old man, he thought he would go and see if the imps would n't take off his lump too. The good old man told him where to go; so he went and hid in the tree, and when the imps came he got out and danced. But the imps said, 'You do not dance well. Shame, old man, shame!' And they took the lump which the other man had had and clapped it on the other side of his face. So he went home with two lumps."

This was a new story to the boys, and they thought it very interesting.

Ginjiro thought up a new story too.

"The story of the wicked badger is in our book," he said. "There was no food in the land where the badgers and the foxes lived. Poor mother-fox was sorry for baby-fox, who cried with hunger. Then said wicked Mr. Badger, 'Mother-fox, I will pretend to be dead, and you can take me to the town and sell me; and when you get the money I will run away!' So mother-fox took the badger to town and sold him. She got the money and bought some food. The badger ran home, and for a time they had plenty to eat. But at last the food was all gone. Then said the badger, 'Mother-fox, it is your turn. You must pretend to be dead, and I will carry you to town.' So mother-fox pretended to be dead, and Mr. Badger carried her to town and sold her. But to the man who bought her he said, 'Take care; that fox is not dead; she is only pretending. Then the man took a club and struck her on the head and killed her. So Mr. Badger had all the money. He bought food and ate it all himself, while baby-fox looked on and cried. At last baby-fox grew up. He was determined to be revenged. So he made the badger change himself into a man and go and bow before the prince. But the prince cried out, 'A badger! a badger!' and ordered the servants to kill him. The baby-fox stood behind a tree and laughed."

There was no one but little Kojiro left to tell a story now, and the air was growing chilly.

"Boys, you had better go home," said an old priest who had been standing near and listening.

"Let Ko tell something first," begged the children.

"I will tell what Saijiro told me," said Ko, drawing close to his friend. "There was once a boy in China named Tsu Loo. He had to go fifty miles to get rice for his parents. But he went cheerfully and never minded the hard work. And afterwards, when he grew up and became rich and honored, he was not so happy as when he was poor and worked for his parents.

"There was another boy whose name was Keang Kih. He lived alone with his mother and was very kind and good to her. A time of trouble arose in the province, and he ran away, carrying his mother on his back. He was very much afraid of meeting robbers, and at last did meet them. They were about to rob him, but when they saw how kind he was to his mother they let him go.

"There was another boy whose father and mother died when he was very young. When he grew older he grieved all the time because he could do nothing for his parents. So he made two wooden images, one of his father and one of his mother, and served them."

The boys all liked Ko's stories. But the darkness was falling over Yamamidzu. Nanjiro had long ago taken the baby home, and all the other boys were ready for their suppers. Saijiro ran over the bridge. His father had eaten his evening meal, and the boy swallowed his rice in silence and went to bed.

CHAPTER XV.

THE GOOD DOCTOR.

The silence of a summer midnight rested over Tokio. It was not dark. The moon rode high in the heavens, and there were lights scattered here and there over the city. Far out in the bay fishermen's torches could be seen, and lamps gleamed from lighthouses and watch-towers. The mosquitoes were holding high festival. Now that most of the people were asleep, it was their time.

But there is never an hour when every one in a great city is asleep; and in Tokio that night there were many who rested not. There were priests in the temples tending the sacred altars, beating the sacred drums, and praying to their idols. There were wicked men abroad, thieves, robbers, would-be murderers, lurking around in the darkest streets and trying to avoid the watchmen, who, striking their staves with bells heavily on the ground, gave evil-doers a chance to escape if they were so inclined. The low haunts of sin and vice were open. Men were drinking, gambling, and committing deeds of shame which they dared do only under cover of the night. There were sick people turning restlessly upon their pallets, and men and women whose hearts were too full of cares and anxieties to sleep.

In one of the mission-houses in the Foreign Concession a light was still burning in the room of a missionary, a man on whose heart rested the burden of human souls. He was bowed in prayer before God in the midst of a great heathen city.

In Fujisawa's house in the Kudan most of the family were sleeping under the great green nets which Japanese use to protect themselves from mosquitoes. Fujisawa himself had gone to the upper room. Mitsu, Chiye, and Kesa had their *futons* under one net in a large room down stairs. Kesa slept quietly between her two sisters. The servants occupied apartments at one end of the large house. The slides were closed, the lamps burned dimly, the busy bustle of the day was over. But through the house, every few moments, there resounded a low cry, a cry of pain, which was immediately followed by tones of soothing tenderness in another voice, the voice of a mother trying to comfort her suffering child.

Before the altar in Mrs. Fujisawa's room candles were burning brightly in tall polished candlesticks. Fresh flowers, fruits, and vegetables were set out on lacquered tables for the gods. On a little writing-table near by were books which the good woman had been reading. They were books of Buddhist doctrines, teaching absorption into the divine essence, the heavenly contemplations, the migrations of the soul—all the vague mysteries of Buddhism. There was the book, too, which Mrs. Fujisawa loved best—a story of the sixteen disciples of Shaka Sama, their devout lives, their peaceful deaths. From this book she often read to Hana, thus quieting her pain.

But now she sat by Hana's side, rubbing her aching limbs, bathing her head, holding her hot, restless hands, and soothing the tired little heart with comforting and loving words.

"Ah," says the Japanese proverb, "mother-love is high as the mountain and deep as the sea."

For thirteen years Mrs. Fujisawa had thus tended this suffering child. Now the disease dreaded most by the Japanese—the *kaké*—had taken strong hold of her, a disease which, beginning in the feet, creeps gradually up to the heart—a slow, sure death. There is no escape, no doubt of the end. Mrs. Fujisawa knew that her little flower was withering fast out of her sight.

"Honorable mother," said Hana, "the doctor says I have *kaké*. If so, I must die."

"*Dogu!* yes, my darling."

"I want to be with the gods in paradise, but I do not want to leave you, *kachan*, nor Mitsu nor Chiye nor Kesa nor the honorable father. I do not know whether I could see you again; and oh, *kachan*, I have thought and thought, but I do not know whether any of the gods love me. I have said Shaka Sama's name over and over so many times, and yet he does not help. *Kachan, kachan*, who can tell me?"

Poor mother! All of her Buddhist books have not told her of love, nor whether dear ones that part in such agony here will meet again in heaven. She cannot help her darling as she sees her drawing near to the shadow of death.

The flickering candles lighted up the golden faces of the gods. There they sat in solemn state amid the lights and flowers, Benten Sama, Yebisu, Daikoku, the beautiful image of Buddha—Hana could look into their faces; kindly, benevolent faces they were, sweet and compassionate in their expression. Surely there was nothing to be feared from them! Surely they would look mercifully upon a child's soul going alone into the dread unknown! Yet the child was unsatisfied, and the mother, who would gladly have given her life for her, was unable to comfort her.

"*Dogu*, darling," she said, "to-morrow we will go to Asaxa to Bindzuru's most holy shrine. You shall pass your hands over his honorable body, and perhaps he will give you rest. We will pray again and again. But, *dogu!* daughter, what the gods will is best. Oh, sleep now, my darling; sleep, sleep."

She lay down beside Hana and sang one of the songs of Old Japan, a song of blossoms and waving trees. The child listened and was soothed. At last both slept.

"I shall take Hana to Asaxa to-day," announced the mother to the family at breakfast.

"Please take me, too," begged Kesa. "It is a holiday, *kachan;* I don't have to go to school."

"*Dogu,* Kesa, you are so rough and noisy; you trouble Hana."

"I will be quiet, honorable mother."

Mrs. Fujisawa sent the servant to order jinrikishas. "Bring old Sankichi," she said.

The man came and prostrated himself before her while she gave her orders.

"Sankichi, I want to take my sick child to Asaxa. Can you take her gently, so that she will not be jarred?"

"I will be very careful, honorable mistress," answered the man.

"Then bring two jinrikishas. Mitsu and Kesa will go with us."

Hana was dressed and carefully wrapped in blankets and lifted into the cart; Mrs. Fujisawa got in beside her; Mitsu and Kesa occupied the other jinrikisha: Chiye went to see her friend Fusa, and the house was left almost as still as it was at the midnight hour.

The coolies drew the carts slowly through the streets. They left the quiet of the Kudan and came out upon the broad Tori, the principal business street of Tokio, and a part of the same great national road along which Yenoske, Saijiro, and the teacher went so often in their journeyings to and fro on the Hakones.

"See, Hana," said the mother, "these houses are like those of the honorable foreigners, with doors and windows."

The child raised her eyes wearily to look at the new houses. Just then a coach passed them filled with Englishmen, and on the sidewalk were a foreign lady and gentleman and a little girl, who wore a white hat trimmed with blue ribbons.

"Oh, Mitsu," said Kesa, delighted, "see the little girl! How I wish I knew her."

"It is the same one we saw at the honorable foreigners' house the day we passed in the boat," said Mitsu. "I have heard of them. They are called Jesus-teachers. They do not believe in our Shaka Sama."

"Chiye and I do not care for Shaka Sama."

"Oh, Kesa," said Mitsu, "you and Chiye must not talk together about the gods. You will grieve the honorable mother and make the honorable father very angry."

"But," persisted Kesa, "the other day old Daikoku Sama fell down and broke his nose, and had to go and get mended. I don't think the gods can help us when they can't help themselves."

Mitsu sighed, but could not answer.

THE GOOD DOCTOR. 173

Just then they were crossing Nippon bridge, the most wonderful bridge of all Japan; for it is the centre of Japan, and, consequently, the centre of the world. From it all distances are reckoned in the empire.

"A long while ago," said Mitsu to Kesa, "there were edicts written on boards which were nailed up here. They said that any one who listened to the Jesus-teachers, and believed in their doctrines, should be put to death."

"I am glad they are not there now," said Kesa, "for I like the Jesus-teachers."

"You do not know anything about them, Kesa," Mitsu said severely.

On went the coolies through the crowded city streets, until at last they came up to the temple. There are always people going to worship there, and when Mrs. Fujisawa and her children got out of their jinrikishas at the gate, they found themselves in a crowd of gayly dressed people who carried new summer umbrellas. It was a holiday. One of the gods was to be carried out in his car. Poor Hana could scarcely walk. Her mother and Mitsu carefully assisted her up the steps, while Kesa danced on ahead.

"Be reverent, my daughter," said Mrs. Fujisawa. "You will anger the great god Bindzuru, and Hana will get no help."

So Kesa stopped her dancing, and worshipped with the others before entering the temple. The old wooden statue of Bindzuru stood near the door. His nose and ears were almost gone and his eyes could scarcely be seen. All of his body was worn smooth by the rubbing of thousands of afflicted ones. "For," said the people, "whatever part of your body is pained, rub the corresponding member of the god's body, and help will come."

Hana and her mother approached the idol and waited for their turn. Another mother stood there with her blind baby. She folded its little hands, made it bow its little head, then guided its tiny fingers to the eyes of the image. A lame man rubbed the god's feet. A weeping woman besought Bindzuru for some loved sufferer at home. Hana's turn came at last. There was something strangely spiritual in her looks. All her faith in the gods had returned. She had come for help and was sure of getting it. With a rapt expression on her face she passed her trembling hand over Bindzuru's body.

"Truly, very sick," murmured the bystanders, nodding to one another as they noted her pale face and wasted form. They saw her lifted, almost fainting, into the jinrikisha. "It is too late," they said.

Mitsu and Kesa took their places. The coolies lifted the shafts and waited respectfully for directions.

"We will go and see Kei," said Mrs. Fujisawa. "Nippon Boshu," i. e. bridge, "first street to the right, number 48."

When the coolies called, "*O tano moshimasu,*"—"I call!" the polite way of announcing one's arrival on a visit—old Kei pushed aside the slides. Seeing who her visitors were, her face beamed with delight.

"Truly, welcome," she said. "A great surprise! Come in."

Hana was laid carefully on a *futon* to rest. The others sat on the floor. Tea was brought, fans were handed round, many compliments were exchanged.

Now Kei had just found a wonderful book. She had been absorbed in it when her visitors arrived, and had laid it down beside the *hibachi*. Her spectacles were still between the pages, and the place they marked read thus:

"And at even, when the sun did set, they brought unto him all that were diseased and them that were possessed with devils. And all the city was gathered together at the door. And he healed many that were sick of divers diseases."

Mrs. Fujisawa saw the book and asked what it was.

"*Dogu,*" said Kei, "it is one of the Jesus-teachers' books."

Mrs. Fujisawa looked shocked. "But the Jesus-teachers instruct their pupils to give up all worship of our gods. How can they be right?"

Kei answered, "*Dogu*, I don't know. But it is the most interesting book I ever read. I have heard how this Jesus, with the Father, God, made the world."

"But," said Mitsu, "we know already how the gods made Japan. What does it matter how the Christians' country was made?"

"It tells some wonderful things about the Jesus-God," persisted Kei. "He could open the eyes of the blind and make the lame walk."

"Shaka Sama did far more wonderful things," said Mrs. Fujisawa. "I have heard how the God of the Christians walked on the water; but Daruma Sama came over from China on a leaf. Hotei Sama floats on the water on his rice pouch. I cannot see but that our gods do just as wonderful things as the God of the Christians."

"*Dogu*," answered Kei, "I don't know about that. I never saw a book like this before, and I mean to read it. The honorable foreign doctor has great skill and good medicines; why don't you take Hana to him?"

"I fear," was the gentle answer, "that no one can do good who despises Shaka Sama and his teachings."

Here the conversation ended. The guests drank more tea and then went home.

Hana grew worse rather than better, and her faith in Bindzuru was sorely tried.

"Take the child to the foreign doctor in the

Concession," said Fujisawa to his wife as one day Hana's low moans reached his ears. Poor Mrs. Fujisawa! It was her last hope. Both mother and child shrank from the Christians and from all knowledge of the Christians' God. But, oh! to have her darling's life spared! So it happened that, one June afternoon, among the many others who crowded the good doctor's dispensary in the mission, Mrs. Fujisawa and Hana awaited their turn and the doctor's decision.

Does any life lived upon earth come nearer to that which the Lord Jesus lived than that of the missionary doctor? Surely, the people crowding about the door of the house where the Saviour tarried in Capernaum were like these who, on that summer afternoon in Japan, waited for the word and touch of his disciple. There were blind and lame and withered. There were those covered with loathsome sores and those grievously tormented with pain. The doctor went from one to another, administering remedies and speaking kindly words. He stood, at last, before Hana and her mother.

"What is it that you want, my good woman?" he asked.

The mother lifted her eyes to that friendly face and was reassured by what she saw there. "My little daughter has been sick and we fear that she will die; and we do not know where her spirit will go. She is afraid. We have heard of your skill and have come to ask you to save her life."

The doctor looked into Hana's worn face, felt her feeble pulse, examined her swollen limbs. The dire disease was there and slowly creeping upward to her heart. All of his skill would avail nothing. His heart yearned over the child, shrinking back even now from the darkness, the uncertainty of death; over the mother, dreading to see her child go into it without her. He bent over Hana as if to examine more closely. In reality he was seeking for some words to meet the need of child and mother. The stillness of the room was broken only by the "swish, swish" of waves against the breakwater and by the soft sighing of the summer wind.

"Do you see the picture on the wall, my child?" asked the doctor at last.

It was a picture of a shepherd leading his flock. In his arms he carried a tender lamb.

"Is it the Jesus-God of the Christians?" asked Mrs. Fujisawa.

"No," answered the doctor, "it is only a shepherd. But the Lord Jesus says that he is like a shepherd. He loves children as a shepherd loves his lambs. He holds them in his arms. He carries them in his bosom."

To the darkened souls who heard the doctor's words this Jesus-God was only one of many gods. But "loves," "holds," "carries;" not one of the Buddhas, not one of the gods of Japan, ever spoke such words as these. The three little words were like three little seeds dropped into Hana's heart. But it was long ere they found strength to germinate. Always, however, she bore in her memory the picture of the shepherd leading his lambs. Her extreme dread of the foreigners was gone from that time.

"But can you help my child, honorable doctor?" inquired the mother anxiously.

"I think I can give her some medicine which will relieve her pain, my good woman. And you must come again."

Kesa was watching for them when they returned home. She was eager to hear what they had seen and what they had done. Had they seen the little foreign girl? Hana was too weary to answer questions, and the mother was never communicative. So Kesa's curiosity remained ungratified.

CHAPTER XVI.

THE STORM IN THE MOUNTAINS.

JUST beyond the Hakones, near the town of Shidzuoka, where the ex-Shogun lives, lies the Oyama range. Within its dark recesses, so say the people, dwells a dread deity whose anger must be appeased by most solemn and mysterious rites, who grants forgiveness to those only who perform severe penances. One sultry July morning, not long after the day on which Hana and her mother visited the missionary doctor, some men were dragging a heavy cart up one of the steepest of the Oyama passes.

There was scarcely a breath of air on the mountain. The leaves were drooping on the trees; flowers and grasses hung their heads. The perspiration stood in great drops on the men's bodies; but they did not stop either for rest or for refreshment. They went on, on with that weary load, deeper and deeper into the heart of the mountain. Climbing, they chanted a wild song, often calling upon the name of the god and striking their breasts. Their breasts were bruised and sore, their feet torn and bleeding, their faces pale and distorted with the violence of their worship. Their hands were cut by the cart-rope.

THE STORM IN THE MOUNTAINS. 181

Never a word spoke they to each other. Over and over again they chanted their prayer.

First of all, bearing the chief weight of the burden, went Yetaro, the Yamamidzu schoolteacher, Saijiro's father. How he panted! Frequently a terrible cough racked his frame. But he did not falter. He was trying his last chance for favor with the gods of Japan. This failing, he had nothing left. At last, however, the weary chanters paused for an instant. But it was only to listen for something. Faintly, from afar off, came mingled sounds as of drums, of gongs, of human cries.

"We near the temple," said one. "At noon we shall worship there."

"Take courage, brother," said a second.

"The great Buddha be praised!" chimed in a third.

The temple which the new-comers gained at last was small. The densest shade, unbroken by a single ray of sunshine, was all around it. Never a ray of hope had entered the hearts of those who worshipped there. Never a traveller had descended that mountain with new peace in his heart. It was an altar of despair, a place of gloom and of the shadow of death.

Up came the weary wretches with their cart before the gate. A priest advanced to meet them and all prostrated themselves.

"It is well, O friends," said the priest. "You

have drawn the sacred car up the mountain. Enter and pray."

Yetaro let go the rope. A sickening sense of exhaustion and of utter misery rushed over his spirit, a loathing of life and of the rites of Buddhism. But he struggled through the gate and went to a fountain to bathe before entering the temple. How terribly oppressive the air was! How difficult for those failing lungs to do their work! How hard for the faltering heart to find strength to worship! Yetaro's heart and flesh were failing. He entered the temple and prostrated himself before the altar. Poor feet, cut and torn! Poor hands, bruised and wounded! Poor heart, broken and without hope! There he lay before the idols, the grim, ugly, unforgiving idols. He had come there, but now he found no words to call upon the god, no strength to beat the drums or sound the gongs. The din around him increased with the ardor of the worshippers.

"Beat the drums!" called the priests. "Shout the name of the god. Call upon him; he is away. Call, call, call!"

But Yetaro heard it all dimly, as at a distance; it seemed to him only an empty, frightful din. A sad hopelessness had seized him. In his weakness there came a thought of his boy playing happily in peaceful Yamamidzu, a thought of the time when Kochi had gone in and out before him, with his bright, merry baby on her back. Then came a memory of sweet running water in his village home and of the lilies Saijiro loved so well, but never a thought of the god before whose shrine he lay. It was all over for Yetaro; the weary pilgrimage of the years was finished; the crying to Japan's gods for mercy would be heard from his lips no more.

While the priests and people chanted the praise of this god a severe storm burst over the temple. Yetaro joined not in the song, but in a lull of the rain went away from the temple with the sound of the chant ringing in his ears. With difficulty he made his way back to the main road. The rain poured down upon him, wetting him to the skin. Little streams swollen into torrents tried to turn him back. He waded through them down, down, away from the terrible mountain to the great highway. He would look upon his boy's face once more and die.

At sunset that evening Yetaro sat at a little wayside tea-house just where the mountain road meets the Tokaido, the great highway between Tokio and Kioto. The heavy clouds had rolled over and were broken into great fleecy masses of white, with borders of gold and tinged with sunset colors, pinks, purples, and blues. The setting sun threw long rays of light over the landscape. Yetaro sat on a bench drinking a cup of tea. For days he had eaten little and was well nigh exhausted. Lifting up his eyes he saw a man coming from the Hakones, a traveller like himself. Yetaro arose and they bowed down to the ground.

"From what place are you?" asked Yetaro.

"Thanks," answered the man, "I have come from Tokio."

"Are you going up to the mountain to pray?" asked the teacher.

"No," answered the stranger, "I worship the idols no more. I have heard the Jesus-teachers, and I want to believe as they do. I do not understand very well, but I have a book from which I read. I am going back to Tokio to learn more." He drew from one of his big sleeves a copy of the Gospel of Mark, Kei's beloved volume.

"*Dogu!*" said Yetaro. "Does it tell about a man who hung on the cross?"

"Yes," answered the traveller; "I will find you the place."

So in the fading light Yetaro and the stranger read together Mark's story of the crucifixion.

"Do you know why he hung there?" asked Yetaro when they could see no more.

"*Dogu!*" answered the man, "I cannot tell very well, but the teacher said it was because we have all sinned, and he bore our punishment."

A great joy shot through Yetaro's heart. His resolution was taken. He would go to Tokio and find the Jesus-teacher, and Saijiro should go with him.

Late the next afternoon Yetaro came into the

village, where Saijiro was having a merry game with the boys. There was a new teacher from Tokio at the Yamamidzu school, and the instruction was no longer confined to the Chinese classics; the boys and girls were taught something besides these. The teacher, dressed partly in foreign style, sat by a table, while his books were neatly arranged in a bookcase instead of being piled up on the floor. The schoolhouse itself had been repaired. There were clean mats on the floor and the roof no longer leaked. There was a blackboard in the hall, and the pupils learned the Japanese syllabary and Chinese characters from that. The girls were delighted with the charts, from which they had object lessons. Even blind Ko's hands were guided around the great globe, as he with the others learned the shape of the world and the relative positions of the countries. Graded readers had been introduced with interesting stories in them; and the pupils learned of Washington, Napoleon, and other noted characters. The Japanese Government had determined that all the people should be instructed in the new sciences.

Saijiro stopped playing when he saw his father and saluted him, bowing down to the ground.

"You will come home with me, my son," said Yetaro; and together they crossed the little swinging bridge.

The boy, eager to prepare the evening rice for

his father, walked on without asking any question as to his journey.

"Saijiro," said the father at last, "in two days you will be ready to go with me to Tokio."

Much astonished as Saijiro was, he merely bowed his head. The father continued his directions. "We will shut up the house and carry what clothing we can with us."

"Shall we be long away, honorable father?" asked Saijiro.

"A very long time, my son. I shall come back no more, and you will remain with the honorable foreigners."

That evening Yenoske learned the teacher's intention of leaving Yamamidzu and going to Tokio. His heart was heavy at the thought, and he stood for a long while in the starlight, leaning against the side of the house and thinking over a plan he had in his mind. At last he went in, and finding his aged father and mother sitting on their mats smoking pipes preparatory to retiring, he said as he prostrated himself before them,

"Honorable parents, the *sensei* and the little master go to-morrow to Tokio. The *sensei* is very ill, and will die and leave the little master alone in the great city. *Dogu!* I crave your honorable permission to go with them. I cannot let them go alone."

"*Dogu! dogu!*" said the old man and the old woman together. "We can ill spare you, Yenoske. Who will take care of us and manage the business?"

"*Dogu*, honorable parents, how can the *sensei* and the child go alone?" questioned Yenoske in his turn.

"It is true," said the father; "as you please, my son. You will return to us by-and-by. Reverence the gods."

"Thanks; a great thank-you," answered Yenoske. "May you rest well, honorable parents. Good night."

CHAPTER XVII.

FROM YAMAMIDZU TO TOKIO.

VERY early in the morning of the second day after the teacher returned to Yamamidzu Yenoske pushed aside the slide of his parents' house; passing softly out, he went to the shed where the horse was chewing a bit of rice straw, and stood for a moment with his arm thrown lightly over the animal's neck.

There was something wonderfully alike in the pair. Yenoske was patient, so was the horse; Yenoske often went hungry, so did the horse; Yenoske asked no questions, neither did the horse. Many and many a mile had they travelled together through summer heat and winter cold, treading rough, toilsome ways and bearing heavy burdens without murmur or complaint. Yenoske's heart was too loyal to allow him to part from his faithful friend without regret. He stroked the animal's mane, looked into his eyes, and then, leaving an extra supply of rice straw where he could get it, turned away and went towards the house.

Strong as was his love for the mountains, for father, mother, and home, he had a yet stronger passion, and that was his love for Saijiro. The boy was his darling, his heart's desire, and his little master. Yenoske had always obeyed every command of the child, carrying him on his back, climbing precipices for lilies, and wading into deep streams for lotus flowers and bulbs. When he left home his last thought was for "Saichan." During his journeys everything that could interest or please the child was stored away in his memory to be related on his return. There was always something for Saijiro stored away in his sleeves or in the bosom of his dress.

This morning Yenoske had his head bound with a blue 'kerchief, and in one hand he carried a broad-brimmed hat. He wore a loose robe pulled up above his knees. He was all ready for his journey. Just as he reached the house the slides were pushed open, and his mother, who had evidently just arisen from her bed, stood before him. Yenoske saluted her.

"Get ready quickly, honorable mother. I hear the little master coming, and it is time to start."

Saijiro had come across the bridge, and Yenoske could hear the sound of his wooden clogs as he came rapidly up the village street.

"Is the honorable father all ready, Saijiro?" asked Yenoske.

"He will meet us at the bridge."

In a few minutes Yenoske, accompanied by his parents, turned away from the hotel and went to the bridge, where they found the teacher waiting for them. It was growing lighter, and they could just see the outlines of the house where Yetaro had lived so long, where Saijiro had spent his childhood, and where Kochi had died. Yetaro gave one backward glance as they stood there, and the little company moved on.

As they passed the temple little Ko joined them. He had been waiting long for Saijiro, and now ran to him and took hold of his hands, sobbing with grief at the thought of losing him.

"Don't cry, Ko. I will come back again and tell you such beautiful stories of what I see in the city," said Saijiro.

"Tell me about the beautiful gods you see, Saijiro; and if you should go to the great Buddha's image which the *bon-sama* has told me about, think of me and tell me about it."

They were going up a narrow mountain path. Yamamidzu lies down on the side of the mountain, so they had to go up some distance before reaching the Tokaido, or great East-Sea-Road, which leads down into the town. The road was steep and slippery, and only the great stones kept them from sliding at every step. Brighter and brighter grew the morning, until at last up came the sun over the mountain, and all the flowers woke to beauty and all the birds to song. Then the inn-keeper and his wife and Yenoske saluted the sun, rubbed their hands, bowed their heads, and prayed. The warm beams poured down over their heads and filled the valley with light. But the sun listened not to their prayers.

Yetaro did not worship, and Saijiro, watching his father, likewise remained silent; but Ko's worship came from the depths of his little heart as he turned his face upwards as though to receive a blessing.

At last they came to the main road and the time of parting. It was a beautiful spot. Just where the two ways met was a waterfall, and directly in front of the waterfall a lovely glade, with rocks and trees and clinging vines. A summer-house was there, and in the summer-house were two ladies, evidently from the city. They were admiring the scenery.

"Beautiful, truly beautiful!" said one.

"For the first time," said the other.

The ladies had on plaid sashes and trailing dresses. They looked curiously at the little party from the village, and covered their mouths with their sleeves as they passed. Their coolies were on the road opposite the tea-house eating their morning rice.

It was in this place near the tea-house that the Yamamidzu friends separated.

"Farewell, *sensei*," said the innkeeper and his wife to Yetaro; and "Farewell, little master," to Saijiro.

Ko's tears were falling again, and he clung to Saijiro.

The old woman wept much when she bade farewell to her son, and even his father wiped his eyes.

"*Saionara;* you have been a good son, Yenoske. Take care of the honorable *sensei* and the little master," said his mother.

"*Saionara*, my son; do n't forget to worship," said the father.

"Be good to Ko, Baba," urged Saijiro, the tears gathering in his eyes.

Down upon the ground they all fell, saying their last farewells and parting with real sorrow. Then, taking little Ko, Yenoske's parents went back to their village. The others, lifting upon their shoulders the sticks to which their bundles were tied, went on under great overhanging trees down towards Odawara. A grand old highway, that, between the two capitals of Japan! Over it the *daimios* used to pass with their trains in the days of old Japan. The Dutch passed along it on their yearly visits to the Shogun's capital.

The morning being so lovely, our travellers went on cosily enough. Yetaro was feeling better, and talked to Saijiro as they walked. Perhaps you would not have guessed that the guttural sound issuing from Yenoske's throat was singing. Yet he was considered a good singer in Yamamidzu. He knew the words of all the best Japanese songs.

The sun grew hotter and hotter. Yetaro's strength was easily exhausted, and at an early hour they stopped for their nooning. A clear little brook flowed by the roadside. They took their blue 'kerchiefs, dipped them in the brook, and wiped faces, hands, and chests. Then stooping down they drank. Seating themselves under a tree, Yenoske opened a box and took out rice and *daikon*. This, with some tea bought from a teahouse near by, was their frugal meal. The spot could not have been more lovely. The trees formed a roof thick enough to protect them from the sun. Soft moss made a couch better than any to which they had been accustomed. The brook ran close by, and all around were flowers and vines. The music of a waterfall sounded in their ears. There were katydids, grasshoppers, and tree-toads about them, but nothing hurtful.

Almost hidden from our travellers by a turn in the road was a little thatched cottage. Near it the brook suddenly widened. Some women were standing in the water washing clothes. Their voices could be heard through the sounds of dipping and pounding. One could almost distinguish what was said. Yenoske and the teacher lay upon the ground resting and smoking their pipes. Saijiro amused himself by watching the women and turning occasional glances upward at the fleecy clouds.

But at last the women finished their washing

and carried the clean clothes away in tubs to the cottage. Some men passed by on their way up the mountain. A fine lady went by on a litter. A traveller, like our Yamamidzu people, appeared and saluted them. He asked where they were going.

"Thanks; we are on our way to Tokio."

"Ah," returned the stranger, "I am just from Tokio. Do you go to see the sights or to pray at one of the shrines?"

Yetaro answered, "No; we are going to look for the Jesus-teachers and find out about one of their gods, one who died upon a cross."

The stranger had heard of the Jesus-teachers, he said. "But I have never listened to their teachings. The old way is good enough for me."

The day was passing. Yetaro and his companions rose to continue their journey. The afternoon grew hot; the way was steep and wearisome. Early in the evening they reached Odawara and went to a hotel. There the occupants were already preparing for the night. As usual, the large gloomy kitchen was in front. Servants were busy boiling rice, cutting *daikons*, frying fish, making tea, and doing a thousand other things. Girls, carrying trays, rice-bowls, and teapots, were hurrying from the kitchen to the upper story, where guests were assembled. Every now and then was heard a loud clapping of hands from the guests, followed by a prolonged "*Hai!*" from the kitchen. There was a splashing of water in a large tank where travellers availed themselves of the luxury of a hot bath. In another apartment blind shampooers were hard at work rubbing and pounding tired travellers.

After seeing that Yetaro and the boy had a room and some refreshments, Yenoske went off with the servants. Candles were brought, green nets were hung, *futons* and pillows were provided, and Yetaro and Saijiro lay down side by side.

Yenoske woke first. "Come," he said, lightly touching the sleeping boy, "it is time to get up and make ready for the journey. Get water for the honorable father and then bring rice and tea."

Saijiro rubbed his eyes. He had forgotten that they were in Odawara. He jumped up and hurried out into the courtyard of the hotel. Early as it was, most of the coolies had gone—some to carry *kagos* up the mountain, some to drag jinrikishas along the great highway, and others still to lead pack-horses up the narrow passes, or themselves, transformed into mere beasts of burden, to bear heavy loads.

The day was sultry. Not a breath of air came from land or sea. Saijiro bathed himself at a fountain, and then begged a basin in which to carry water to his father. A girl gave him one, and also a blue cotton towel.

Yetaro was up when Saijiro reëntered their chamber.

The servants brought rice and tea, and Yetaro and Saijiro ate breakfast.

"Honorable *sensei*," said Yenoske, stepping just inside the room and stooping in a reverential manner, "shall you take a jinrikisha? *Dogu*, the way is long, and you are weak!"

The teacher shook his head.

A few minutes later they started on their journey, still going toward the East Sea and the great city Tokio. Yenoske had spoken truly. It was a long way and a weary one. The sun poured his fiercest rays upon their unsheltered heads; the sand of the road burned and blistered their feet. Not a tree along the highway for shade and coolness; not a green field to invite them to rest and refreshment. There were few travellers. Once a party of pilgrims passed on their way to Mt. Fuji. Yetaro shuddered when he saw them.

"It is all of no use, my boy," he gasped, as he saw Saijiro looking earnestly at the men in their white dresses. "I have done it, and I know no peace."

Once Yenoske urged him to go and rest in a temple inclosure; but Yetaro would not enter.

"I have done it all," he reiterated. "I am on my way to the Jesus-teachers."

At noon they came to a quiet river rippling

brightly along on its golden sands. Yenoske went to find a boat, leaving Saijiro with his father. The teacher looked very white. Indeed, Yenoske had gone but a few steps when Saijiro was calling after him: "Oh, Yenoske! what is the matter with the honorable father?"

Yetaro had fainted. Yenoske brought water quickly, and, some men coming up, he was lifted into a boat that had just arrived. The rest, the cool breeze, and some rice procured on the other side of the river revived the dying man. Slowly, slowly they went along the Tokaido, and in the evening they came to a little town where Yenoske said they must remain a while.

"To-morrow night," murmured Yetaro, "we shall be in Tokio."

The little village at which they had stopped stood in the midst of some rice-fields. The Hakones were scarcely visible; but all around were foot-hills, green as emeralds and covered with trees, maples, cedars, and pines. Around one of these hills, the one nearest the hotel, wound a beautiful stream. Flowers bloomed in the hotel garden. The air was cool and pleasant. How different it was from crowded, noisy Odawara!

"Oh, honorable father, isn't it nice!" said Saijiro, as they sat at the open slides of an upper room eating their supper.

The sun had gone down, and the soft evening light gave the landscape a red tinge. Saijiro had never before seen rice-fields when the grain was ripening. His eyes were delighted with the rich green.

When Yetaro lay resting under the mosquito-net, Saijiro and Yenoske stole out for a walk over the fields. One of the hotel girls offered to accompany them. The three went together over a narrow path leading through the rice-paddies. The ground was very wet, and frogs were trying to see which one of them could make the most noise. The girl suggested that they should go to see the waterfall. Already the boys could hear the sound of it. Yenoske's heart gave a great bound. It was like home, his home in the Hakones. But Saijiro looked rather contemptuously at the baby waterfall, scarcely higher than his head.

"Do you call that a waterfall?" said he. "Why, in our country we can't see up to the heights from which the water tumbles."

"And where," asked the girl, "may your honorable country be?"

"*Dogu!* it is in the Hakones. We are going to Tokio to find the Jesus-teachers. The honorable father wants to learn their doctrine."

"Two of the Jesus-teachers stopped here seven days ago," the girl said. "They were on their way to the Hakones. They told us about one God, and sang some songs about him and a happy land. But the song said that the land was far, far away, and I do not know where it can be. I like this country well enough."

The speaker was dressed in a blue calico. Her sleeves were tied up, that she might not be impeded in her work. She had a round, rosy face and well-developed limbs. She leaned against the hillside, while Saijiro lay at her feet looking at the rice-fields. Yenoske sat by the little waterfall. He loved its music. Ts'koi lay curled up in a heap near his master. Smoke, tinged with the sunset red, rose from different parts of the rice-paddies. Thatched cottages of farmers made the scene more picturesque.

The last day's journey was over rice-fields and under shady trees, until they came to the lower land near the sea and the great plain on which Tokio lies. There was no smoke rising from high chimneys, no domes or minarets or towers, to indicate the neighborhood of the large city. They came upon it suddenly in the evening, entering by way of the Kudan.

The teacher looked long and earnestly over the city as they stood on one of the heights above Fujisawa's house. "The Jesus-teacher lives over by the bay," he whispered.

His strength was fast failing. The boys could see that he was very pale and haggard in the twilight.

They passed Fujisawa's door. The whole

family stood there making their *saionaras* to Kei, who had been dressing the ladies' hair.

"Kesa," said Chiye, "see that poor sick man, with the boy and servant and that funny yellow dog."

In truth Yetaro was very ill; and at last, his strength failing utterly, he sat down on the steps of a small temple. Saijiro hung over him in some alarm, while Yenoske went for water. Just then old Kei came up to them. Now the Japanese will often pass dying persons in the street, leaving them to their pain and woe without so much as giving a word of sympathy. It is strange that the same religion which teaches them not to tread upon a worm nor to torture a fly should be so indifferent to human life and suffering. But a man is only a man; and a worm may be an ancestor or some great and holy person in this vile form! Kei had been reading too much of the gospel, and its truth had made too deep an impression on her heart, not to be touched at the sight of the dying man and the distressed boy.

"What is it?" she asked of Saijiro.

Yetaro opened his eyes.

"*Dogu!*" said Saijiro, "this is my honorable father; he has travelled a long way, and he is very ill."

"From whence did you come?" asked Kei.

"Thanks; from the Hakones."

Just then the sunset light was gilding those

mountain-tops, making a long bright line along the horizon.

"We have come to find the Jesus-teacher," added Saijiro. "My father wants to know of the doctrine."

Then Kei's heart was touched indeed. Yenoske came with the water and Yetaro was somewhat revived. A coolie was called, and the sick man was lifted into a jinrikisha.

"Take me to the Jesus-teacher," he said; "I have no time to spare."

Slowly went the little procession through the darkening streets, that seemed endless to Saijiro, and on down to the mission-house on the bay. The coolies drew the cart up before the gate, and Kei asked for "the honorable missionary doctor." He came immediately.

"*Dogu!*" said Kei, making her bow, "I have found a sick man who has come all the way from the Hakones to learn of your doctrine."

The doctor saw at a glance that poor Yetaro's hours were numbered.

"Make ready a room in the servants' quarters," he said. "Give the stranger some refreshments, and I will come."

Yetaro was lifted out of the cart and laid on a pallet in one of the servants' rooms. He took a little tea and then asked impatiently for the doctor.

The doctor came soon and sat down beside

him. "What is it, my friend?" he asked kindly, administering some strengthening draught.

"I am dying," said Yetaro, "but I wish to know of your teaching. I have worshipped the Japanese gods in vain. I have wasted the years of my life in going from shrine to shrine."

"*Dogu!*" ejaculated Kei, who stood near. The man's story was like her own.

"I have stood on Fuji's top," continued Yetaro, "I have prayed to Isuye," a holy shrine. "I have fasted and chastised myself, have made and kept most solemn vows. *Dogu*, I have had no rest. I want forgiveness for my sins. *Dogu*, I have been very wicked!"

Then came a violent fit of coughing, followed by a terrible exhaustion. Again the doctor administered a stimulant. The tears rolled down old Kei's cheeks. Saijiro and Yenoske were with the servants, taking their evening meal.

"I was taught the principles of Confucius," continued Yetaro at last, "respect and obedience to parents and all maxims of truth and right. But I was unkind and rough to my parents; I cared nothing for them, but only for *saké* and gambling and all sorts of wicked things. One night, when drunk, I quarrelled with one of my companions, and in my anger I killed him. When I knew what I had done I fled from the place, and no one pursued me. *Dogu!* the people care little about a man who may be found dead by the wayside; and that one was a stranger and had no near relatives.

"But the dreadful deed sobered me. I became a student, and was industrious and temperate. Especially did I study the doctrine of the gods to find some way to wash away my sin. But my guilt has ever been present with me. I had no rest. Often I longed to go back and confess my sin to the officers of my own country. But I did not. At last I married, and when my boy was a mere infant I went to live in Yamamidzu. I was often impatient and irritable with my wife. Our food was scanty and poor, and at last she died, worn out with suffering and sorrow. I have done all I can to get peace and pardon for my sins in the Japanese way, and now I have come to ask of the Jesus-doctrine, and if I may be forgiven. And I want my boy to be brought up in the way of truth and right.

"Once when he was on the Tokaido travelling down to Nagoya, a foreigner met him and gave him a book. It had this picture in it." Yetaro took from his breast the little book and showed the picture of the crucifixion. "Ever since I have wanted to know about the man on the cross. A man in the mountain told me something about it a few days ago. I am dying; but oh, tell me about the man on the cross! Can he forgive me? Can he forgive me?" Gasping for breath, Yetaro fell back on his pallet.

The missionary, Mr. West, had come in, and had listened with deep interest to the sick man's story. Kei stood wiping her eyes in one corner of the room. Saijiro crept close to his father and took his hand. Yenoske stood with the servants at the door. Some one brought a candle, and its flickering light shone upon Yetaro's head as he lay on his pallet. The doctor administered a stimulant and beckoned to the missionary to draw near. His eye fell upon the little book, which he recognized as one he himself had given to Saijiro when he first came to Japan and was travelling to Nagoya.

"My friend," said he, "I will read of the Man who hung upon the cross, and of one who was crucified with him, and will teach you the prayer of this one, who was a thief and perhaps a murderer."

Yetaro held the little book in his hand while the missionary read the evangelist Luke's account of the thief upon the cross. The sick man repeated after the missionary the prayer of the penitent one, who, acknowledging the justice of his punishment, said with faith, "Lord, remember me when thou comest into thy kingdom." And eagerly did Yetaro listen to the Saviour's gracious answer, "To-day shalt thou be with me in paradise."

"He came from heaven, the beloved Son of God, and died to save sinners; he died that we might live; he bore our punishment in our stead, because he loved us. Do you believe this, Yetaro?"

The sick man bowed his head.

"Do you believe that he died for *you*, Yetaro?"

Again he nodded assent.

"Let us pray," said the missionary.

The servants bowed their heads. Yenoske fell prostrate to the floor. Saijiro clung fast to his father's hand. Kei drew nearer to hear the words of the prayer.

"Oh, thou blessed Saviour, thou who didst hang upon the cross that our sins might be forgiven, have mercy upon this poor soul who has been so long seeking thee. Reach down and take this poor wandering one unto thyself. Grant him all he wants—forgiveness of his sins, the peace that thou alone canst give, life and blessedness with thee for ever."

A restful look came into Yetaro's eyes. "I have found him at last," he said, "the Man who hung on the cross. I only ask now that you teach my boy. He will repay you as well as he can."

The promise was readily given.

Yetaro sank rapidly and soon passed away, and Saijiro was left an orphan in a great city.

CHAPTER XVIII.

THE CHAPEL SERVICE.

It was Sunday morning, the beginning of a warm summer day. Aka had risen early from her pallet. Her heart was too sorrowful to let her rest long. The woman who had come to live in the house after Rinjiro's death had been more than usually unkind the day before. She often left her heavy baby to the weak and weary Aka's care. Aka loved the little one. She would carry him away into her room, and laying his cheek to hers would listen to his baby prattle. But her health was so delicate it seemed sometimes as if she could not bear the care of him. Her trembling frame tottered under his weight.

Now Aka slipped quietly out of the house and stood for a moment in the street. The sun had just risen. Old Fuji was hidden behind clouds and mist. The storm which had broken so relentlessly over the teacher was still raging on its summit, although all was so calm in the fields below.

Aka looked towards Fujisawa's house and her heart went out towards little Kesa, just then soundly asleep by Chiye's side. "My Rinjiro's little bride," she thought. "How handsome and happy they would have been together!"

Then she turned and went to the temple. The court was quite deserted; but within priests were chanting a solemn dirge and the deep tones of a bell could be heard. Aka said her prayer at the steps and threw her money into the box, then she walked into the cemetery and straight towards a well-known grave. Birds were twittering in the boughs above her; doves hopped around her feet. Her tears fell on the stone which bore Rinjiro's new name, as she stood and thought of him. With a wooden dipper that lay near the grave she dipped out the water from the hollow in the stone; then she filled the hollow with beautiful flowers and poured fresh water over them.

Look, Aka! the sun rises over the hilltop and gilds the temple roof. For you a new morning is dawning. This very day you shall catch the first glimmer in your darkened soul of the Sun of Righteousness.

She stole into the house on her return as quietly as she had crept out and went to her own room. Here everything was neat and pretty. In one corner a little table held some books which she had been reading. The books were a novel, one of the long Japanese novels in many volumes, each volume consisting of two books. Nothing of this insipid sort could comfort Aka's aching heart, but still she must do something; time hung heavily on her hands. So on this Sabbath morning she took up the seventeenth volume of her novel and tried to become interested in it.

In the meantime the household of the Fujisawas had begun the day. Very early the servants were all astir. They drew water, kindled charcoal, swept mats and verandas, and opened slides. There is no such thing as sleep while all this is going on or after it is done. So at a little past seven a pleasant bustle began. Chiye and Kesa slipped on their blue cotton dresses, washed ther. Mitsu came into the family room, and soon faces and hands, and went to salute father and mo- after Hana appeared there. Hana had improved somewhat under the foreign doctor's treatment; she suffered less pain.

The servants brought in breakfast. Each member of the family had a little lacquered table on which were tiny cups and dishes. The meal consisted of rice and tea, with some salt fish and pickles. They chatted together pleasantly as they ate.

"Soon you will go to the foreign school," said the father, addressing Chiye and Kesa.

Chiye's eyes sparkled. Kesa bowed.

"We have a request, honorable father," said Mitsu. "We wish to go to the Christian temple this afternoon. This is the rest-day of the honorable foreigners. If you please, we beg."

"*Dogu*," said Fujisawa, "I do not know.

You will not find it interesting, and the day will be very hot. What is it, Hana?" he asked, noticing that the child had turned pale and clung to Mitsu.

"Oh," said Hana, "I like the good doctor and his sweet little daughter; but, *dogu!* they do not love our Shaka Sama. They teach the people to worship their god in Shaka Sama's place. And they never pray to Bindzuru."

"I never heard them say anything against Shaka Sama," cried Chiye. "And I do n't think that Bindzuru has helped you much, Hana. Besides, I think he is very ugly, with his eyes and nose all rubbed off and his feet nearly gone. Yesterday mamma's beautiful Benten Sama fell down and her head rolled off."

"*Dogu!*" ejaculated Mrs. Fujisawa, who avoided discussions with Chiye.

"Well," said Fujisawa, "do as you please."

He went up stairs to smoke and a brother officer dropped in to talk with him, for Sunday was now a day of rest in Japan, and there were no official duties to perform.

In the little house at Nippon Boshi sat old Kei reading her wonderful book. "Strange! Wonderful!" she murmured, perusing for the twentieth time the story of the cross. The slides were pushed back so that she could see what was going on in the street. Crowds of people were going towards the bridge, and other crowds were going from it. Hours passed. Still Kei sat reading, more and more absorbed. She thought too of the man who had come from the mountain. He was to be carried that very day to the grave. She thought of the orphan Saijiro.

Aka, still reading her novel, heard a childish voice at the door. She called, "Come in." The slides were pushed aside and there was Kesa's bright face.

"Welcome, Kechan," said Aka.

"Mitsu's compliments," said Kesa, "and she would like to have you go with her to the Christian temple this afternoon."

"Give Mitsu my thanks and tell her I will go; and," Aka added, "I will ask Baba to go too."

Baba, Aka, Mitsu, Chiye, and Kesa all enjoyed the jinrikisha ride over to the Concession. Old Baba, who rode with Chiye and Kesa, asked many a question about the foreigners and the school as they were rolled rapidly through the streets of Tokio. Aka and Mitsu had common sorrows to draw them together and talked in a low tone.

All of the missionary teachers, Dr. and Mrs. Fielding, with their little daughter, and Mr. West and Miss Wilton, were at the mission-house to meet any who might come and show them the way to the chapel. They knew the Fujisawa party and greeted them warmly.

Baba had never been in a foreign house before. "Magnificent! Exceedingly fine!" said the old lady when she saw the high ceilings, the carpets and furniture.

On the mantel-piece was a picture, and near it were some flowers in vases. Baba thought the picture some god of the Christians, and before Mrs. Fielding could prevent it the old lady was prostrate before it, muttering Buddhist prayers.

"Oh, don't do that!" cried the doctor's wife in dismay. "That is a picture of my sister in America. Besides, we do not pray before pictures."

The old lady rose with an apology, and Mrs. Fielding showed her the photograph and told her of her dear young sister in America.

Kesa had brought a beautiful lotus-flower for Marion, and it was duly admired before being placed in a large vase. Others gathered from time to time, and quite a large party went from the mission-house to the chapel. Kei was among the number.

"I rejoice much at seeing you," said Kei when she spied Aka, Baba, and Mitsu. "The teaching is very good."

The missionary looked down from his pulpit that day upon two hundred upturned faces. There were people of all ages and all classes. There were old *babas* and *jisans* (grandmothers and grandfathers), babies in arms, and little toddlers whose bells tinkled as they moved in their seats. There were mothers and fathers, sons and daughters, all come to listen to the new teaching. Officers, artisans, merchants, and coolies mingled together; and apart, at one end of the room, was a group of Buddhist priests. It was an interesting scene. So thought the young missionary as he began his simple sermon.

"Dear friends, I have just returned from a visit to the Hakone Mountains. I thought them very beautiful, but it seemed strange to me to find no sheep there, no shepherd leading his flock to the clear streams or watching them feed upon the sunny slopes. It was not like this in the country where Jesus lived. There many a strong man found occupation in tending sheep. Shepherds there watched over many flocks by night and by day. They found pasture for them and water in the wilderness. They helped the weak ones and carried the lambs in their arms. They defended them against lions and bears and wolves. They would give up their own lives for the sheep. Nay, they even called each sheep by its name, and each sheep knew its own shepherd and followed him. Now I will read you what the Lord Jesus calls himself in the tenth chapter of the Gospel of John."

Mr. West then read slowly and distinctly the verses he had referred to.

"Dear friends, the Lord Jesus is the Shepherd

and his people are the sheep. There are many weak ones among them whom he leads and helps. Little children are the lambs of the Lord Jesus. Beloved, I hear so many voices calling you. There are so many false teachers, so many who pretend to be shepherds, but are not. They call you to go this way and that, until you are bewildered and do not know where to turn. There is but one Shepherd, but one way. Beloved, I pray you to listen to that voice and walk in that way."

Then followed the reading and explaining of another passage of Scripture, to which the audience listened attentively. There was comparatively little disorder. Once a man coming in went up and shook hands with the preacher; others who came late saluted their friends. A man occasionally went round with a stick and poked up any who had fallen asleep. The meeting closed with an old, familiar hymn. The people stood and sang in their own language "There is a happy land," and then quietly dispersed.

"Kechan," said Aka as they walked away, "I should like to ask the teacher some time more about the Good Shepherd. I wish Rinjiro had known Him."

The sun had gone down and the yellow moon had come up from the sea. Old Kei sat in her upper room. Before her was a row of idols, and Kei was gazing earnestly at them. There was Daikoku with his round, jolly face, Yebisu with his fish, an image of Bindzuru, some household gods, a beautiful gilt figure of Benten, and some pictures. Kei looked at them long. Tears gathered in her eyes and rolled down her cheeks. She had trusted to these gods so long and had spent so much time in trying to please them.

Presently she took a square of cloth and tied all the idols up in it. A moment later she was in the street going towards the river. It was a glorious night. The canals were golden in the moonlight, the river ran in bright ripples down to the sea. Kei went quietly along the darkest, narrowest streets, and at last reached the river. In a lonely spot, where she was hidden by some buildings, she dropped her bundle down, down into the deep, mysterious water. There was a heavy splash. She shuddered a little, but soon turned, and with a firm step and a lighter heart went home.

CHAPTER XIX.

A COUNTRY BOY IN TOKIO.

To Saijiro and his faithful friend Yenoske a room in the servants' quarters had been assigned when Yetaro died. "Take time and rest, my boy," the missionary had kindly said. For Saijiro had gone to the doctor after the funeral, had stood before him respectfully, and said,

"Honorable doctor, we have no money. We have to work. My father wished me to learn your doctrine and to go to your school, and Yenoske and I will work for my education."

There was something noble in the appearance of the boy. He was tall and manly, and seemed to bring a breath of his native mountain air with him, so fresh was his complexion, so bright his eye, and so straightforward his look.

"All in good time, my boy," answered the doctor. "Take time and rest."

Is it not pleasant to note the workings of God's providence, the little links in the great chain which binds us to his throne? A few months before, in far-off Pennsylvania, a mother and her boy sat talking together of that boy's future.

"I will be a missionary, mamma," said the

eager boy, "a missionary in Japan. But it will be so long before I can go. I can hardly wait, mamma, I can hardly wait."

And now there had come to the doctor's wife a letter from that same mother. It read thus:

"Dear friend: I may never look into your eyes nor feel the pressure of your hand nor listen to the tones of your voice, but my very soul goes out to you when I read of your good work in Japan. My husband is a clergyman in this place, and our church is deeply interested in missions. We have been blessed with seven children. A few weeks ago our eldest boy, a bright, happy lad of thirteen, was taken from us after an illness of a few hours. We have six children left, six sweet, loving little ones. But there is a vacant place in my heart. My boy had chosen to be a missionary in Japan. It was his constant thought. Dear friend, we want to take into our hearts a Japanese boy. We want to love and educate him for our Harry's sake."

All of the thirteen years during which Saijiro had been growing up on the mountain Harry Rindberg had lived his happy life in the little town in Pennsylvania. And now that he had been taken away, the mother's heart yearned for some better monument to the boy's memory than any marble could afford.

"Surely the Lord's hand is in this," said Dr. Fielding as he read the letter. "Saijiro shall be

Mrs. Rindberg's boy. May he comfort her for her lost Harry!"

"The God of the Christians has sent you a mother, my boy," he said to Saijiro.

The boy lifted his eyes in surprise and Yenoske bowed low. Then the doctor told of Harry, and of the mother's wish for a Japanese boy to be to her as a son in her lost one's place. Saijiro could scarcely comprehend, but from that time his heart went out to his "mother in America." Yenoske was taken as a servant in the doctor's family. The coolie who had been the under-servant had left, and Yenoske gladly took his place.

"But," said the doctor as he unfolded his plans concerning them, "take a day or two and see this wonderful city before you begin to work."

So early the next morning Saijiro and Yenoske started off to explore Tokio. What New York is to one of our rustics, Tokio is to a country boy in Japan, and Saijiro greatly enjoyed the sight-seeing. The canals looked silvery in the pale light just before the sunrise, and the air was still and warm. The sea-breeze had not yet sprung up over the city. Fuji's outlines were dimly visible, and more than once Yenoske turned his eyes in the direction of the Hakone Hills. Yenoske loved his mountain home and often longed for its wild, free life. But his devotion to Saijiro remained unchanged, and he never once thought of going back.

They made their way down towards the Tori, choosing to go to the railroad station and see the train go out. They were astonished at the long row of foreign-built houses with their pretty colonnades.

"What a fine jinrikisha you have," said Saijiro, addressing a coolie who sat upon the ground beside his cart.

"*Dogu*," said the man, "it is a fine *karuma*," cart, "but it is very heavy."

"Is it hard work to pull it?" inquired Yenoske.

The man answered, "Yes; and sometimes for two or three days I have no customers. I like to draw the honorable foreigners; they pay three times as much as the Japanese do."

"But do they beat you?" asked Yenoske.

"*Dogu*, they never beat me. I like the Jesus-teachers; they are always kind and reasonable."

Just then the man spied a foreigner crossing the street, and started towards him. Saijiro and Yenoske saw the stranger stop the jinrikisha. They wanted to hear what was said.

"How much to go to the station?"

"Two *boos*." A *boo* is twelve and a half cents.

"That is too much. One *boo*," said the foreigner, holding up a finger.

After considerable parleying the two compromised for one *boo* and a half. Even that was too much. But the gentleman got into the cart and was borne off towards the station.

By this time the sun had risen. The streets were filling with people. Some clouds had gathered overhead. These who met and saluted said it was going to rain. The two mountain boys passed through a great fish-market which interested them exceedingly. Fish, except mountain trout, was rare enough in their home in the heart of the Hakones. Some sailors passed them carrying an immense shark.

"What is that big fish?" Saijiro asked.

Even Yenoske had never seen a shark before, and so could not answer.

They followed the three men, and when these had deposited the shark upon a board and were preparing to cut it, Saijiro put his question again.

The men answered it, adding, "Where did you come from, little master?"

"From the Hakone Mountains."

"Where did you get the shark?" now inquired Yenoske.

"*Dogu*," replied one of the sailors, "we have been out all night on the bay. It was rough, and we caught nothing until we speared this big fellow."

The boys continued their walk around the market. There were oysters, clams, and crabs. There were fine salmon from Hakodate and tiny sardines from the more southern coasts. Saijiro admired the *tai*—a species of carp—and *bora*, with their beautiful, delicate scales, and looked with interest at the seaweed, mosses, and curious cuttle-fish.

Having passed through the market, the boys found themselves presently on a bridge which crossed a large canal. A number of boats were being propelled slowly up the canal towards the castle. There was a long line of house-boats fastened by staples and ropes to the shore. A great many people were crossing the bridge, some in jinrikishas and some on foot. All of these had to make way for a Japanese soldier, who urged his horse carelessly and rapidly through the crowd.

"*Dogu*," said a lady whose jinrikisha the horse had grazed in passing, "these foreigners make us a great deal of trouble, teaching our people to ride like that."

Just after the boys had crossed the bridge it began to rain. Those few clouds had gradually covered the sky. A heavy shower fell on Tokio. The *jinrikiyas* pulled oil-paper covers over their carts. Women drew their skirts up over their heads and ran laughing along. Those who had babies stopped under the projecting eaves of the houses.

"It will be over soon," said Yenoske as Saijiro shook the drops from his hair.

Sure enough, by the time they entered Shiba the sun was shining brightly again, and all the wet tree-tops were resplendent in its beams. The boys went up to the great gateway, and after admiring it entered the inclosure. Of all the temples of Tokio, this is the most beautiful. Saijiro and Yenoske walked up the broad flagging to the temple steps, but not to worship. Some thoughts were in their minds which made them hesitate. "What is this place?" Yenoske asked of a priest, who in yellow robes and with shaven head was hurrying by them, an incense-box in his hand.

"*Dogu!*" answered he, surprised, "do you not know? This is Shiba, where the Shoguns are buried."

The boys stood in a broad avenue. Grand forest trees bent over them, through whose interlaced branches poured the rich sunlight. Under these trees grew violets, ferns, and mosses. Not a sign was at hand of the large city they had just left. They might, indeed, have been deep in the solitudes of their own mountains. The little temples dedicated to the Shoguns were of the most exquisite workmanship, the gates of many of them being of solid bronze. Beautiful Shiba! Never before had Saijiro seen anything like it. Taking off his shoes, he went into a temple. Over the altar were dainty lilies and pomegranates, made of gold and suspended by golden chains. The ceiling was of inlaid work, and the floor of wonderfully polished wood.

From Shiba the boys made their way to the

railway station, where Saijiro was soon intensely interested in the cars. There were foreign ladies and gentlemen waiting in the station to take the next train for Yokohama.

"Why does n't the young master ride down to Shinagawa?" asked an official who was standing near. "It is only a few miles and costs but a few *sen*."

So Saijiro and Yenoske followed a crowd of Japanese into a third-class car. They were all packed closely together; but it was an open car, and they had plenty of fresh air. The rapid motion almost frightened the two friends at first. They had scarcely had time to become accustomed to it when the train stopped, and they had to get out.

Every precaution is taken for the safety of passengers, and of people crossing the tracks, in Japan. A sentinel is posted at every crossing, and wherever it is possible the road goes either under or over the track. The boys carefully examined the "iron road." They went upon a bridge which crossed it and stood looking at the forts. An old man observed them, and drawing near, entered into conversation with them. The forts were very pretty, appearing like little green islands in the blue waters of the bay.

"*Dogu*," began the old man, following the direction of Saijiro's gaze, "those forts were built when the honorable foreigners first came into the country with their great iron ships. "*Dogu!* how frightened we all were. Honorable grandfather died with fright."

Saijiro looked concerned. The "honorable foreigners" certainly did a great deal of mischief.

"The ships," continued the man, "were anchored right off there. We saw them very early one morning; they seemed like black mountains in the mist. Some fishermen hastened ashore to tell us what they were. Then we kindled fires, to show that the country was in danger, and every one was terribly distressed. The thunder and lightning from the cannon made us terribly afraid. Oh, what a calling upon the gods there was! Honorable grandmother sat all day counting her beads. We set off to the ships in our *sampans* to sell vegetables and fruits. But the foreigners would not let any one go aboard."

"But they did n't really hurt any of the Japanese, did they?" questioned Saijiro.

"*Dogu!*" said the man, "no; but there has been a great deal of trouble since."

The boys now made their way slowly back to Tokio. They had seen quite enough for one day.

That afternoon the Fujisawas had some company. Dr. and Mrs. Fielding, with their little daughter Marion, came to make them a long-promised visit. The coolies who had drawn the jinrikishas from the Concession to Fujisawa's door were just about to call, "*O tano moshimasu,*" when the slides were pushed open, and Kesa's bright face appeared.

"You are very welcome," said she.

The guests stopped a moment to exchange their heavy shoes for slippers. No one wishes to tread with shoes on spotless white mats. Kesa stood quietly by until the visitors were ready, and then conducted them into the parlor, where the family were assembled. Pleasant were the greetings exchanged.

Mrs. Fujisawa directed her servant to bring in tea. The girl handed each cup on a little tray, getting down on her knees to present it. Then a beautiful bowl was brought and placed before Mrs. Fujisawa. This was filled with ice-cold water. Near it was set a dish of pears which looked like russet apples. These the lady of the house peeled daintily and cut into small pieces, letting them fall into the ice-water. Then with chopsticks she presented a piece to each guest. They found them refreshingly juicy and cold.

The children soon went into the garden to play among the flowers.

"How old are you?" Kesa asked of Marion.

The little American answered, "I am ten."

"And so am I," cried Kesa.

The fair skin, blue eyes, and light, curling hair of one child presented a great contrast to the olive complexion, dark eyes, and straight, black locks of the other. Yet they were not altogether unlike. Blue eyes and black eyes both had the same look, at once fearless and earnest; and both children were well developed physically. Each in her own way presented a picture of childish health and beauty.

They stood for a time upon the knoll, gazing at the distant mountains.

"Old Fuji is almost hidden to-day," said Marion. "We cannot see the mountains of the Kadzusa range at all. But what a pretty garden you have, Kesa, and how nice it must be to play here."

They wandered at last into the little summer-house where, eight years before, Kesa and Rinjiro had been playing when Kei came and told her plaintive story of Nantaro and her weary search for him. On a shelf in one corner were some broken toys, and on a little table Daruma himself reposed in solemn state.

"I played with them when I was a baby," said Kesa, pointing out the toys, "and that Daruma Sama was Rinjiro's."

"Where is Rinjiro now?" asked Marion.

"*Dogu!* he is dead and finished. He was my husband, or he would have been if he had lived."

But such grave thoughts do not long occupy the minds of children, and these were soon playing again, bright, happy, and careless. When tired, they went indoors to look at some pictures.

"What is this?" asked Marion.

The picture she held represented a man dressed like a prince, with a princely feast spread before him. Beside him sat a beautiful woman in a court dress. Behind the pair were two fishes dressed as servants and with heads bowed respectfully. Before them was a row of fishes, waiting as if to receive orders; while two other fishes seemed to be coming up from the depths of the sea, one bearing a table, and the other a covered dish.

"Oh, we have a whole set of those pictures," said Chiye. "They illustrate the story of Urashima."

"Tell me about it," urged Marion. "I love to hear stories of Old Japan, and these pictures are very pretty."

The first of the set showed a fisherman in a little boat. In one hand he held a tortoise, which he was just putting back into the sea.

"That man," said Chiye, "is Urashima. Long, long years ago he lived in a fishing-village on the coast. One day he went out in his boat to fish. He let down his net and caught a tortoise. Now the tortoise lives a thousand years, and Urashima, seeing that this was a young one, thought it would be a pity to deprive it of its long, happy life; so he dropped it back into the sea.

"The next picture shows Urashima asleep in his boat. A beautiful young lady has risen out of the waves to sit with him in the boat while he is still sleeping. On awaking he was naturally astonished at the unexpected vision. To his surprise the young lady told him that she was the tortoise whose life he had spared. As a reward for his kindness he might now be her husband and go down with her to her beautiful palace under the sea. Urashima agreed. So they went down, down to the promised dwelling. The leaves of the trees there were of emeralds, the fruits were rubies, and the dewdrops were pearls. They lived in perfect happiness until Urashima began to think he must go home and see his aged parents; he imagined he had been away only a few weeks. 'You may go,' said the beautiful princess, 'but you must take this box with you. Do not open it, for if you do you will never find your way back to me.'

"Urashima took the box, bade farewell to his lovely wife, and rose slowly, slowly out of the sea. At last he found himself on his own shore and stood looking about for his cottage. But everything had gone. An old man came up and spoke to him. 'What are you looking for, young man?' 'Alas,' answered Urashima, 'can you tell me where Urashima's cottage is?' 'Urashima's cottage! Why, Urashima was drowned in the sea three or four hundred years ago.'

"Then Urishama was sad and could only think of hurrying back to the palace where the lovely princess waited for him. But he did not know the way back. He thought of his box. 'I will open it. Perhaps I shall find the way then.' So, forgetting the command of the princess, he opened the box. A great white cloud arose from it. Urashima found himself shrivelling, his strength going. In a few minutes he was dead. So he never got back to that palace under the sea, though the beautiful princess waited long for him, though the emerald leaves, the ruby fruits, and the pearly dewdrops shone and gleamed as gladly as of old."

"That is the prettiest Japanese story I have ever heard," said Marion. "It is a little like our Rip Van Winkle."

"Tell us that," begged Kesa.

But Marion's father and mother had finished their visit and were calling to her, and the *saionaras* must be said.

"How nice it was, mamma," said she, nestling close to her mother's side in the jinrikisha as they rode.

CHAPTER XX.

SCHOOL DAYS.

"BE very careful, Kesa, and do study more, child. The teacher at the school says you are so idle and careless."

Thus spoke Mrs. Fujisawa to Kesa as she and Chiye stood waiting for the jinrikishas which were to carry them to the foreign school. Chiye was radiantly happy, and Kesa was not unwilling to go with her favorite sister to the school, although she was not fond of study and the teacher's complaint was but too well founded.

The girls were dressed with care and taste, as befitted the daughters of the high officer Fujisawa. Their dresses were of a delicate, soft gray, with which their red sashes contrasted prettily; and the lovely crapes at the neck and in the hair were of the most charming shades. Each had a *futon*, with a warm wadded covering, a wooden pillow, and a little table, besides books and clothing. A coolie was loading a cart with their things, and the jinrikishas were being drawn up the street.

"There come the carts," said Chiye, spying the vehicles as they came around the corner.

"*Saionara*, honorable mother. Again on the

sixth day," said the girls, prostrating themselves before their mother.

"*Saionara*, my daughters; may the gods protect you," said Mrs. Fujisawa, sighing when she remembered that both children had positively refused to carry idols with them to the school.

"*Saionara*, honorable sisters," and again before Mitsu and Hana Chiye and Kesa were prostrate.

"*Saionara, saionara*," responded the sisters, who would be lonely enough through the long days of the week.

"*Saionara*," said the servants, who were standing in a line to witness the departure.

Then the girls, almost hidden by the immense bouquets they carried, got into one jinrikisha, and Fujisawa, carefully holding a lacquered box, took his seat in the other. It was a lovely September morning and the girls enjoyed the ride down to the mission compound.

Children had come in jinrikishas from all parts of the city, and all carried presents for their dear teacher—flowers, eggs, and beautiful lacquer and china ware. The children were all bright and happy, glad to get back to school after the long summer vacation. Miss Wilton received them lovingly and listened with sympathy to their accounts of the way in which they had spent the summer.

"I have been to see my aunt in Yokohama," said one.

"I have visited the mountains," said another.

"And I went across the bay to the Kadzusa Hills," said a third.

"Ah, there come the Fujisawas," cried Fusa, Chiye's friend, as she saw the three jinrikishas.

Miss Wilton hastened to meet them.

Fujisawa alighted from the cart and bowed. "For the favor of many days ago I thank you," he said.

"You are truly welcome," answered Miss Wilton.

"For my daughters I beg your honorable care. They are very stupid girls and do not learn well. If you please, I beg your kind consideration and your honorable attentions."

"Thanks, Mr. Fujisawa; I will gladly accept the charge," said Miss Wilton, who already had noticed Chiye's bright intelligence and Kesa's winning manners.

"Truly, a small present, scarcely worthy of your consideration," said Fujisawa, presenting a pair of exquisite bronze vases.

The girls bowed gracefully and presented their flowers. The house was already one mass of blossoms. Lilies, chrysanthemums, and hydrangeas all bore testimony to the love of the pupils for their teacher.

"If you please, I wish my daughters to learn English," said Fujisawa, when Miss Wilton had thanked them for the beautiful gifts. "They will come hereafter, as you wish, on Sunday mornings, and remain until Friday evening. I will accompany them myself or send a servant for them."

"You know that we teach them the Bible and send them to church," said Miss Wilton.

"It is well," answered Fujisawa. It made little difference to him what they were taught concerning religion.

"You have a friend here," said Miss Wilton to Chiye, when Fujisawa had bowed himself away.

Chiye smiled. "Yes, my dear friend Fusa. We have sworn an eternal friendship; we are always going to the same school, and we shall never, never be separated."

The teacher was amused. Chiye's words reminded her of American girls and their eternal friendships. But she called Fusa and told her to show the girls the dormitory and their apartments; so they all went off together. Fusa led the way into a spacious, well-ventilated room, where each girl was assigned a small compartment, separated from the others by fixed screens. A servant brought up the bedding and other things, and Fusa helped the Fujisawas arrange everything nicely and then took them down to the school-room. This was furnished with foreign desks and chairs, and Chiye's eyes fairly shone as she noted the blackboards, maps, and pictures on the walls.

SCHOOL DAYS.   233

"I will study so hard that I will soon be able to go on with you in your English classes," she said to Fusa.

"Have you read any English at all?" asked Miss Wilton of the Fujisawas.

"No, honorable *sensei*. We have read only Japanese and Chinese," they answered. But while Chiye was put into the lowest English class, she was far ahead of all the other girls in Chinese, and had to study alone.

There were no classes that day, and when the girls had been examined they were sent off. Chiye went up to her room with her precious book, and Kesa wandered out into the garden.

She walked about in a listless way at first, but soon her attention was arrested by the sound of children's voices, and she peeped through the hedge which separated the doctor's yard from the school compound.

Marion Fielding was working in her garden, and near her was a boy of seven, her motherless cousin Carroll. He wore a white suit and a broad-brimmed straw hat; a shower of golden curls fell on his shoulders; and Kesa thought she had never seen anything so charming as his whole appearance. She could not understand what the children were saying, but thought it must be something connected with the flowers.

"Marion *san!*" she called at last. *San* is a respectful address, like Sir or Madame.

Marion looked up to see Kesa's eyes fixed upon her, and greeted her warmly. "Come and see my garden, Kesa," she said, turning quickly from English to Japanese.

Kesa was soon standing by Marion and Carroll. "Why do you work yourselves?" she asked. "Old Oto takes care of our garden. Does not the honorable father allow you servants?"

"Oh, yes, but we love to work with the flowers. They are the dearest flowers on earth to us —these that we plant and take care of ourselves."

"How do you like the school, Kesa?" asked Carroll. "Is your lesson hard?"

But Kesa made no answer. She had a vague feeling that she ought to be with Chiye, studying her lesson; but it was pleasanter in the garden, and she stood looking in a dreamy way at the bright water, the trees, and the flowers, and watching Marion and Carroll as they dug, planted, and watered.

Yet all the while her little heart was not idle; deep impressions were being made; and when the doctor's wife came out of the house and stood by her little daughter, and Marion eagerly explained to her what she had been doing, Kesa noted the mother's full interest and sympathy and turned away with an indefinite feeling of sorrow and unrest. This child had a warm, loving heart, and the rather cold and indifferent manner of her mother—a genuine Japanese—never seemed to satisfy its cravings.

"Where have you been, Kesa? And have you studied your lesson?" asked Chiye, as her sister entered the dormitory.

"No, sister."

"What have you been doing?"

"Nothing, sister."

"Kesa, the honorable father will be much displeased if you are so idle. Sit down, and I will show you about the lesson. See, I have already learned one page."

One page! Poor little Kesa! Would she ever know what was on that page?

But Chiye was patient and helped her, until she could read and translate with tolerable ease, "The girl has a doll."

"We are to begin school to-morrow, and we must learn our lessons," said Chiye.

"Did you bring Daikoku Sama and Benten Sama with you?" asked one of the new girls of Kesa in the afternoon. They were in the dormitory, sitting on a mat. The windows were open, and they could see some boats out on the water.

"No; I don't like them, and the people here don't have images," said Kesa.

"But I have," said the girl; and taking Kesa to her compartment and drawing aside a curtain, she showed her little shrine on which sat the gods of luck.

"Oh, Chiye, Riki has Daikoku Sama and Yebisu Sama with her," said Kesa.

"Well, she will not keep them long. All of the girls bring their idols with them, but they soon throw them away," said Fusa.

The next morning school began in good earnest for Chiye and Kesa. By six o'clock the girls were all up, and then came a time of washing, dressing, and airing *futons*. Then some of the girls knelt and prayed to the unseen God; one or two offered their devotions to the idols which they had brought; and a large girl, Haru, saluted the sun.

"To whom shall we pray, sister?" asked Kesa.

"*Dogu*, I should like to pray to the true God, but I do n't know what to say, Kesa."

"How did the teacher pray last night, Chiye?"

"He asked the true God to bless us and make us happy, for the Lord Jesus Christ's sake."

Kesa knelt by her sister's side while Chiye prayed: "Oh, true God, bless us and make us happy, for the Lord Jesus Christ's sake."

"I think that will do, Chiye," said Kesa, as they rose from their knees.

They followed the rest of the girls into the dining-room, where they found, each on her own little table, a bowl of rice, steaming hot, and a cup of tea. Kesa sat by Chiye and was just taking up her chopsticks to begin eating, when her sister called,

"Wait, Kesa."

Kesa saw all the girls bowing their heads and waited while an elderly woman, who resembled Kei in appearance and dress, said a simple grace.

"What did Kotu say, sister?" asked Kesa.

"She thanked God for giving us this food," said Chiye.

"I think that was very nice," rejoined Kesa, and then took up the chopsticks and soon made way with the rice.

After breakfast the girls had time for a walk beside the bay. At nine they all went into the schoolroom, where the day's exercises were begun with singing, prayer, and Bible-reading. The Scripture lesson occupied half an hour, and all listened attentively to the native teacher's explanation of the story of creation.

All of the servants came in and sat near the door. Yenoske tried to understand, but thought the subject very puzzling. He knew that the world was beautiful and that he loved it, but he cared little as to how it was made or who made it.

Then came the English classes. When each reading class was dismissed the girls composing it were sent to the translation teacher, who saw that they understood what they read. These classes occupied the time until twelve o'clock, when there was an intermission of two hours.

The noon meal was like the breakfast, except that the girls had also fish with sauce and a dish of greens stood beside each rice-bowl. They always had greens or Japanese "sugar potatoes" or lily and lotus roots for dinner.

The girls had their Chinese writing and Japanese and Chinese reading lessons in the afternoon. They wrote in the dining-room at the same little tables on which they had their rice-bowls at meals.

At four all assembled in the schoolroom, and after a hymn and some words from their teacher they were dismissed.

After this a half-hour was spent in Bible study by those who especially desired it. Chiye quickly joined this Bible-class, but Kesa preferred going out to play with the younger girls, and most of the day scholars went home.

Again in the evening the boarding pupils assembled around the large table in the study-room, where, after worship, they had talks with their teacher. It was hard at first to get them to talk freely, but they were learning to come to her with their petty grievances, with their questionings about things which they did not understand, and with their pleasures as well as their sorrows and perplexities. Miss Wilton knew all their homes and could talk with them of father, mother, brothers, and sisters, thus drawing them close to her with her intelligent sympathy. She thought this evening hour the very pleasantest of all the pleasant hours of the day, and so thought the girls.

Many a day passed thus for Chiye and Kesa; many a day thus came and went for their devoted teacher.

"I thought, when I had made the one great sacrifice, that that was the end of little worries; but I find that life is the same in the mission-field as anywhere else," said Miss Wilton one day to the doctor's wife.

"Yes, life is made up of little things here as well as in America, dear Miss Wilton," answered Mrs. Fielding. And the teacher soon learned to go cheerfully through the routine of school-work and to bear bravely all the annoyances which fell to her lot.

Chiye soon left Kesa far behind in her studies. Miss Wilton gloried in the older sister's rapid progress, but she loved the little Kesa. The child had an irresistibly winning way of giving a bright upward glance at her teacher's face when she had spelled or read a word, and she had not been long in the school before Miss Wilton noticed her sweet, clear voice rising above all the others when the girls sang their hymns.

"I often make them sing, 'I am so glad that our Father in heaven,' in order to hear that child's voice ring out, 'Jesus loves even me,'"

Miss Wilton said one day, when Mrs. Fielding had been speaking of Kesa and her own increasing interest in Marion's little friend.

In the meantime Saijiro was making good progress in his English studies in the boys' school in the adjoining compound. He also studied Chinese and Japanese and was gaining knowledge of the Scriptures. His ambition was to write a letter to his "mother in America;" and bravely did he work over the English alphabet, and tried to hold his pen in the English way. His room-mate was a studious, thoughtful youth, named Harukichi.

"I wish to study and be a teacher of the Christian doctrine," he said to Saijiro one day.

"And can you not, Harukichi?" asked the boy.

"*Dogu!* the honorable parents will not hear of it; if I do it, I may not go home nor look upon their honorable faces again. When I went home last summer I begged them to let me become a Christian teacher; but honorable mother's honorable tears fell fast, and she beat her breast and tore her hair. What will your honorable parents say, Saijiro, if you wish to be a Christian?"

"*Dogu*, I have no honorable parents, except my mother in America," answered Saijiro.

The conversation dropped, but Saijiro knew that the Chinese Bible was Harukichi's favorite volume. Day and night he studied it, and one

SCHOOL DAYS. 241

day Saijiro, coming in unexpectedly, found him engaged in earnest prayer.

"Have you no image which you worship?" asked Saijiro.

"No; I worship the Christians' God," Harukichi answered.

Yenoske, all this time, was faithfully discharging his duties as under-servant in the doctor's family, carrying wood, bringing water, performing the most servile tasks with the cheerfulness and readiness which had always characterized him. Often his eyes turned longingly and lovingly to the long line of the Hakone Hills; but he never complained or spoke of his yearning for his mountain home. And he gained from his mistress that which she said seemed to her the highest of all titles—that of "faithful servant."

One morning, late in September, when the girls went to take their exercise on the beach, they noticed that the clouds were very dark overhead and that the waves were breaking into white caps. Thousands of ugly-looking black bugs, which had their homes in the crevices of the rocks of the breakwater, came creeping up on the shore and on the sides of the mission-house.

"Ah, a *taifu!*"—great wind—said the girls; and some of the little ones began to cry. In truth, a typhoon is something to be dreaded. These terrible winds sweep the coast of China and Japan once a year, always in the late summer or early fall; and woe to the ships which are caught in their centre!

When the girls first noticed the approaching storm the fishermen were hastening into the river with their boats. Right gallantly did the frail-looking little *sampans* ride the waves, never taking in a drop of water, but always high and dry on top of the billows. Bravely did the boatmen work their oars, and beautifully did the sailboats bend to the wind and allow themselves to be driven into the harbor. In came all the fishing-boats, all the pleasure-craft, all the junks, all the *sampans*—a whole fleet of vessels running in front of the gale into the safe river. Outside rode some men-of-war, tossed like cockles by the fierce waves.

Higher and higher rose the billows; darker and darker grew the clouds. The waves leaped over the breakwater and at last dashed on the second-story veranda of the mission-house. Tiles, fence-rails, gate-posts, everything that was in the least degree loose, flew about like so many feathers before the wind. Oh, the creaking and groaning of the rafters, the sound of the rushing, roaring waters, the rough voice of the howling wind!

There was no school that day; but in the evening Miss Wilton sent word to the girls to gather in the study-room, and soon came to them, accompanied by Makichi, the venerable teacher who conducted the Bible exercises in the schoolroom every morning.

"Ah, a great storm! Have you feared, my children?" asked Makichi.

"Truly, yes, honorable *sensei*."

"I have come," he said, "to read you a story of the Lord Jesus when he was in a storm on the Sea of Galilee."

The girls listened while Makichi read these sweet words of the evangelist Mark:

"And there arose a great storm of wind, and the waves beat into the ship, so that it was now full. And he was in the hinder part of the ship, asleep on a pillow: and they awake him, and say unto him, Master, carest thou not that we perish? And he arose, and rebuked the wind, and said unto the sea, Peace, be still. And the wind ceased, and there was a great calm."

"It is very beautiful," said the older girls.

"But," asked one, "does the God of the Christians do everything himself? Has he no servants? Our Hachiman Sama has horses and doves. Inari Sama has the fox. And there are the Thunder-god and the Pain-god and so many others."

"The book of God," answered Makichi, "this Bible which I hold in my hands, tells us that the winds, the rain, the frost, the snow, and the thunder are all the servants and messengers of the great true God who made the heavens and the earth. By-and-by you will study philosophy and learn how God uses these things, become acquainted with some of the laws by which he regulates them." Then Makichi prayed with the girls, and they went to bed calm and peaceful in the midst of the storm.

The next morning the wind had ceased, all the clouds had rolled away, and out shone the sun, seemingly brighter and more glorious than ever. The sea and sky were alike of a deep blue. All the little fishing-boats, all the junks and *sampans* and pleasure-craft, came out of the river and danced on the waters. Japan was beautiful, all fresh and green, and the hearts of the people rejoiced. The girls crowded on the upper veranda of the mission-house to see Mt. Fuji. There it stood, a grand white cone rising far above the other mountains.

"It *is* beautiful," said the missionaries. "No wonder the Japanese, from their standpoint, worship it, the grandest thing in all Dai Nippon."

"But to worship at its top cannot make people holy. Only the blood of Christ can wash away our sins," said a Christian girl.

CHAPTER XXI.

MIDWINTER IN TOKIO.

WARM September gave place to golden October. October passed, and November's cold, dreary days came. It rained a great deal, and the children had to go to school in jinrikishas covered with oiled paper. And now it was far on in December and nearing the happy Christmas and New Year's time.

"Next week," said Kesa, as she sat by Hana's side one Friday afternoon when she and Chiye had returned to their home after the week in school, "there will be a great feast of the Christians."

"What is it?" asked Hana.

"They call it Christmas, and it is in honor of the birthday of Christ."

"What will the Christians do?"

"The boys of the school are going to get trees and berries, and the teacher will have Chinese oranges, nuts, and other foreign things for us. We are learning some songs for Christmas, but they are in English, and you would n't understand them, Hana."

"Do you understand them, Kesa?"

"Not very well. But oh, Hana, Marion *san*

has such a pretty new hat with a red feather in it, and a new cloak! She says that her grandmother in America sent them to her. And the teachers all have new clothes, and every one is happy for the holidays."

"Well, and aren't we getting new things for the holidays too, Kesa? Tell me about your book."

"Well, I read a story about a lazy man who went and sat down in the sun. Hana, I think that is very foolish. How could a man go and sit down in the sun?"

"I don't know how he could get up there," said Hana.

"It is in the honorable foreigners' book," said Kesa.

"We will ask Chiye," said Hana, "and she'll tell us about the Christmas hymns. You don't seem to understand anything very well, Kesa."

In truth, poor little Kesa was blundering along in the dark. Chiye was kind to her, but often failed in giving needed help, chiefly because she did not realize that it was needed.

The child learned the letters and words in a mechanical way which deceived her teachers, who were far from suspecting how little she understood or how often the bright eyes were filled with tears as she tried to study. But she was naturally merry and happy, and quickly forgot her troubles when playtime came.

Chiye, on the other hand, grasped everything, so when Hana, a little later, asked her about Christmas and the hymns, she was able to explain them.

"They are hymns," she said, "about the infant Jesus, who was born in a stable in a town called Bethlehem. There were shepherds watching their flocks at night, when the angel of the Lord came down and told them that Jesus was born. And then a great many angels came and sang and told the shepherds where to go. And they went and worshipped the holy child."

"Sister, there is something about a star," said Kesa.

"Oh, yes. Some wise men in another country wanted to find the infant Jesus, and a star went before them and stood over the place where he was. And the men went in and gave gifts."

"*Dogu!*" said Mrs. Fujisawa.

She and Hana remained firm in their Buddhist faith, although they liked the Bible stories, and the lives of the "Sixteen Holy Disciples" had somewhat lost their charm.

The girls had to leave home early Sunday morning in order to get to the mission in time for the Sunday-school, which was held from half-past nine until eleven. Then the boys and girls had time for study and rest until the hour for afternoon service. The girls had of their own accord organized a noon prayer-meeting, and very sweet and simple and full of faith were the petitions which they put up.

Long before two o'clock that afternoon people began to gather together for the service. Kei, whose interest in her wonderful book was increasing, came from her little house near Nippon Boshi. Aka, Mitsu, and the *yashiki* Baba were there with their Testaments, and Fusa gladly welcomed her parents for the first time.

The church was a low wooden building with high windows, and furnished with benches. A table served for a pulpit; this was on a platform covered with neat Chinese matting. At the side of the platform was a good-sized cabinet organ. The warm sunlight poured through the windows. There were flowers on the table, and everything looked cheerful and pleasant.

The services were long; the Japanese seemed to expect this; it was not worth while to come so far and then go away immediately. Sometimes a little child would grow restless and trot around the church, the little bell it wore tinkling as it went hither and thither. Sometimes a drowsy person would fall asleep, when one of the ushers would poke the offender with a long stick.

The sermons were simple expositions of the gospel with many texts interspersed. "Sow the word, the pure word of God, and ask his blessing on it," said the missionary. And the people listened attentively, while the truth sank deep into many a heart.

On this Sabbath before Christmas the story of the Babe of Bethlehem was told to the people; and many an eye brightened with interest as they listened.

When the prayer after the sermon was ended, Mr. West said, "We will sing 'Rock of Ages.'" Old Kei sang with all her heart,

> "Nothing in my hands I bring,
> Simply to thy cross I cling."

Had she not gone with offerings—even the very best she possessed—to the idol shrines? Had she not cut off the long black tresses from her head and hung them up in the temple? Had she not gone on toilsome pilgrimages and made many prayers in weariness and painfulness? And all to no avail. And now she stood up and sang the sweet words which have been the comfort of so many weary hearts, and was happy.

The people lingered after the service to greet one another and to talk; and many said that the doctrine was good, and many thanked God for his blessings to them.

Of all the people who went away from the church that afternoon, none had listened more closely than Chiye Fujisawa; no one had tried harder to understand them than Kesa; no one was more respectfully attentive than Saijiro; and no one was more puzzled than Yenoske.

In the evening the boys and girls gathered together to receive Bible instruction in the mission chapel on the girls' compound. They repeated verses and studied a simple catechism.

One would think they would have wearied, but that night, when Miss Wilton was sitting by the fire, thinking that the day's work was over, she heard a timid knock at the door.

"Come in," she said.

It was Chiye who had knocked; and when she and the other girls had come and crowded around their teacher she said, "Oh, *sensei*, we want to know more; please, please teach us more."

The girls and boys had a happy Christmas at the mission. They sang around the tree, which Saijiro and some of the other boys had brought from a garden near Tokio, and pretty gifts were distributed among them. They called the day the "birthday of Jesus," and most of them knew the meaning of the hymns and the reason why such pretty presents were given them. "As the Father has given to us the great gift of his Son, so do we present gifts to one another."

Saijiro was one of the boys who carried around the candy-bags and Chinese oranges to the girls. Kesa looked up to thank him as she took hers, and for the first time their eyes met.

And now it was time for them to separate for the two weeks' vacation; so in the gathering twilight of the late winter afternoon, and with the prayers and the blessings of the teachers, the girls and boys dispersed to their homes.

Mrs. Fujisawa had been more than once to her door to look for her children, and was glad to hear the welcome sound of the jinrikishas.

"I have a Chinese orange and a bag of foreign candy for you, Hana," said Kesa.

"A very great thank-you," said Hana, reaching out her hand to take the treasures.

"We are going to take our teachers presents on New Year's day," said Kesa.

"I wish I could send the doctor's good wife something," sighed Hana.

"So you shall, darling," said the mother, and brought her a piece of beautiful crape.

"Thanks, honorable mother," said the sick girl, and laid it away to give to Kesa on the New Year's morning.

The year opened beautifully in Tokio. There was scarcely a cloud in the sky all day, and the winter flowers, the camellias and jonquils, and the red berries were glorious. The missionary ladies and children had gathered in the parlor, which was tastefully decorated with flowers and berries.

"Holidays are the homesick times," said the doctor's wife, drawing her little daughter closer to her. "I feel sorry to think that my Marion has missed the winter joys of the home-land: the gathering together of the happy band of relatives; the snow-balling, sleighing, skating; the nuts and apples around the fire; grandpa's and grandma's kisses and welcomes. But she shall know them some time."

"Yes, these anniversaries are the hardest days of the year," responded Miss Wilton, who was also thinking of the dear ones at home.

But their thoughts were diverted by a shout from Carroll, and looking from the window they saw a long line of jinrikishas, filled with laughing, happy girls, coming along the *Bund* (levée), bound for the mission. The girls wore bright new sashes and hairpins, and each one carried some gift for her teachers and friends.

"Happy New Year!" they all shouted at once, as they alighted from the jinrikishas and saw their friends, who had hastened out on the veranda to meet them.

"Happy New Year!" responded the missionaries, and the merry girls were conducted into the parlor.

Daintily and gracefully they presented their gifts.

"Will you condescend to stoop down and accept a little token from me?" said one, offering a beautiful lacquered box.

"May I lift up a small, poor gift to you?" said another, presenting flowers and eggs.

There were cups and balls for Marion and Carroll, and boxes of confectionery, silks, and crapes for the ladies.

"My sick sister Hana sends this to you, and begs your honorable acceptance," said Chiye, handing the doctor's wife Hana's exquisite piece of crape.

"Thank your sister very much for me, Chiye. How is she?" said Mrs. Fielding.

"Thanks, she suffers less pain."

"And she does not yet believe in the Christians' God, Chiye?"

"*Dogu*, she loves to listen to the stories of the Lord Jesus, but she also loves Shaka Sama. She does not know which to believe."

"But she has the picture of the shepherd and the lambs that you gave her, and often looks at it," said Kesa.

"Many, many thanks for your coming and your gifts," said the ladies as the girls rose to depart.

"We should like to have you remain longer, but cannot keep you from your own homes," said Miss Wilton.

The girls left with bows and *saionaras* and many good wishes.

"That is the most beautiful Japanese child I ever saw," said Mrs. Fielding, as Kesa Fujisawa waved a *saionara* from her jinrikisha.

"The Japanese do not consider her pretty," answered Miss Wilton. "But these Fujisawa girls both look you in the eye, and it is seldom that any of the others will do that. They seem like American girls to me."

"I am going over into the city to a prayer-meeting to-night," said Harukichi to Saijiro one cold winter afternoon during the vacation.

"Ah, I should like to go with you," said Saijiro, and one or two of the other boys begged permission to be of the party.

Harukichi was glad to have them accompany him and readily granted permission.

Yenoske, hearing of the meeting, asked if he might go too. So in the early evening quite a little company started from the mission-house to go to the prayer-meeting in the city. The night was cold and dark, and all were closely muffled and carried lanterns. Their wooden clogs made a sharp, ringing noise on the stones, and as they walked they talked together in low, musical tones.

"Ah," said Makichi, "I remember well the days when those who wished to study with the honorable foreigners stole over these walks at night, one at a time, in order to avoid the notice of the officers."

"Yes," answered a friend; "and you were threatened, Makichi. Did you not feel afraid?"

"*Dogu*, the flesh is weak, and sometimes I did tremble; but I know I should have had strength to endure even the horrors of a prison."

They were walking through the Foreign Concession and came at last to the bridge which divides it from the city proper.

MIDWINTER IN TOKIO.   255

"This is where the guards were stationed in the olden times. *Dogu*, one night some anti-foreign outlaws broke through and got into Tokiji" (the Foreign Concession). "What a time that was!" said Makichi.

"Yes," answered the other, "the honorable foreigners could not go out unaccompanied by guards."

They passed the gate and entered a wide street. Lanterns hung from the houses on each side. A blind shampooer was walking along, now and then blowing his shrill whistle. Another man was trundling a cart and crying out, "*Sojiura*." This is a kind of soup of which the Japanese are very fond. A few children were playing in the street, and occasionally a man or woman passed by. Every one was muffled and carried a lantern. The coolies who drew the jinrikishas found it difficult to keep their lanterns burning. The wind would often extinguish their lights, and then they would go on without any until stopped by a policeman.

On went the little company of believers through the great heathen city, until they came to the Tori. There all was life and activity. The lanterns made a beautiful display as the swiftly-moving crowd shifted from place to place. The cries of the fishmongers, the *sojiura* men and the sweet-*sake* venders, the whistle of the *amas* (shampooers), the appeals of the story-tellers, and the strange sounds of the coolies as they toiled under their heavy loads, all made a deafening uproar.

The teacher led the way quickly across the Tori to one of the back streets, and passing through a dark, narrow alley, they stopped at the entrance of a large house. They were evidently expected, for some one from within quickly admitted them and led them through the kitchen to a room in the rear.

Here were gathered about seventy people. An elderly man, evidently the proprietor, rose to greet the company from the mission, and the rest of the people bowed. There were three or four large *hibachis* in the room filled with glowing coals. Over these sat some old people, warming their hands. Some fine-looking young men with Bibles sat in one corner, and in another were some young women and children. Three or four blind men sat by a little table, and near them was a thoughtful-looking priest in yellow robes. There was no light in the room save that thrown out by the coals in the *hibachis* and the flickering flames of three or four tallow candles.

"Dear friends," said Makichi after the opening services, "we have come together for a prayer-meeting. This is the first one we have had in this neighborhood, and many of you have come to pray to the Christians' God for the first time. We do not have to call loudly to him. We do not have to beat drums or ring bells or strike on the ground with our staves. Neither do we have to repeat his name over and over, and so gain merit. He tells us that he is our Father and that we are his children; and prayer is asking him for what we want, telling him our troubles, begging him to relieve our distresses and pardon our sins, and thanking him for mercies, through our Lord and Saviour Jesus Christ.

"Now I know that some of you here to-night have wants and cares, that you need God's help, and that you also have many mercies for which you can thank him. I see old Maka crying bitterly. My friends, her sorrow is a heavy one. We all know that her beloved son is in prison for committing a crime. Can the Lord help Maka? Oh, yes; he can give her strength to bear her troubles. And prison walls cannot keep out the Lord Jesus. He can visit poor Jujiro in his cell and can turn his heart to Him. Listen to what he says to those who were thieves : 'Let him that stole steal no more; but rather let him labor, working with his hands.' And here is another text, 'The blood of Jesus Christ his Son cleanseth us from all sin.' Dearly beloved, there is hope for a thief. Let us pray for Maka and her son."

The woman stopped her sobbing to listen while one of the Christian men poured out his heart in her behalf.

"And now," continued Makichi, "I hear that

Rosuki has lost some of his worldly goods and that his heart is sorely troubled."

Rosuki bowed.

"Dear friends, listen to what the Lord Jesus says to such:

"'Lay not up for yourselves treasures upon earth, where moth and dust doth corrupt, and where thieves break through and steal; but lay up for yourselves treasures in heaven, where neither moth nor rust doth corrupt, and where thieves do not break through nor steal; for where your treasure is, there will your heart be also.' Let us pray for Rosuki."

Harukichi led in a short, fervent prayer; and as he prayed the hearts of the people were drawn upward to the glorious inheritance of the saints.

"And poor Riki"—again the teacher spoke—"has lost her two darling children, the joy and the pride of her heart. Ah, how lovingly the Lord speaks to the bereaved mother! He says, 'Suffer the little children to come unto me, and forbid them not: for of such is the kingdom of God.' Rejoice, O friends, for Riki is going to start on a pilgrimage to the land where her babies have gone, to the land where Christ, the Good Shepherd, leads his flock beside the still waters and in the green pastures.

"I know there are those here whose life is a toiling for daily bread, and sometimes they know not where they shall find house or food or clothing. Dearly beloved, the Lord speaks also to you, and says:

"'Be not anxious for your life, what ye shall eat or what ye shall drink; nor yet for your body, what ye shall put on. Is not the life more than food and the body than raiment? Behold the fowls of the air: for they sow not, neither do they reap nor gather into barns; yet your Heavenly Father feedeth them. Are ye not much better than they?'"

And thus the meeting went on, and some hungry souls eagerly seized the bread of life; thirsty souls drank joyfully of the pure waters. The weary, the sad, the burdened ones listened gratefully to the words of Jesus.

"Thanks, oh! a great thank-you," said the listeners when Makichi ceased, and then the company quietly dispersed.

Another week, and the girls all gathered back to the school.

One evening when Miss Wilton had gone to her room after worship she was startled by a succession of shrieks from the girls' dormitory.

"They must be on fire; nothing else would make them scream so," she thought, as she rushed, terrified, from her room. But when she reached the dormitory she found the room totally dark and the children huddled together in a corner. Some of the older girls had hurried up from the study-room on hearing the screams, and were trying to pacify the little ones.

"What is it?" asked the startled teacher.

"Hono saw a ghost, a terrible monster dressed in white, and with fire coming out of its eyes; and we were all frightened and put out the lamps."

"Light the lamps again," said Miss Wilton.

"Now, Hono, take your lantern and go around with me, and we will see if there is anything to make you afraid in the room."

Into every corner and cranny peered Miss Wilton, followed by the trembling Hono with her lantern. There was nothing unusual to be seen, nothing to alarm any one; and after a while all settled down quietly for the night.

The next evening, when the time came for their talk, Miss Wilton referred to their last evening's alarm and asked an explanation. "If any one was trying to frighten Hono, I want to know it. Mitsuye, was it you?"

By way of answer, Mitsuye rose and threw herself down at her teacher's feet.

"Oh, get up, Mitsuye. That is not the way we do in America," said Miss Wilton. "But I am glad to have you tell me what you did."

"*Dogu! dogu!* forgive me; your condescending forgiveness I crave," said Mitsuye.

"Think, Mitsuye, how you frightened Hono

and put all the little girls in a panic; and you might have done more mischief."

Mitsuye promised never to do such a thing again, and the teacher sent her to her seat.

"Now see at what a foolish thing you were alarmed," said Miss Wilton, turning to the other girls. "It was simply Mitsuye trying to frighten Hono. When will you girls learn not to believe in *bakemonos?*"

"Japanese mothers and nurses tell such stories to the children to frighten them and make them keep still," said one of the girls. "And sometimes children sit and tell ghost stories until they are so frightened that they scream and run from the house."

"Well, there must be none of it in the school," rejoined the teacher. "The Bible tells us of strong and holy angels who are God's messengers, and whom he employs for the good of those who trust in him. It also tells us of evil spirits; but they are all under God's control, and if we trust him all will be well."

Then the girls learned this verse, which tells of God's care for his children: "He shall give his angels charge over thee, to keep thee in all thy ways. They shall bear thee up in their hands, lest thou dash thy foot against a stone."

CHAPTER XXII.

SPRING BLOSSOMS.

The sweet springtime had come again and Japan was full of flowers. The girls and boys had all been to "see flowers," and the vases in the mission-house and school were filled with beautiful blooms of peach and cherry.

"Good morning, Harukichi. Oh, a great thank-you!" said the doctor's wife as the young man, followed by Saijiro and Ts'koi, came up and presented her with a flower-pot in which grew both pink and white blossoms from the same stalk.

"I thank you," said Mrs. Fielding. "What an exquisite branch!"

Turning then to the mountain lad she said, "Well, Saijiro, so that is your dog, is it?"

"Yes, *sensei*," answered Saijiro, making a low bow.

"How do you like the school?"

"Thanks, honorable lady, I am glad to learn."

"But still you would like to see your own mountain home?"

"*Dogu*, yes, *sensei*. I want more than all to see little Ko."

"And who is Ko?"

"He is my friend, and he is blind."

"Poor little fellow!" said Mrs. Fielding. "Is your little friend going to be an *ama?*"

"No, *sensei*, he wishes to be a priest. He loves Shaka Sama."

"I wish we could tell him of the Lord Jesus, Saijiro."

"*Dogu, sensei,* Yenoske and I talk about it. Yenoske did not care anything about Jesus until he knew that he opened the eyes of the blind."

The school-bell was ringing, and Saijiro, bowing, went off to school.

Harukichi had many things to trouble and perplex him. When he left the ladies he turned and went across a small court to the room which Mr. West, the missionary, occupied.

"Come in," said Mr. West in answer to Harukichi's knock; and the young man entered the well-known apartment and stood before the missionary.

It was a pleasant room, one window looking towards Mt. Fuji and the sunset and the other commanding a view of the river and the bay. There had been many long, serious talks in that room, and many prayers had gone up from it.

"Sit down, Harukichi. Is there something you wish to say to me?" inquired the missionary.

"Yes, *sensei*," answered the young man. "I have studied the Bible long; I love its teachings;

I know that they are true. But I love and honor my parents, and they hate Christianity."

"Your father is a wealthy man and has a beautiful home, I hear, Harukichi."

"Yes, *sensei;* and when I asked his honorable permission to be baptized and to become a teacher of Christian doctrines he was very angry and threatened to disinherit me."

"But can you not make up your mind to endure losses?"

"Yes, *sensei*. It is not that so much as the honorable mother's grief and tears that I dread. *Dogu*, she thinks some terrible evil will happen to all of us if I become a Christian. It frightens her."

"I think I understand about it, Harukichi."

"It is very hard for me to know what to do, *sensei*."

"Yes, Harukichi, I know it is hard. But what says your own heart?"

"My heart, *sensei*, is no good guide; sometimes it says one thing and sometimes another."

"Then, Harukichi, you must ask guidance of One better than your own heart. Let us go to God in prayer," and they knelt together.

"Dear Lord," prayed Mr. West, "thou seest before thee this young man who desires to walk in thy way. Thou knowest how many obstacles there are in his path; thou knowest how many times he will stumble and falter in it. Show him thy will; teach him thy way. Bless his ignorant parents and soften their hearts. Oh, Shepherd, leading thy flock, cause *this* soul to follow thee."

"Thanks, *sensei*, I will think," said Harukichi as he left the missionary; and Mr. West kept him in his thoughts and in his prayers all day.

Suddenly in the evening of that day of flowers and sunshine there came a great earthquake. The solid ground shook and trembled and the mission-houses rocked like ships upon the sea. Doors and window-shutters were burst violently open, bells were rung, and small articles were thrown down from tables and mantelpieces.

The terrified girls ran from the dining-room, where they were eating their rice, out into the open air. The missionaries, who were also at tea, stood up and held on to their plates, dishes, and lamps as well as they could. A feeling of faintness and terror came over each one as the shocks continued.

The disturbance lasted only for a moment or two, but it was enough to make them all realize the uncertainties of earth; and the girls were still pale and trembling when they gathered in the study-room for evening worship.

"We will take the earthquake for our lesson to-night," said Miss Wilton. "You were afraid, girls."

"And you also, *sensei*, and the honorable doctor's wife and the honorable children?" questioned the girls.

"Yes," answered Miss Wilton, "we did fear. It is a terrible feeling to have the ground suddenly give way under you. But we have a beautiful Psalm, part of which I will teach you soon. What do you think causes the earthquakes, Chiye?"

"*Dogu, sensei*, the Japanese have a foolish notion that the world rests on the back of a turtle, and that when the turtle moves the earth shakes!"

"What do they say the turtle rests on?"

"That I do not know, *sensei*."

"The ancient Greeks and Romans had a fable that the sky rested on the shoulders of a giant named Atlas, and that he became so weary of the burden that he tried once to induce some one else to assume it for him. How different is our God, who made and upholds all things by the word of his power and never falters or wearies."

"*Sensei*," said one of the girls, "Tokio was almost destroyed by an earthquake once, and a tidal wave swept over this part of Japan and even washed the head of Dai Butsu."

"Yes, I often think how carelessly we live here day after day, when at any time we may be swallowed up in the depths of the earth," said the teacher.

"We never think of the earthquakes until

they come, and then for a little while after," rejoined one of the girls.

"What is the best thing to do, *sensei?* Kei told us one day when we had a slight shock to go out on the roof, and when the house fell we would be on top."

Miss Wilton smiled. She tried to imagine these excitable girls sitting quietly on the roof in the event of such a catastrophe! But she answered, "The best place, in case a house falls, is a doorway, I am told. Some persons advise carrying out of doors a plank or a door, to bridge over any fissures caused by the cracking open of the earth's crust. But the plank might be too short to be of any service. It is hard to know what to do."

"What do the honorable foreigners say about earthquakes, *sensei?*" asked Chiye.

"They have a great many theories, but it is not known yet exactly what causes them. We know, however, that Japan is composed of volcanic islands and that there are fires under us; volcanoes form safety-valves for these fires; and any volcanic country is subject to earthquakes."

Then the girls learned the following verses from the forty-sixth Psalm, and went off quieted and comforted:

"God is our refuge and strength, a very present help in trouble.

"Therefore will not we fear, though the earth

be removed and though the mountains be carried into the midst of the sea;

"Though the waters thereof roar and be troubled, though the mountains shake with the swelling thereof."

"Bring me some water, Yenoske," said Carroll Fielding in a quick, peremptory tone, not at all befitting a little child of seven.

Yenoske obeyed, and Carroll took the water without a word of thanks, drank what he wanted, and then threw the remaining contents of the cup on Yenoske's feet.

"Ah," thought the patient young Japanese, "these young Americans are rude. The little master never did so."

"Carroll, come to me," now called the doctor's wife from the veranda whence she had watched these proceedings.

The child slowly and sullenly walked towards the house.

"Why do you speak so to Yenoske, Carroll?"

"He is only a Japanese coolie, auntie."

"Yenoske is worth a great deal to me, Carroll, and I do not wish you to speak or act in that way to any Japanese."

This little Carroll Fielding was a hard child to manage; he was passionate and full of self-conceit, never willing to obey, and always thrusting in his opinions. The day thus begun proved a peculiarly trying one for his aunt and himself; and when at last in the evening Mrs. Fielding left him asleep in his crib, she felt utterly discouraged and dismayed.

"I do not know what to do with him," she said to her husband, as they sat together on the veranda.

"Dear Mary, let us leave the child in God's hands. He can subdue his heart," said the doctor.

"I am afraid he will have to suffer, then."

"Yes, Mary, but the Father loves him and will do all things well for him."

The next morning the doctor went off on a missionary tour, and the children stood and waved to him from the mission-house as far as they could see the jinrikisha.

The school-bell was rung at nine o'clock, and Carroll went, as usual, to his aunt for lessons. He was quiet, she thought, but at recess went out to play. Missing him soon from the garden, however, Mrs. Fielding went to look for him, and found him asleep on the parlor floor. It was something unusual for him to sleep in the morning, and Mrs. Fielding felt a vague sense of uneasiness, though she scarcely knew why. She called Yenoske, who laid him on a sofa, where he was left to finish his nap. And so it was for two or three days.

"What is the matter, Carroll?" his aunt would ask; and the reply invariably would be,

"Nothing, auntie;" and he would get up and go on with his play.

"Come and look at Carroll," said Mrs. Fielding to her husband on the evening of his return from his three-days' trip. "He seems languid at times, and I am uneasy about him."

The doctor bent over the little bed. The child was sleeping quietly, but his fair hair was very damp and his hands were very white. "Why, Mary!" the doctor exclaimed; and the troubled expression of his countenance deepened as he examined the boy more closely.

"Oh, what is it, Richard? I did not think he was *very* sick. He has just been a little languid, but he has had his lessons and has played most of the time."

"Mary," said the doctor, drawing her to him, "a few days ago we resolved to leave this child, for whom we have had so many anxieties, in our Heavenly Father's hands. Mary, he is going to take him to himself; in a few days our boy will be safe at home."

The doctor left his wife and went with saddened heart to stand for a moment at the bedside of their own little daughter.

Mrs. Fielding went and knelt by Carroll's side. She could not think, she could not pray. Only she took one of the little waxy hands in hers and laid her head on the pillow close to that of the sleeping boy.

Could it be possible?

"He is not sick. He is not sick," she repeated again and again to herself. "He never complained of any pain, and he has been playing and happy all the time."

The little bed was moved to Mrs. Fielding's room.

"How came I here, auntie?" asked the child with a bright smile the next morning.

"We feared you were not well, Carroll," answered the doctor.

"But I am well, uncle." And he sprang up and dressed, and came in to breakfast looking so bright that Mrs. Fielding whispered, "Were you not mistaken, Richard?"

"No, Mary, there can be no mistake. Is he not always this way early in the morning?"

"You may omit your lessons, Marion, and go to play with Carroll; and when he is tired, come in. I have something to tell you." And the children went out into the garden. They went around to the side of the house and took their little spades, while the mother watched them from the window. The picture they made was one she remembered for years and years. Snatches of the conversation were wafted in through the open casement. At first it was all about the flowers.

"I am going to have chrysanthemums in my garden, and in the fall they will be so pretty," said Marion.

"Oh, I can't wait for chrysanthemums; I must have something that will bloom right away. I told Yenoske to make haste and bring me some lilies," said Carroll, digging earnestly with his little spade. "I love lilies," continued Carroll. "Saijiro has often told me of how Yenoske gathered lilies for him on the mountains."

Carroll's aunt had sometimes said that his love for flowers was a very pleasant and hopeful trait in his character. It was, indeed, a passion with him. Mrs. Fielding had often given him a bunch of flowers when his hot little temper had gained the mastery and his impatient little heart was boiling over with rage; and the sweet influence of the fair blossoms would calm him when nothing else could. Sometimes, too, they would miss him at sunset, and find him alone, drinking in the beauty of the evening sky. "Don't speak, auntie, don't speak," he had called one evening when Mrs. Fielding had thus discovered him; and he moved his little hand and turned again to the rich coloring of the west.

The children's prattle went on; and still the mother sat at the window, watching as it were a dark cloud coming up to overshadow her darlings, who were as yet in the bright sunshine, all unconscious of the approach of darkness.

"My papa is going to take me to America soon," said Carroll, with one foot resting on his spade.

"And my mamma is going to take me," chimed in his cousin; "and in the winter we are to have apples and nuts by the fire."

"I am to have a sled and skates," said Carroll. "But, oh, let us go in and rest, Marion; I am so tired!"

A deathly sickness and languor had seized the little fellow and he went with difficulty into the house. His aunt met him and he was lifted on to the sofa.

"Bring your chair, Marion, and sit by us," said Mrs. Fielding when Carroll's faint turn had passed off, leaving him weary and restless. "I heard you talking in the garden, dear children, about going to America and to grandpa's house."

"Yes, mamma, and Carroll wants a sled and some skates."

"But suppose, my little Carroll, that you were to go to a better country than America and a safer, happier home than grandpa's."

"What country is better than America, auntie?"

"I mean heaven, my darling, and our Father's house on high."

"But, auntie," and the child lifted his eyes to her face with a frightened expression, "that means dying."

"Yes, darling, I know we call it dying, but in reality, if we love the Lord Jesus Christ, it is only going into God's beautiful country, where the flowers ever bloom and where all is beautiful, pure, and good. My little Carroll must trust himself to the Saviour, and there he will never be naughty or passionate any more. He will always be happy and good."

"Oh, mamma, *must* he go?" cried Marion.

"Papa says so, darling, and he knows. Don't sob so, my daughter. If the Lord Jesus, who loves little children, wants to take Carroll, will he not be willing to go? and shall we not be willing to let him go, darling?"

Then the doctor came in with strong words of comfort, and they talked of Christ and of heaven until he and they grew happy in the prospect.

During the days that followed Carroll was the happiest, brightest, and bravest of them all. He talked cheerfully of his new home, he gave his little treasures away, he repented of all his naughty ways and gave himself to Christ with all his heart.

"I should like to see Yenoske," he said one day; "and, auntie, may I give him my little Testament?"

Yenoske was called and went quietly to the bed. The sight of the pale little face among the pillows almost broke the heart of the sympathetic Japanese.

"I beg your pardon, Yenoske, for all the naughty things I have done, and will you keep my little book?"

"*Dogu*, little master—" but Yenoske could say no more.

One day Marion wandered into the garden, and soon Kesa, who thought much about the dying boy, was at her side.

"Must Carroll die?" she asked.

"Yes, Kesa, papa says he must."

"Is he afraid, Marion?"

"No, Kesa, he is glad."

"What makes him glad? My sister Hana is always afraid to die."

"He is going to a beautiful country full of flowers and sunshine, and the Lord Jesus loves him and takes care of him."

Kesa treasured all this in her heart to tell to Hana. She was learning better lessons than those in the books.

It was at sunset that Carroll entered the land of everlasting day. He bade them all good-by, folded his little hands, and quietly went to sleep.

"He is safe now, Mary," said the doctor; and in spite of their weeping there was a deep peace in their hearts, a feeling that the Lord Jesus was specially near and tenderly assuring them that it was well with their little one.

The school children attended the short and simple service in the mission-house parlor. How restful seemed the reclining of the little body compared with the cramped sitting posture of the Japanese dead; how peaceful the crossed hands holding the lilies that Saijiro and Yenoske had brought; how sweet the expression on the little face!

Mr. West, the missionary, read in Japanese "Suffer the little children to come unto me, and forbid them not; for of such is the kingdom of God."

"Dear friends and children," he said then, "this child, whose body is lying here, gave himself to God, and He has taken him home. Jesus, the Good Shepherd, carries him in his arms and holds him in his bosom."

After a few more words and a prayer all sang in Japanese the hymn beginning,

  "Jesus loves me! this I know,"

and soon Carroll was taken away.

Not long after Carroll's death Aka, Mitsu, Chiye, and Harukichi joined the class of candidates for baptism; and so the days went on, and all were growing in knowledge.

CHAPTER XXIII.

"MUSHI."

The most unpleasant season of all the year had come in Japan. It was that which the Japanese call "*mushi*," a time of heat and constant rain, a time when everything is damp and mouldy and every person is sick and miserable.

"I cannot take up my shoes to put them on in the morning without finding them covered with mould. Nothing can be aired on account of the constant rains, our pillows are so damp and musty that we can scarcely bear to lay our heads on them, and rice kept for a day will be full of worms. We have to kindle great fires in our bedrooms and sitting-rooms, every closet door and bureau drawer is left open, and we never think of making up a bed until night." Thus wrote Mrs. Fielding to a friend in America one rainy Monday morning during the "*mushi*" season.

Marion was standing at the window looking rather disconsolately at the falling rain. The extreme heat and excessive dampness made every one feel thoroughly uncomfortable. The Sabbath had been so stormy that very few of the girls had come back to school, and Miss Wilton had begun her week's work with a few boarders who had not gone home on Friday at all.

"There is a jinrikisha, mamma," said Marion, "and it is coming here."

The jinrikisha stopped and Kesa stepped out, carrying a bunch of red lilies and a little cage.

"Why, Kesa, did you come alone in this pouring rain?" asked Mrs. Fielding.

"Thanks, Chiye is with me. I came to offer these flowers and this cage of fireflies to Marion *san*. Please graciously to accept the poor gift."

Marion took them with thanks, and Kesa went to school.

"How sweet she is, mamma, and I like the flowers; but the poor fireflies! I hate to have them crowded together in the cage. What is the reason, mamma, when the Japanese are so kind to insects, that they will catch and confine these fireflies every year?"

"That is a question pretty hard to answer, daughter. But I must go on with my letter, or it will not be ready for the mail."

Marion carried her cage into a dark closet and amused herself for a while by sprinkling water over it; this caused the fireflies to emit a bright light which illuminated the closet. Then she made a hole in the top of the cage and hung it where the insects could crawl out. She had a number of such gauze cages which had been given her from time to time, and also some, of exquisite workmanship, made of bamboo. The bamboo cages had contained singing crickets, of which the Japanese are especially fond, and which had been given to Marion with directions how to feed them with cucumbers. But the poor crickets never lived very long in their pretty cages, and their singing soon came to an end.

Then Marion was constantly the recipient of white mice and gold-fish, gifts which always distressed her, as invariably the fish died and the mice came to an untimely end.

"I like flowers, eggs, and pictures, or pretty lacquered boxes and teacups, but I don't like live presents," she would say.

At last, however, the doctor had a fish-pond made and committed it to the care of the Japanese servants, who understood it; and the fish were as contented on the mission premises as they had been in the Fujisawa pond. As for the mice, Yenoske was very fond of them, and made them a house near his own room and fed them with his own hand.

One morning during the *mushi* Yenoske came into Mrs. Fielding's sitting-room and said, "Please, honorable mistress, I have something to say to you."

"Very well, Yenoske, say it right out then. Don't tell me that your mother is sick or dead and that you wish to leave."

"Please, honorable mistress, my honorable

parents are well; but"—here Yenoske looked rather conscious and foolish—"I wish to return for a time to my own country."

"Why, Yenoske, I shall be sorry to lose you. You have been a good, faithful servant. And what will become of Saijiro?"

"*Dogu*, honorable mistress, I shall not be away long. I wish to look upon the faces of my honorable parents; and, *dogu*, I wish to get a wife."

Mrs. Fielding could not complain of any lack of directness in the manner in which the last announcement was made. She smiled and said, "But surely, Yenoske, you do not wish to go in all this rain!" for all over Japan the rain had been pouring almost incessantly for three weeks, and there was no immediate prospect of a change.

"*Dogu*, I will wait until the rain is over, honorable mistress; but I wish to send a letter to a go-between and have the honorable bride ready, so that I need not be kept away very long."

"But can you live with your wife in your small room, Yenoske?"

"*Dogu*, it is a beautiful room, honorable mistress, and we are only too fortunate."

"Very well, Yenoske, I wish you success and much joy."

So it happened that one day, about two weeks later, Yenoske bade farewell to Saijiro and his friends at the mission-house, went out of the city and travelled along the great highway to Odawara. Saijiro longed to go too, but it was thought best that he should not, so he contented himself with sending a great many messages to his friends in Yamamidzu, especially to Ko.

Oh, how Yenoske's heart thrilled as he stood at the foot of the mountain, staff in hand, all ready for a climb! What long breaths he took of the pure mountain air! How like music to his ears was the sound of the waterfall! How he sang of the trees and the flowers! The only thing that marred his happiness was that he had heard not a word from his go-between, and knew not whether his fair one had accepted him. But still with swift feet he climbed the mountain, often leaving the highway and jumping from rock to rock.

At last he came to the turn of the road, and, looking down the mountain path, saw the houses of Yamamidzu. He ran quickly down into the village, passing the old shrine of Inari, where he had so often stopped to pray. He had not yet become a Christian, but he had lost his reverence for Inari and his fear of him, and could pass the fox-god without stopping.

All this time he had seen nothing of the villagers, but at the end of the street he now saw the old priest coming towards him.

"*Dogu*, Yenoske, you are welcome. How is the little master? We have heard that the honorable *sensei* is dead and finished," said the *bon-sama*.

"Thanks, the little master is well; and the honorable teacher is buried in the Buddhist cemetery in Tokio."

"Does the little master go to school?"

"Thanks, yes; he is learning many things of the honorable foreigners and is happy. But tell me where I can find Bokichi."

"Ah, Bokichi is in his home," answered the priest, smiling; and Yenoske went on.

But out from the temple came Kojiro, running; he had heard Yenoske's voice. The child could scarcely speak from excitement, so anxious was he to hear from Saijiro.

"The little master is well, Ko," said Yenoske, taking him by the hand; "and he told me to tell you how the honorable teachers tell him of Jesus, who cured the blind."

"*Dogu*," said Kojiro, "I wish they would come and tell me about him."

"They have sent some books, and some day they are coming themselves," answered Yenoske.

The two were hurrying up the street to the little inn, where Yenoske stopped to go in and greet his parents. Then he hastened to find Bokichi, the go-between.

"*Dogu*, the honorable Yen consents and is ready," said Bokichi.

In truth, the bright, happy Yen of the mountain was the one whom Yenoske had selected as his bride. The old *baba* was dead, and Yen had come to live in Yamamidzu.

"Thanks for your kindness; you have attended to my business well," said Yenoske.

In the evening the villagers, the blushing Yen among them, crowded around Yenoske on the temple steps. Close to his side crept little Kojiro, eager for news of his friend. The old priest had been in Tokio, and asked something about the city. Yenoske told them of the foreign-built houses in the Tori and of the foreign cars and omnibuses which run up and down the wide streets.

"*Dogu*, it must be very dangerous to the Japanese. Are children killed?" asked one of the villagers.

"I have never heard of a child having been killed," answered Yenoske. "They have Japanese grooms to run in front of the horses, and they lift the children out of the way."

"Tell us about the iron road with iron horses breathing out fire. Have you had a ride on it, Yenoske? and were you terribly frightened?" asked the landlord, Yenoske's father.

"The little master and I rode a few miles once," answered Yenoske.

"*Dogu! dogu!*" said the mother.

"Very wonderful!" said the father.

"We went very fast, and sat on wooden benches and held on tightly."

"Are the honorable foreigners good to you, my son?" asked the anxious mother.

"Very, very kind, honorable mother. I have never known such kind masters. They tell us that the 'Jesus-books' teach them to be kind and good to all. *Dogu*, I cannot understand the doctrines well, but they are good."

"Tell us about the *sensei*," said the priest.

"He believed in the Jesus-book before he died. He looked happier than I ever saw him look before."

"My son, be careful. Our gods may be very angry. It is better to be safe and to reverence the gods of your fathers, and not to neglect the worship of your honorable ancestors," said the mother.

"*Dogu*, honorable mother, I am not a Christian; I cannot understand the doctrines well enough yet. But I know that they are all good. And when the little foreign master died they said that he had gone to a happy country to be with their God, and that they too were going there some day and should see him. And he gave me a book;" and Yenoske took the little Testament out of his sleeve.

"*Dogu*," said the mother, taking hold of the book carefully as though afraid of it; "I don't know; but be careful."

A few days after this there was a wedding in the village. All of the village girls went and escorted the pretty bride with her newly blackened teeth to the inn, where Yenoske, a happy bridegroom, waited with his parents. Yen was warmly welcomed into the family and the usual ceremonies took place. Then came a feast of *sake*, sweetmeats, and soup for the villagers.

The following morning the happy pair trudged away, Yenoske carrying the luggage—two bright paper boxes, each swung on one end of a pole—on his shoulders. The strong, hearty mountain girl walked by his side, and on the fourth day they came to Tokio.

"Ah, Yenoske," said the doctor, "you are back; and this is your wife?"

Yen had been instructed to shake hands with the foreigners and put out her right hand timidly.

The missionaries all came out to greet them, and Saijiro ran over from the school to offer his congratulations and hear from the village.

The servants had a feast and Yen began housekeeping in her small room. A *hibachi*, two *futons*, with coverings and pillows, two paper boxes containing the trousseau, some small utensils and dishes, and some pictures completed the list of household goods.

And now the school term was about to close and the girls and boys were getting ready for their examinations.

Chiye had long since entered the Third Reader

class with her friend Fusa. Kesa had plodded through the First Reader and had just begun the Second. Saijiro had almost finished the Second Reader, was able to write to his "mother in America," and had developed a wonderful quickness in mathematics.

The few months at school had changed them all. New intelligence was expressed in their faces. They had learned a great deal, thought a great deal, seen a great deal, and were vastly improved.

"What does your father say, Chiye?" asked Miss Wilton, when Chiye came to her one day and expressed a desire to be baptized with Aka and Mitsu.

"He said that we might receive baptism, *sensei*, if we said nothing to him about it and did not let him know just when it was done."

So on the Sabbath before school closed Aka, Mitsu, Chiye, and Harukichi were admitted into the church through the ordinance of baptism. Not one of them all gave evidence of a more intelligent and loving trust in Christ than Chiye. Harukichi, looking on her sweet face, loved her, and purposed in his heart that some day, God willing, he would make her his wife. But of that Chiye knew nothing.

CHAPTER XXIV.

HARUKICHI AND CHIYE.

There were very few at the prayer-meeting in the mission chapel on the Wednesday evening after school closed. The pupils had scattered for the summer vacation, some of them going far into the country. Harukichi and Saijiro were there, and after the meeting they lingered to speak to the missionary.

"So, Harukichi, you leave us to-morrow," said Mr. West kindly.

"Yes, *sensei*, and I ask your honorable permission for Saijiro to accompany me as far as Oji."

"Certainly, Harukichi; and may God be with you and bless you."

"*Saionara*," said Harukichi.

"*Saionara*," responded Mr. West, with a warm grasp of Harukichi's hand.

Harukichi was going home. Before him lay the hard task of informing his parents of his public confession of Christ and his intention to study for the Christian ministry. The struggle had been sore, but was now over. He was ready to meet his father's anger, ready to give up all his earthly hopes, ready even to bear the sight of his mother's tears.

Before sunrise the next morning Harukichi and Saijiro were on their way out of the city. Their road at first led them along the river bank. They passed the great temple Asaxa, where Hana had been taken to rub the god Bindzuru.

"I cannot think how I ever worshipped those idols," said Harukichi. "Last night when Mr. West prayed with me and begged our Heavenly Father to watch over and protect me, I thought how absurd it would be to pray thus to Shaka Sama. We were always afraid that the gods were angry with us, and the idea of their loving us never entered our heads."

"Yes; my honorable father spent all his life in trying to turn away the anger of the gods," answered Saijiro.

"I have heard of your father, Saijiro; he died a Christian."

The sun was just rising over Tokio, coming up out of the Eastern Sea. Some laborers, going out to their daily toil, stopped when they saw the sun and stood facing it with clasped hands and bowed heads. One man caught the reflection in a pail of water which he carried, and stooping over worshipped that.

"O Saijiro, I *must* give my life to teaching them better things," said Harukichi.

"But is n't it better that they should worship the sun than those images?" said Saijiro.

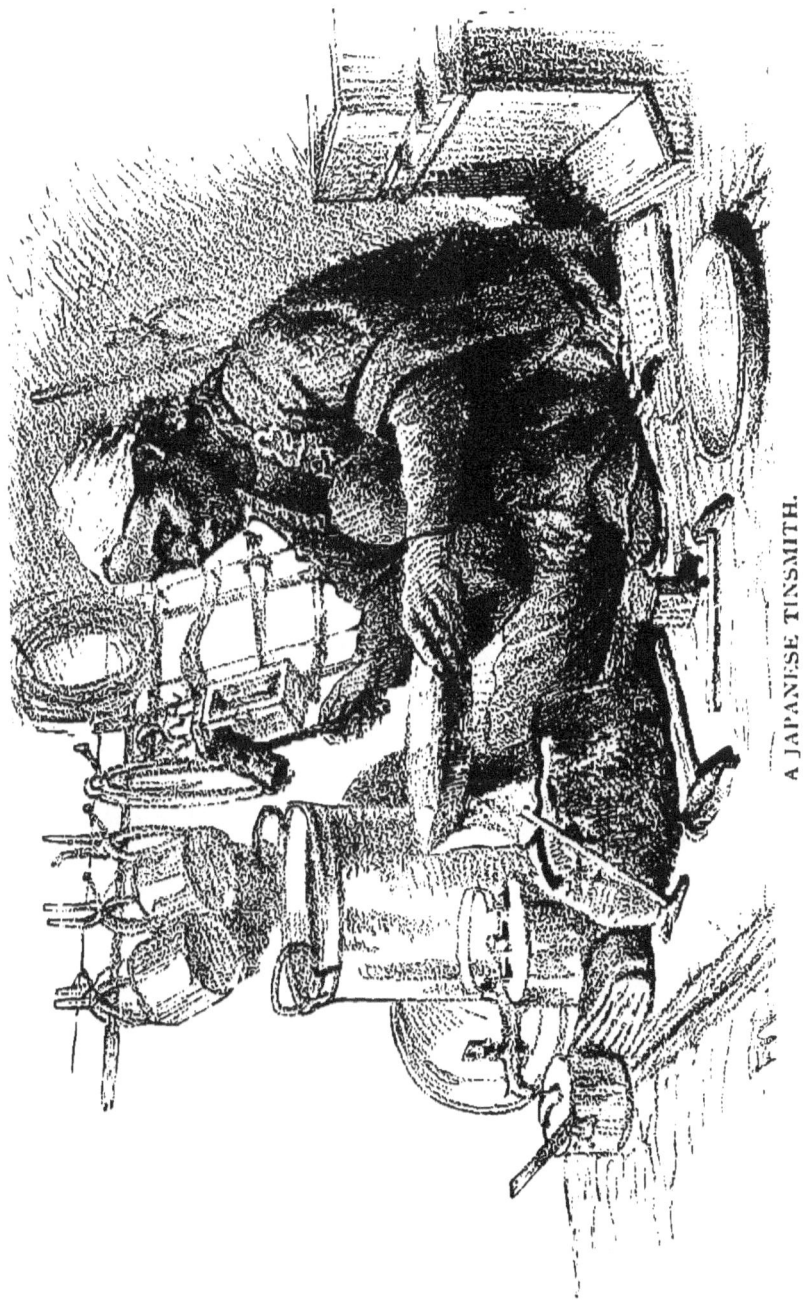

A JAPANESE TINSMITH.

"They must go higher than the sun, Saijiro, to the God who made it."

Then the man with the pail of water, observing that they did not worship, asked, "Honorable masters, how is it that you do not worship the sacred luminary?"

"We are Christians, and we worship one true God. He made the sun, and we worship him," said Harukichi.

The man shook his head and said, "I do not understand," and went away.

Harukichi and Saijiro followed the path across the green, beautiful fields to Oji. In the midst of rice-paddies were every now and then clumps of trees, and under the trees thatched farmhouses. The people were just beginning to stir. Men and women were performing their morning ablutions on the verandas and by the brooks, and naked children were playing around. Some jinrikisha men were getting their carts dusted and their blankets cleaned and aired before going out to seek for customers. They looked up anxiously at Harukichi and Saijiro, but the rich man's son, who had always been accustomed to take the finest jinrikishas and *kagos*, now felt that he must save his money, so he shook his head and walked on.

The friends walked quickly on, enjoying the summer morning, and at last came into the village. They walked down its one street, with the clear stream on one side of them and the long row of hotels on the other, never heeding the invitations to stop and rest which were urged upon them. Reaching the end of the village, they sat down on a bench at a tea-house and took a cup of tea.

"*Dogu*," said Harukichi, feeling really sorry to part from the bright boy who had been his companion all through the winter, "I wish I could ask you, Saijiro, to come and visit me this summer; but, *dogu!* I have no home; the honorable father will not receive me, and the honorable mother will be ill with grief."

Saijiro did not know exactly what consolation to offer. "But you will come back to the school, Harukichi," he said at length.

"Yes; I must find some work, and I must study to be a Christian teacher. But now you must go back, Saijiro, and I will go on to Nikko."

"Ah, I have heard that it is very beautiful at your home, Harukichi."

"Yes, Saijiro, Nikko is a beautiful place. Oh, if you could see the trees, the waterfalls, the flowers, and my honorable parents! Oh, they have been so good to me, Saijiro; I cannot bear to displease them!"

"Why do they hate the Christians so, Harukichi? I think the Christians are good and kind; and what they tell us is not foolish, like the stories of our own religion."

"I hope the honorable parents will know better some day, Saijiro. But now good-by; I must go on alone."

So they parted, Saijiro to go back to the lonely schoolhouse in Tokio, and Harukichi to the sacred mountains of Nikko.

For several days he travelled slowly along the great highway. At night he stopped at the humblest inns; he contented himself with the cheapest food. Sometimes he would bathe his weary feet in a spring by the wayside; sometimes he lay down to rest on the soft moss under the grand old trees. He had always before travelled with servants, and had commanded all the luxuries possible to travellers in Japan. He had gone home to receive the fondest, proudest greetings from father and mother; now he expected only anger and tears. But Harukichi enjoyed these days of solitude on the highway. A sweet peace filled his breast, and as he went he often sang the hymns of the church and read the loved stories of the Saviour's life on earth.

Oh, you in more favored Christian lands who have never yet had to leave "house or brethren or sisters or father or mother or wife or children or lands" for Christ's sake and the gospel's, you do not realize the blessedness of the "hundred-fold" reward which those who are called to such surrender receive even in this life.

Going up the magnificent avenue which leads

to Nikko's temples, Harukichi met a friend, and under the great archway they saluted.

"Welcome home, Harukichi. The father and mother will greatly rejoice," said the friend.

Gently and firmly Harukichi answered, "Koskiki, I have become a Christian, I have been baptized, and I fear there will be no rejoicings."

The friend looked concerned, and said, "*Dogu*, I fear the honorable father will be very angry."

Harukichi bowed and they passed on, the friend going down the mountain and Harukichi still ascending it towards Nikko.

The temples of Nikko are the finest of all Japan. Marvellous are the gates of bronze, exquisite the gildings and carvings, magnificent the stone pavements and the lanterns. In the solemn shades priests are ever attending to the duties of their ritual, gliding in and out in their white and yellow robes; never-ceasing prayers are made, and incense continually fills the temples. Harukichi passed them all by without stopping and went around the mountain-side to his own home. It was almost dark when he reached the house, and no one had observed his approach.

The house was situated in the midst of beautiful gardens. At one side a waterfall from the mountain fell over the terraced grounds into a pond, where were innumerable gold and silver

A JAPANESE MANSION.

fish. Clumps of trees were scattered here and there, and all the summer flowers of Japan were blooming in the gardens. The house was large and arranged with a view to the comfort and pleasure of its occupants. There were rooms in the upper story affording the most advantageous outlook upon the beautiful view presented in every direction. From one point the highest peaks of Nikko were visible, their tops almost veiled in mist. From another one had a sight of the waterfall, from its start on the rocky mountain to where it fell into the fish-pond. Another point revealed the winding road down the mountain, with trees and vines and sunny slopes between. There were tea-houses in the gardens, and arbors and shady retired nooks, into some of which one had to climb by means of steps cut in the solid rock. Harukichi stood and looked on the familiar scene for a moment; tears came into his eyes and his courage suddenly failed. He turned away and entered a little grove. The last rays of the setting sun touched one spot far up in the tree-tops, making a golden glory in the midst of the darkness.

Harukichi knelt, and bowing his head prayed thus:

"Dear Lord, I am a poor ignorant Japanese, weak and sorrowful. Give me strength to tell father and mother that I have learned to love thee and am determined to serve thee. Soften their hearts and turn them unto thee. And now, O Lord Jesus, give me strength."

And strength was given. Harukichi walked firmly to the house. The father and mother were sitting in the family room, waiting for the dinner to be served. Harukichi entered and prostrated himself before them.

"Welcome, my son," said the father.

"A very great happiness," said the mother.

"How are your honorable healths?" asked Harukichi, raising his head, but immediately lowering it again.

"Thanks, we are well. And your honorable health, my son?"

"Thanks, I am well," answered Harukichi. Then he sat up and waited respectfully to see what would come next.

"You have come home now to remain, my son," said the father. "You need not to study any more."

"Thanks, no, honorable father; I have not come home to stay. I have been baptized as a Christian, O my father, and am going back to study to be a teacher of Christianity to my people. Pardon me, O honorable parents, and still receive me as your son."

Then came angry expostulations and rebukes on the part of the father and bitter weeping from the mother. She thought it shameful, this ignorant Japanese woman, that her only son should forsake the religion of his fathers and follow other teachings.

"I hate the Christians," she said; "they teach children to disobey their parents. Oh, my son, I fear the wrath of the gods. And will you no more worship at the ancestral tablets, no more go up with me to the holy shrine, no more read with me the holy doctrines of Buddha? *Dogu! dogu! dogu!*" The poor woman rocked to and fro in her agony.

"See," said the father, "you are crushing your mother with sorrow."

Harukichi had risen and stood upright. "Honorable father," he said, "one of the chief commandments of the Christian religion is, 'Honor thy father and thy mother.' But when the commands of God are different from those of our earthly parents, we are to obey God. It grieves my heart to see my mother's tears, but, honorable, beloved parents, my resolution is taken; I am a Christian and shall remain one."

Then said the father, "You know my will. Go out from my house and come back no more, nor expect anything from me, until you repent of your evil and return to the faith of your ancestors."

Harukichi bowed and went out. Some of the servants, meeting him, saluted him with joy; he answered them kindly and passed on down the mountain-side. He cared not for shelter or refreshment, but throwing himself down under a tree on the soft moss, slept an uneasy sleep until the morning.

A few days after, weary and travel-worn, he stood before Mr. West in his study at Tokio.

"So, Harukichi, you have come back," said the missionary.

"Yes, *sensei*, the honorable father has driven me from his home. Now I must work, so that I can go on with my education."

The missionary gave him copying to do for the summer, and when school began he took charge of some of the small boys. It was a great change, but he bore it bravely, and the little ones loved him.

The days passed on, and Chiye and Kesa had been nearly two years in school. Kesa was now in the Third Reader, and was beginning to understand a little better and to take a greater interest in her studies. Chiye had gone through book after book in her eager thirst for knowledge, and was now a member of the most advanced class in the school. Never had the devoted teacher enjoyed a class more than this one in Moral Science. The discussions on the various subjects brought up by the text, of right and wrong, of conscience, responsibility, and other matters, just suited and pleased the thoughtful girls; and of all of them Chiye Fujisawa was the brightest and the most beloved.

One day as Miss Wilton was passing through the hall her quick ears caught the sound of suppressed sobbing, and as she turned around she discovered Chiye weeping bitterly in a corner.

"Why, Chiye, what is the matter?" she asked, hastening to the girl.

"*Dogu, sensei*, I have been very wicked; I called Haru a fool, and she will not forgive me."

"I should think she would find it hard to forgive, Chiye. You must be careful. It is well to speak out just what you think sometimes, instead of trying to cover up unpleasant truths, as the Japanese do; but one must remember to be kind and not hurt any one's feelings."

Only a few evenings after this, when the girls came to say good night, the teacher missed Chiye from among them.

"Where is Chiye Fujisawa?" she asked.

"*Dogu*, she is very sick; blood comes from her mouth when she speaks, and she feels very ill." The doctor was summoned, and looked grave.

For days after that Chiye Fujisawa lay on her pallet, thus suddenly stricken down in the midst of her young, strong, vigorous life, never again to know perfect health, always to be more or less a sufferer, but always cheerful, patient, and loving.

Kesa, in her own sweet way, would comfort Chiye, not by words, for this quiet little maiden had few of them, but by her presence, never being contented to remain long away from her beloved sister. Sometimes Miss Wilton would be ready to chide the child for restlessness and inattention in school, and the words would be arrested by the wistful look in Kesa's eyes.

"Will you take your book and sit by Chiye?" she would ask.

Then a glad light would come to Kesa's eyes and she would slip off to the dormitory. Hour after hour, if permitted, she would stay there, patient and gentle, never seeming to weary, never wanting to play.

The father and mother came and went as they could. Miss Wilton thought Fujisawa cold and indifferent. But he deeply mourned the fate of his favorite child, and his heart grew more hard and bitter.

Old Kei came often and sat with Chiye, and one day Meguchi stole into the room and sang low lullabies, such as the women sing to their sleeping infants; and Chiye listened and was soothed.

Miss Wilton missed Chiye in the schoolroom. She had never known before how she had depended upon her as a leader among the girls, how many hopes were centred in her as a helper in the Christian work. She had always been bright, active, and strong. Her fearless way of speaking the truth and her honest methods of dealing with every one had been a relief from the weak, vacillating characters of most of the other girls.

One evening, before the lamp had been lighted in the sick-room, Miss Wilton stole quietly in and sat down by Chiye's side.

"*Sensei*," murmured the young sufferer.

"Did you know it was I, Chiye?"

"Yes; I shall always know when you are with me."

"I was thinking that when I came over to Japan and first saw the shores of this pleasant country, I was a perfect stranger and knew no one. Now how different it would be if I should go back to America and return here again. How many pleasant anticipations of meeting dear ones I should have! And I think, Chiye, it is something like our looking forward to the heaven of which we are told. We already know some who are with the Lord and who are waiting to welcome us there."

"Yes, *sensei;* I know Carroll and Rinjiro, and there is Saijiro's father."

"But best of all the Lord Jesus, Chiye. Just as you felt my presence when I came in and sat by you without speaking, so do we feel at times his nearness; and we will be no strangers in the land whose Prince is our own familiar friend."

Haru at first had kept away from Chiye, but one day she came to the teacher and begged to be allowed to help with the nursing.

"Have you quite forgiven her, Haru?" asked Miss Wilton kindly.

Haru's eyes filled with tears. "See," she said, holding up before Miss Wilton a beautifully-embroidered *furushiki* or kerchief, "Chiye worked night and day to get this done for me; I almost think it made her sick to work so hard; and I never thanked her." Haru was crying bitterly by this time.

Miss Wilton led her to Chiye, and on returning after a time found her sitting by Chiye's side, happy and at peace.

So, through the long days of sickness and nights of pain, a sweet, restful atmosphere pervaded the sick-room and even made itself felt all over the mission building.

At last there came a day when Chiye was taken home. She begged to be laid by Hana's side; she had something to tell Hana.

"Are you very sick, sister?" asked the younger girl.

"Yes, Hana darling."

"Are you going to die, as I am?"

"I do not know. But, oh, Hana, I am not afraid. I should go into the country where Carroll is, and the Lord Jesus would be with me."

"I wish I were not afraid, sister."

"You need not be, darling. If you were one of the lambs you would not be afraid to follow the shepherd, would you?"

"No, sister; I often look at the picture, and the shepherd's face is so kind and the country where he is tending his flock is so fair."

"Chiye, the honorable doctor has forbidden you to talk," called the anxious mother.

Hana turned away and slept; but she never forgot that Chiye was not afraid to die.

There came a letter soon after this to Fujisawa; it was from the aunt in Nagoya, and begged a visit from Chiye. Thinking that the change might do her good, Fujisawa consented, and Chiye was carried up into the bracing air of the Hakones. After spending some time at the springs, she was taken down to Nagoya.

When Chiye went away Kesa almost made herself sick with crying. The parting with her favorite sister was her first real sorrow. Miss Wilton noticed her loneliness and gave her more thought and care. The child appreciated this at once, and soon learned to love her teacher with all the fervor of her little undisciplined heart.

CHAPTER XXV.

THE DISMANTLED SHRINE.

It was Friday afternoon. The week's work at the school was done, and the girls were getting ready to go to their homes. Already several jinrikishas were waiting at the gates.

"Kesa, can you come to me and hear a letter from Chiye?" called Miss Wilton.

Kesa ran quickly to her teacher.

"Has your jinrikisha not yet come?"

"No, *sensei*," answered the child; "please condescend to read me the letter."

Miss Wilton put her arm around the little girl, drew her to her side, and then read slowly and distinctly Chiye's English letter.

"Dear Teacher: I love you very much. I hope you take great care of your body and not get sick. I thank you, I am much better. No more bleeding come from my lungs. I thank God for this. I want to get well and teach poor ignorant Japanese the way of the true God. My aunt will not believe. She lets me read the Bible to her at some time, but she too much like the doctrine of the Japanese. Pray for her. She is very strict Buddhist woman, like my mother. Dear teacher, I feel for my sister Hana. She is going to die, and she does not know what she believe, and she fear to pain the honorable mother's heart if she believe in true God and on our Lord Jesus Christ. Will you not pray for her and teach her better? And I fear for my little sister Kesa. She think not much of anything. She very careless and do many wrong things. But she in school. I talk with my sister Hana before I came away. I tell her I not afraid to die, but she does not know where she is going.

"Dear teacher, my heart feel dark and sad sometimes. But I try to think that God will hear my prayer. I think next year I come home, but I think I not see my sister Hana any more. Nagoya is a nice place. My aunt's house near a beautiful castle. But it a great Buddhist place. The people worship so much. They go early in the morning to the temple, and I can hear the bell-ringing and praying in the temple. Then my heart feel sorry.

"Dear teacher, I want missionary come here. I want to see all the girls, but more than all I want to see my little sister Kesa. Dear teacher, I send you my love and my love to all the girls. I hope you write me soon.
"CHIYE FUJISAWA."

Kesa's eyes had filled with tears while Miss Wilton read the letter. "I am going to try and be a good girl, and to think more about what I am doing," she said.

Just then she spied her jinrikisha and old Meguchi, and soon after was rolling through the streets towards the Kudan.

"Hana is very sick to-day, and she is looking for you; she has been wanting you all day, Ke-chan," said Meguchi.

So when Kesa had saluted her mother she went to Hana and sat down by the *futon* on which the sick girl was lying.

"Please read to me, Kesa, about the Shepherd," said Hana.

Mitsu often read and talked to Hana. What Carroll had said about the sinless, painless, joyful country to which he was going, where the Lord Jesus was the Shepherd of his flock, had been talked about again and again. Aka, too, would talk with Hana and read to her from the Japanese New Testament. And Hana listened to them both. But, strange to say, she rather turned for help and comfort to the little sister, the heedless, careless child who, Chiye said, thought so little and did so many wrong things.

"Have you learned anything more about Jesus?" No one knew it, but this was the question that Hana put week after week to Kesa, as she came home on Fridays. And Kesa listened, for Hana's sake more than for her own, to everything that was said about the Lord Jesus; and when they were alone she would tell Hana that she had heard this and that of him. He had said that if a man believed in him he should never die. He had raised Lazarus from the dead and had healed the sick daughter of the Syrophœnician woman. The stories comforted Hana, and they fell like seed into Kesa's own heart.

Kesa sat patiently by Hana's side and read of the Shepherd who gave his life for the sheep, until she was called to the evening meal. It was dark and the candles were lighted. Fujisawa was away on some business, and the mother was occupied with Hana, so Kesa and Mitsu ate their dinners together.

"A letter came from Chiye to-day to the *sensci*," said Kesa.

"And how is Chiye?" asked Mitsu.

"She is better, and she sends her love. How can people send love in a letter, Mitsu?"

"Kesa, you ask such foolish questions sometimes," said Mitsu.

"But the Japanese send 'compliments, compliments,'" persisted Kesa, "and the honorable foreigners send love. Do you think, sister, that the Japanese love their children as well as the honorable foreigners do?"

"*Dogu*, Kesa," said Mitsu, not knowing what else to say, and scarcely daring to meet those earnest eyes.

But Kesa did not wait for an answer. "Marion's mother takes her in her arms and kisses her, and calls her her darling and talks to her;

and they make gardens together, and she helps Marion with her dolls, and—and— But my mother never calls me her darling nor talks to me nor helps me with my dolls. Japanese dolls are not like American dolls, are they, sister? Their clothes are sewed on them, and we don't play with them as the American girls do. *I* should like to be an American girl and to have a doll that I could love and a mother who loved me."

"Kesa," said Mitsu, astonished at this outburst, "you have had everything you have wanted all your life, and it is a shame to say that the mother does not love you."

"Oh, I didn't mean that," said Kesa.

"And see," continued Mitsu, "how for so many years the mother has given up everything to Hana. She never goes out; for two years she has had no new clothes; she gets no rest at night. Kesa, how can you say that Japanese mothers do not love their children? You are an ungrateful girl."

A dim sense of not being understood passed through Kesa's heart, but there the conversation dropped.

The mother and daughters spent the evening together in Hana's room, and at about ten o'clock Mitsu and Kesa went to bed. Mrs. Fujisawa busied herself for a time in making preparations for the night. She shook up the pallet and arranged the pillow. Hana had a comfortable pillow which the doctor's wife had sent her, and had long ago discarded the wooden one. Then Mrs. Fujisawa gave Hana her medicine, and after that she got down in a corner of the room to mend a dress to be ready for Kesa in the morning. Hana lay quite still for a time, and her mother thought she was asleep; but she was looking up at the shrine where the candles burned and where the flowers filled the vases. There was the gilded image of Benten Sama, and there the jolly faces of Daikoku and Yebisu. There were little imaages of other gods also, and pictures and scrolls.

Hana looked at them long and earnestly and then called, "Honorable mother."

"Yes, my darling;" and the mother hastened to the pallet.

"Honorable mother, I have something to ask."

"And what is it, my child?"

"I want you to take away the images; I cannot bear to see them any more. Mother, mother, please take them away."

Take away the idols, dismantle the shrine before which the mother had prayed during so many years! Surely some terrible calamity would happen to her if she did!

"Oh, mother, mother," pleaded the girl, who saw her hesitation, "I cannot bear to see them. I am going to die, mother, and I cannot die looking at them. I want to have the Lord Jesus with me when I die, mother. I know he could come even if they were here; but oh, mother, please take them away."

Mrs. Fujisawa, trembling and crying, went up to the shrine and began to take down the images. She carried them carefully into an inner room and set them up in a corner. What would the gods think to have their images so dishonored!

But the ancestral tablets were left and the flowers and the candles and the incense-boxes.

"Oh, take them all away, mother," still pleaded the girl. "I cannot worship the spirits of our ancestors; they cannot help me. O mother, I am going to die, and I cannot die in peace. Oh, do not cry so, mother; the gods will not hurt us; and I am going to be with Carroll and with the Lord Jesus in the Christians' paradise."

With sobs convulsing her whole frame the poor mother took away the flowers and put out the candles. Then she took from the altar the offerings to the idols and removed the altar-cloth.

The sick girl watched her with eager eyes until it was all over and there was nothing left, not even the boards of the altar, to mark the place of worship. Then the books were put away, the books which Mrs. Fujisawa had read so often, and in their place were laid some copies of the Gospels.

"Now, honorable mother, come and lie down by me."

Mrs. Fujisawa laid her pallet down by Hana's, and the girl put her arm around her. "Dear mother," she said, "we have prayed to them so many years and they have done us no good. Now I have peace; I believe in the Lord Jesus, and he has forgiven my sins. Will the honorable father allow me to be baptized?"

"*Dogu*," said the poor puzzled mother, who felt as if everything was sliding away from her, "I do not know."

"Oh, mother, I can go to sleep now; I have peace."

They were the last words that Hana uttered. When the morning came the poor suffering life on earth was over and Hana had gone away.

Miss Wilton, sitting by her window, saw Kesa coming in a jinrikisha with a servant. She hastened to meet her and drew the sobbing child into the house.

"My sister Hana is dead; she died last night. But oh, before she died she had all the idols taken away, and she believed in the true God!"

"I am glad, Kesa. Her pain is over. Wait and I will go with you to your house."

Miss Wilton, sitting by the sorrowing mother, heard with tears in her eyes the story of Hana's last evening upon earth. She tried to comfort the mother and to lead her also to the Shepherd in whom at last her suffering child had trusted; but her mind seemed singularly darkened, and the teacher on leaving her felt discouraged and sad, not knowing what a deep impression her tender sympathy had made in the heathen woman's heart.

Kesa sat beside her mother, holding her hand, and Mitsu and Aka were in the room. All strove to lead Mrs. Fujisawa to some comfort. But "I do not know; I do not know," was still her cry.

Soon old Kei came to pour out her tears. How changed the home was! It seemed only a few days to Kei since it was full of merry, laughing children. Tama had long since gone to her northern home and had a little family growing up around her, Chiye was away on the other side of the Hakones, Hana was dead, and Kesa was almost all the time away at school; so there was left only the quiet, saddened Mitsu.

Fujisawa was summoned to his home and reached it late in the afternoon. Life seemed too much of a disappointment to him in respect to his children. Tama, to be sure, had done just as he had willed, and was prosperous and happy; but after all he had an idea that her life did not amount to much. Mitsu was a poor, weak creature, sad and suffering, and a Christian. His pet and pride, Chiye, would never make the scholar he had hoped; his plans for her were frustrated. Hana was lying dead in the beautiful home. The bright chrysanthemums were blooming in vain for her. And Kesa? Well, she was still a child; she should do what he pleased; she should not be allowed to act as the others had done—forsake her mother's religion and follow strange doctrines. She was too young yet, he thought, to be much influenced by the Christians. He would take her away from school soon and marry her into some high family, for she was fit to be a princess, he said to himself, and his heart filled with pride. He knew something of the admiration that this beautiful Japanese child excited among foreigners, and yet he had hardened his heart into almost hating her. Grief and disappointment had no softening effect upon this father's heart. He was growing cold and bitter, and all his hardness and coldness and bitterness seemed likely to find a vent in tyrannizing over his youngest child.

Kesa meantime was sitting disconsolate, and with vague wondering thoughts in her heart, by the side of the fish-pond, bright sunshine over her and bright flowers all around her. Oh, if Chiye were only at home! she thought. She and Chiye could talk together. If her mother were only like Marion's mother and her father like Marion's father! Where was the "happy land" to which Carroll and Hana had gone? And the Shepherd of whom they spoke so confidently, did he care for her? Kesa sobbed in her perplexity and did not hear a soft footstep behind her, and did not know that her teacher was near her, until she found herself taken into those loving arms and tenderly soothed and comforted.

"My little Kesa," said Miss Wilton, "why do you cry so? Is it because Hana is dead? You know how great her pain was and how hard it was to bear, and are you sorry because she has gone to the country where there is no pain and where no one says, 'I am sick'?"

"No, *sensei*," sobbed the child, "I was crying for myself. It is so lonely."

"But I am here, my little Kesa, and God loves you."

Oh, the wistful, questioning look in those dark eyes! Miss Wilton's heart yearned in unexpressed tenderness over the child, and she seemed to come under the shadow of the cloud that was overhanging Kesa herself. "Kesa," she said, "I must go. But remember, dear, that I love you, and above all, that our Heavenly Father loves you."

Kesa heard the jinrikisha wheels as she was carried away. But the little girl felt comforted and went and sat down quietly by her mother's side.

Hana's body was given up to the Buddhist priests and buried near Rinjiro in the old Buddhist cemetery, under the same trees that overshadowed Rinjiro's grave. Aka and Mitsu often went to carry flowers there and sometimes Kesa went with them.

Kei for more than a year had been an active Bible-woman in the employ of the missionaries. She seemed absolutely untiring in her work, coming home after a long day's tramp over the city as fresh as when she started, eager to tell where she had been and to whom she had spoken. Neighborhood meetings for prayer and Bible-reading were often conducted by Kei under the superintendence of one of the missionaries.

Once Mitsu went with Aka to one of these meetings and prayed with the women. Fujisawa heard of it and sternly forbade her doing so any more. "I will not have a daughter of mine doing such foolish things," he said. And Aka's husband, too, was angry.

The two friends wandered in sadness to the cemetery the next day.

"What can we do, Aka?" said Mitsu sorrowfully. "The teachers tell us that we should work now that we are Christians, and we want to teach our people."

"Well," said Aka, "I have thought that we can do much by talking quietly to any who come to us. Baba listens now. She is too old and feeble to leave her bed, and sometimes when no one else is there she will let me read one of the Bible stories. And there are other women in the *yashiki* who listen, and a man who says he believes."

So Aka and Mitsu spoke many a word of peace that winter in a quiet way.

Kesa attended school regularly, and Chiye lived rather a lonely life in Nagoya, longing for school and home.

One evening after school had closed and when the missionaries were getting ready for a summer trip to the Hakones, Saijiro appeared before the doctor looking as though he wanted something.

"Well, my boy," said the doctor.

"Oh, please, *sensei*, may I not go with you? I will go as a servant, only I want to see my old home and the people. But, dear teacher, I want more than all that you should talk to the people about the true God; and I want to tell Ko about how the Lord Jesus opened the eyes of the blind, and that he'll be able to see in heaven."

CHAPTER XXVI.

MISSIONARIES ON THE HAKONES.

<blockquote>
"Aitchu, Aitchu, Aitchu,
Aitchu, Aitchu, Aitchu."
</blockquote>

THIS unmeaning musical refrain in a minor key sang the coolies carrying *kagos* up the steep road which leads to Hakone. It was a summer morning, and the missionaries, after an uncomfortable night amid the heat, dust, and noise of Odawara, were charmed with the mountain solitudes, the tumbling waterfalls, the great trees, and the birds and flowers. Beside the *kagos* which contained the ladies of the party walked and leaped Saijiro. He carried a long staff and jumped from rock to rock, growing more and more excited as he neared Yamamidzu. The doctor and Mr. West were also walking.

"I have just been thinking," said Mrs. Fielding to her husband, "of the universality of inarticulate sounds. The bark of a dog, the neigh of a horse, the moo of a cow, are unmistakable wherever you may go. The leader of that grand orchestra of birds would have no difficulty in making himself understood in any land. That crow who seems to be delivering a speech on top of the farmhouse yonder might fly to England or India, make the same address, and be equally well understood. And a cat concert here is fully as good as one in our own land."

"Yes," answered the doctor, "the animals certainly were not included in the confusion of tongues at the tower of Babel. And I love to listen to the great voices of nature and remember that they are the same as at home. The sea thunders along the coast here just as it does on the other side; the wind whispers to the trees in the same tones; the rain has the same patter; the waterfall makes the same sweet music. Sun, moon, and stars tell of the glory of God here just as they do at home. We are not strangers in a strange land. It is our Father's country and we are always at home."

"I never realized before coming to Japan how little we need speech for the bare necessities of life," said Mr. West, who had joined them and was listening to the conversation. "We can make known our animal wants without it. We can even express sympathy, love, hatred, and a thousand other things without it. But, oh! what a gift from our Heavenly Father it is, and how thankful we should be for our own rich language, through which every sentiment of the human heart can be made known. Even on the printed page we can read words that thrill and burn, that bring tears from the eyes and laughter from the lips."

There burst upon the ears of the talkers a strain of sweet music and words of a Christian hymn. The ladies behind them were singing in their *kagos*. In a moment all had joined—Mrs. Fielding with a rich alto, the doctor with his deep bass, and Mr. West with a fine tenor. Sweet and clear, loud and strong, sounded the words in the solitude.

> "Oh, how beautiful their feet upon the mountains
> The tidings of peace who bring
> To the nations of the earth who sit in darkness
> And tell them of Zion's King!"

The coolies stopped their wild chanting to listen and kept step to the rhythm of the hymn. Then followed hymn after hymn, and at last the coolies begged to be taught one. So they learned one verse of the little hymn, "Jesus loves me," and sang it very well by the time they reached the turn in the road which leads down to Yamamidzu.

"Oh, *sensei*," said Saijiro, with eager entreaty in his eyes, "may I run down the short path to the cottage?"

"Go, Saijiro," said the doctor, smiling at his excitement.

Down bounded Saijiro and soon entered the village. It looked just as it did when he left it. There was the temple, and there the swinging bridge, and over there the little house, unoccupied now and all crumbling into ruins. He turned into the temple grounds and almost ran over the old priest.

"*Dogu!* It is Saijiro, the young master," said the priest. "How is your honorable health, and how are the honorable ladies?"

Saijiro in his eagerness to see Ko had forgotten that his first duty in Yamamidzu was to go to the inn and bid Yenoske's parents prepare for the travellers.

The priest's inquiry reminded him, and with a bow and "Thanks" and "Tell Ko to come to the hotel," he sprang lightly on up the street into the courtyard of the inn and stood before Yenoske's mother. The old lady almost overwhelmed him in her delight. "The little master, the little master has come! A great boy! A fine young gentleman! A great happiness! An unexpected pleasure! A very, very great happiness!"

In came Yenoske's father, in gathered the people who had seen the boy coming up the street, and who hastened to get news from Tokio.

"*Dogu!* the honorable teachers, four ladies and two gentlemen, are on their way down the mountain and will stop here to-night," said Saijiro.

Then the old lady was at her wit's end and really frightened. "But the food and the beds for the honorable foreigners!" she gasped when she had recovered a little from her first astonishment.

"Oh," said Saijiro, "they have some bedding

A JAPANESE BARBER.

and some food. Only give them room and they will be all right. But hasten, honorable mother, for they come soon."

Oh, the excitement of the Yamamidzu people! What bustle there was in the little inn! Such a pushing of slides and sweeping of floors and shaking of *futons* and polishing of wood-work! The *hibachis* were filled with fresh coals and rice was put on to boil. Children were sent all over the neighborhood to look for fresh eggs. Saijiro's *senseis* had come from Tokio, the people who had been so kind to him and to Yenoske! All the village turned out to do them honor, real gratitude mingling with the curiosity that was felt.

Yenoske's father, the landlord, hastened to the barber's to have his hair neatly dressed, then donned his best coat and went to the entrance of the village to welcome the guests. All of the men, women, boys, girls, and babies were there, with smiling Saijiro and happy Ko at their head.

When the missionaries appeared, coming down the mountain into Yamamidzu, low bowed the landlord. "Welcome, truly welcome, a very great welcome. Thanks for your kindness to my son. Truly, it is wonderful, truly! I never knew anything like it before. Come to my humble residence. Come and partake of rest and refreshment."

Then low bowed the people and all the children as the travellers passed. There were five *kagos*, one for each lady, Mrs. Fielding, Marion, and Miss Wilton, and two others who had joined the party. And there were coolies carrying baggage and the two gentlemen walking.

At the hotel were Yenoske's mother and several other old *babas* and *jisans*, all smiling, bright, and happy, to welcome Yenoske's master and mistress and Saijiro's teachers. And when the travellers were seated on the mats in the best room in came the priests and teacher to pay their respects. And then arrived the children who had been sent for eggs, and who tendered them with compliments as presents; and some brought flowers and some carried grasses and leaves. The old mother's attention was divided between preparing rice and tea for her guests, thanking them for their kindness to Yenoske, and apologizing for her poor accommodations. In truth, the hotel did not afford many comforts for tired foreigners. There were no chairs, no tables, no beds, little food, and plenty of fleas and flies.

But the scenery made up for all deficiencies in these respects. The travellers were seated almost over the rushing, rapid river, and two miles from them towered the mountains, still holding lilies like those that Saijiro had loved so from his babyhood.

"So, Saijiro, this is your home," said the doctor, "and this is Kojiro. Come to me, my boy, and let me see those eyes."

Kojiro lifted his sightless eyes to the doctor, who looked at them long and earnestly.

"Oh, honorable doctor," said the boy, "Saijiro has told me how the Jesus of whom you teach could open the eyes of the blind by a touch. Can *you* do so, honorable doctor?"

"No, my boy," said the doctor; "the Lord Jesus could do that because he was God and could do all things. But I think, if you could go with me to Tokio and submit to some pain, I might, with the blessing of the Saviour, make you see."

Oh, the joy that filled Ko's heart!

"I will see your parents, Kojiro," said the doctor. "You must be patient."

And now dinner was served, and how fortunate were those who were able to see the honorable foreigners eat! Knives, forks, and spoons! how could they use such things instead of simple chopsticks? And the bread! A piece was handed to the observers for examination. What a curiosity it was! And butter! Oh, horrible to put such grease on the honorable bread! But the honorable foreigners could make way with rice and eggs; and right hungry were they after their morning on the mountain; so they did full justice to the meal, which was certainly the best the place could afford.

Next came a delightful walk, with Saijiro for a guide, down the street to the temple, and down the steep descent to the stream. How beautiful was the waterfall, how sweet and powerful the fragrance of the flowers! But nothing could tempt the ladies across the little swinging bridge; so Saijiro and the two gentlemen went over and stood in the little decayed house where Kochi had lived and died, where Saijiro spent the happy days of his earlier life, and where the teacher had bowed in prayer and suffered such penance for so many years and from which he had gone out never to return. There was Inari's deserted shrine. No tapers burned there now, no flowers bloomed on the altar; but the mountain was unchanged still, and Saijiro leaned his head against its hoary side and felt like a child returning to his father or as one who has found again a faithful friend.

"Where can we meet the people this evening to talk?" asked Mr. West as the early evening shadows began to darken around them.

"It is pleasanter outside," said Saijiro, "by the river-bank."

So when the moon came up and all Yamamidzu lay glorified under its beams a little company gathered on the river-bank. The priests, with yellow robes and shaven heads, stood a little apart from the rest. The school teacher had come as near to the missionaries as possible. Children with babies on their backs and children without babies pressed a little timidly near their mothers. Venerable old men and women stood or reclined at full length on the ground. Saijiro, with Ko ever at his side, stayed near the doctor; and in strong contrast to the Japanese appeared the missionary ladies and Marion.

"Dear friends," said Mr. West, "we want to have a little talk this evening. I want you to feel free, and to ask questions if you will. Saijiro has begged us to come and see you and to stop over this night on our way up to Hakone; and we are glad, very glad, to do so, and thank you for your kind welcome to us."

The people all bowed.

"We were glad that the teacher Yetaro came to us before he died, to hear of the true God and of forgiveness through his Son Jesus Christ. You all know how sorrowful Yetaro was because of the great crime he had committed, and how for many years he sought forgiveness and peace from the Japanese gods, but found none. At last he came to us and heard of the Lord Jesus who died upon the cross to save sinners. He believed in him and found peace. We are glad too, friends, to have Saijiro with us. God, our true God, has raised up for him a mother in America, who loves him and is going to educate him in the place of her own dead boy who three years ago went home to heaven. We are glad, too, to have our faithful servant Yenoske and his wife Yen from your mountain home; and we thank you again for your kind welcome. And now we want you to let us take the boy Ko, who has never yet seen the light of the sun nor looked upon the flowers he loves so much, and with the blessing of our God we want to try to make him see."

Ko's father and mother called out their thanks and all the people bowed.

"Now, friends," said Mr. West, "we would like to sing some of our Christian hymns and read to you a few words of our Christian Book and pray to our God before we go to rest. These words will not hurt you, but you can think upon them, and we hope they will sink into your heart. Dear friends, are you not sometimes sorrowful? Our Lord Jesus says that any one who is sad may come unto him and rest. Are you not sometimes cold and hungry and miserable? Do not your wrong thoughts and words and acts fill your life with troubles? Our Book tells us of a blessed country to which we shall go when we die, if we believe on the Lord Jesus Christ and obey the commandments of our God, where we shall never more hunger or thirst, where no cold, piercing wind ever blows, and where the sun shall no more scorch us. Do not sickness and pain come to you? and do not your loved ones go away into the shadows of the tomb and leave you here weeping? I know they do, for Saijiro's mother and father have gone, and so has old Baba who cared for Saijiro in his childhood, and so have many of your little babies. Our Book tells us of a land where God gathers all those whose sins are forgiven for

Christ's sake, and where we shall always be happy and with the Lord. Dear friends, listen to some of our Christian hymns, and do not be afraid."

Then the missionaries sang to the people; and the people listened, and at last tried to learn the words of "Jesus loves me" and "There is a happy land." And then Mr. West read the story of blind Bartimeus, and the people thought it wonderful. Then followed a short, simple explanation of the Christian doctrine and a prayer commending these sheep scattered thus upon the mountains to the Good Shepherd's care. The people listened attentively, and many thanks were expressed to the missionaries, who went back to the inn.

"This is the hardest part of travelling in Japan," said Miss Wilton to Marion, as they were shut up in the close room prepared for the night; "I hate the odor of those green curtains, and never did like to sleep on the floor."

The missionaries had their own pillows, which they used as jinrikisha cushions by day. They spread sheets over their *futons* and crept under the curtains; but with heat and fleas the night passed miserably enough, to the older people at least. Early in the morning they were up and off, going the roundabout way up the mountain to Hakone. Saijiro remained to spend a few days in Yamamidzu and to help prepare Kojiro for the journey to Tokio.

The missionaries passed the deserted tea-house in the recess of the rock where Yen and her grandmother had dispensed tea and sweetmeats to travellers. They visited the hot springs and saw the miserable wretches who were gathered there.

"How dreadful it all is!" said the doctor's wife one day as they had turned, heart-sick and weary, from the sight of the terrible ravages of disease and evidences of depravity which were exposed on every side. "I do shrink from such close contact with sin and misery. Richard, sometimes I wonder how you can go about so among these people, and not dread to minister to their foul bodies and their yet fouler souls. I know that it is the Lord Jesus who helps you. It is his Spirit within you that gives you this love and grace and patience."

The missionaries spent a lovely summer day in Hakone by the side of the lake. Several times during the day a crowd gathered around them to be taught, or some man would come alone and ask to be instructed.

"I am so glad to know these mountains better," said one of the stranger missionary ladies; "I have looked at them so often from my house in Tokio. Now I know what they contain—the waterfalls, the mountain streams, the sunny slopes, the deep ravines, and above all, Hakone and its lake."

"Yes," said Miss Wilton, "this lake always

MOUNTAIN GIRLS.

reminds me of the Sea of Galilee. And those workmen making ready the way for the emperor, did they not remind you of the prophecy, 'Behold, I will send my messenger, and he shall prepare the way before me'?"

Ko was never tired of hearing Saijiro tell and read the stories of the Saviour's healing of the blind.

"Oh, Saichan," he said one day, "have the Christians an image of him, and can I pass my hand over his face?"

"They have no image of their God," said Saijiro. "They worship him by faith; they believe in him."

One day, after the missionaries had returned to their home and the doctor had made everything ready, a successful operation was performed and Ko's eyes gained the power of vision. They let him take off the bandages one evening when the sun was setting. Like a ball of fire, but with its light tempered by the mist, it was sinking into the sea when the boy's eyes were first permitted to look upon it. He gazed for one moment; then turning to Saijiro, he asked,

"Is it God?"

"It is the work of God, dear Ko," answered the doctor. "See; it has gone."

CHAPTER XXVII.

THE MIDNIGHT PRAYER.

Friday afternoon had come again and Miss Wilton's busy week in school was over. The girls had gone to their homes. The last one from whom the teacher had parted was Kesa Fujisawa, whose jinrikisha she had stood watching until the coolie had turned a corner and was out of sight. Something between a sigh and a prayer rose to Miss Wilton's lips. Then seeing the doctor's wife alone on the veranda she joined her, and the two sat in silence for a time, watching the water and listening to the never-ceasing song of the waves as they beat against the shore.

"How strange," said Miss Wilton, "that the most restless thing in the world, this heaving ocean, should be the most restful to us! I often come out here wearied almost to sickness, after a day in school, and only a few moments spent in watching the water, feeling the ocean breeze, and listening to the sound of the waves will make me feel strong again and ready for anything."

"Yes," answered Mrs. Fielding. "The words of the old hymn my mother used to sing, and sings yet, I suppose, often come to my mind:

"'There shall I bathe my weary soul
    In seas of heavenly rest.'"

"I sometimes wonder," said Miss Wilton, "whether we do not educate these girls beyond their surroundings; that is, if the education they receive here does not make them discontented with their own homes."

"Are you thinking of any one of the girls in particular?" asked Mrs. Fielding, noticing the expression of Miss Wilton's face.

"Yes; of that pretty child of the officer Fujisawa's—Kesa. When she first came here I thought her the most modest, most lovable Japanese child I ever saw. She and her sister were more like American girls than any others in the school. The little one was never very forward in her studies, but always happy and bright. Lately she has changed and seems irritable and moody, and I cannot find my way into her heart. I have been to the house often to see them. The father is silent and stern towards Kesa; the mother, since Hana's death, has been sadly failing in health herself. Mitsu is a good girl, but not a very strong character. And so the child has no one to understand her, and something is wrong, something is fretting and jarring her sensitive spirit."

"It is a solemn thing to touch human souls," said Mrs. Fielding. "But, dear Miss Wilton, sometimes I see a shadow over the heart of my own darling which I am not quite able to soothe away. It is true that every human soul must bear its own burden, and we must remember that the Shepherd of whom we speak so often to the Japanese loves these wandering ones better than we do. I have to say that to myself again and again. 'God is light, and in him is no darkness at all.'"

"Thanks, dear Mrs. Fielding, for your words."

The darkness was gathering around them, and the two ladies separated. But far on into the night the teacher turned and tossed on her bed with the burden of the child's soul on her heart. Something in the pathetic depths of the eyes turned to her as she said good-by had touched her beyond expression.

"Dear Lord," she prayed, "I know that thou who didst die on the cross for such as this one dost love her better than I, and that her soul is infinitely more precious to thee than it is to me. Give me grace to yield her up to thee. Teach me to trust thee for her, and for all those whom thou hast given into my charge. Oh, Lord, forbid that through my carelessness or neglect any one of them should be lost!"

"Marion," said Mrs. Fielding the next day, "you are often with Kesa Fujisawa; do you think she feels happy now?"

"Mamma," answered Marion, "I think sometimes Kesa wants to be loved by her mamma and papa as you and papa love me."

"Poor child!" said the mother; "you must try and comfort her, darling."

Marion Fielding was to go home to attend school soon. Kesa knew this, and her heart was sad at the thought of parting from her friend. She did not care much for the Japanese girls, and Marion was often her only companion.

The doctor rightly thought that his little daughter ought to know that there are such things as pain and sorrow in the world, and that she should learn how to meet and comfort the suffering. So he often had her in the visiting-room of his dispensary at the time when the women and children were most apt to assemble there. Marion had early learned to go about among them, directing the frightened children, reassuring the timid mothers, and speaking a word here and giving a touch there. The Japanese loved her, and she in her turn learned many a lesson in the dispensary among the sick, the blind, and the maimed.

Her mother wondered at times if she did right in permitting her childhood to pass in this heathen land, with no playmate of her own nation. But she equally dreaded sending her away, and so kept the child, trusting to the sweet home influences to counteract any injurious effects of too much intercourse with the Japanese. Only once, in her earliest childhood, had Marion visited the home-land, and she had scarcely any recollection of her grandfather's house and of the uncles, aunts, and cousins who loved her there. Now the time had come when the parents felt that she must spend some years in her native land. So she was to go with her mother, to remain three years, while the mother would return the next summer.

Kesa was Marion's chosen playmate among the Japanese. "She is a good little girl," she would say, and never could Mrs. Fielding's closest questionings draw anything from her save in evidence of Kesa's gentleness, truthfulness, and purity. So during Kesa's four years at school the girls had many a play together.

Kesa wondered at first why Marion should love a doll and tend and dress it as if it were a child. She thought that perhaps there was something more lovable in a foreign doll than in one of the Japanese dolls, and in her heart of hearts she longed to have one like Marion's. But the reticent child never told her desire. Only in secret at home she tried to fashion a doll something like the pretty "Daisy," and made it a dress after the pattern of Daisy's dresses. Long afterwards, when Kesa had gone from her father's house, and Mrs. Fielding was trying to comfort the sorrowing mother, Mitsu brought the poor uncouth doll to her and told her of the child's longing; and the doctor's wife sighed as she thought of the little girl's unsatisfied yearning, and said regretfully, "If I had only known, I would have given her one like Marion's."

One pleasant June Sabbath Marion Fielding stood at the schoolroom-window looking for Kesa. She knew that when the next Sabbath dawned she and her father and mother would be far out on the ocean, every moment taking her farther and farther away from her dark-eyed friend. The girls were already beginning to come over the commons to the school, most of them carrying flowers, and all looking bright and happy, as though glad to get back.

"There she is, mamma. I know the old jinrikisha and Meguchi," said Marion at last, hastening to meet Fujisawa's daughter.

Kesa had not only lovely flowers, but a beautiful lacquered box and handsome crapes to give to Marion. "The mother, Mitsu, and Aka send these with their compliments," she said, "and wish you to accept them and take them to America with you."

"*Oki arigato*"—a great thank-you—responded the American girl. "Will not Aka and Mitsu be at the church this afternoon, Kesa? You know that Saijiro, Yenoske, and Yen are to be baptized, and mamma is so happy to see them enter the Christian church before she goes away."

"They will be here," said Kesa, and the girls went into the house.

Saijiro was now a tall, studious boy of seventeen. He had almost completed the course of study in the boys' school. Harukichi was still his faithful friend, and Saijiro had decided to follow in his footsteps and preach the gospel to the Japanese.

Yenoske had long ago been promoted to the position of dining-room servant in the doctor's family. Yen was as smiling as ever, and her baby as bright and rosy as though it had been born in America. The hearts of Yenoske and Yen had been touched by the Spirit of God, and, forsaking their old beliefs, they had accepted the Saviour as theirs. Yenoske's devotion to his "little master" was unchanged, and when Saijiro had decided to receive Christian baptism Yenoske had begged that he and Yen might be admitted into the church at the same time. Ko, full of love to every one, and especially to the Lord Jesus, who had opened the eyes of the blind, stood at Saijiro's side.

Mr. West, as he looked on the little group from the mountain, gave thanks in his heart to the Good Shepherd who thus had led his sheep. Very solemn and touching was the engagement of those who had been servants of idols to be faithful and earnest in serving the Lord.

"I cannot believe as quickly as Chiye did, Marion," said Kesa a little sadly, as the two girls went out of church together after the communion.

"But you will some time, Kesa."

"I hope so; I will try to be good. I wish I were going with you."

"You will write to me, Kesa, and I will write to you, and tell you all about America and grandmamma's house. And three years will pass away quickly, mamma says."

But Kesa's heart was heavy with sadness and loneliness. She kept close to Marion's side during the last few days of her tarrying in Japan. Together they carefully packed away the old doll Daisy and her wardrobe. Together they tended the flowers, some of which Carroll's hands had planted, but whose blossoms he never saw.

The day before the steamer sailed Marion whispered a request to her father. He smiled and said, "I will see, daughter," and went away. Some hours after he returned, and in answer to his child's questioning eyes said, "All right, darling."

"Oh, papa, did you really see the officer Fujisawa, and did he say Kesa might go to Yokohama?"

"Yes, daughter," said the doctor, replying to both questions at once; and Marion ran off to tell Kesa that she was to go with her to the ship.

A sorrowful group gathered in the mission chapel the morning that Mrs. Fielding and Marion went away. The old teacher, Makichi, conducted the morning worship, and amid the tears of servants and friends he read Paul's address to the Ephesian elders, with the touching words at the close:

"And when he had thus spoken, he kneeled down and prayed with them all. And they all wept sore and fell on Paul's neck and kissed him, sorrowing most of all for the words which he spake, that they should see his face no more. And they accompanied him unto the ship."

Exquisitely touching was the venerable man's prayer as he thanked the Lord for sending such missionaries to Japan, and begged for the divine protection in behalf of those who were about to depart and for their safe return in due time to the people who loved them.

Mrs. Fielding and Marion bade their friends farewell with tears. They felt like turning back and saying, "We will remain with you," but it was necessary for them to go, and amid tears and prayers and flowers which were showered upon them they left the shelter of the mission-house.

Soon Kesa and Marion were seated by the car window looking out upon the landscape as the train hurried along.

"There is Fujisan," said Kesa as she spied the top of the mountain.

"How I wish we had something we could both look at while we are separated," said Marion.

"Well, there are the stars," responded Kesa.

"Yes, and the sun and the moon," said Marion.

THE MIDNIGHT PRAYER. 337

"But I have the English Bible you gave me, Maichan, and you have my Japanese Testament, and they are better than anything else."

"Yes," answered Marion. "But see how pretty the fields are, Kesa, in their bright summer dress. I do love them so. I wonder if America is as pretty as Japan."

It was only ten o'clock when the party reached Yokohama, and they started immediately for the ship, which lay far out in the harbor. After getting through the custom-house they had a ride in a Japanese *sampan* far over the bright waters. The bay was full of life that morning. The sound of the hammer was heard from many of the vessels as work went on preparatory to going to sea again. A ship under full sail was just coming into port after a long voyage around the cape, and a steamer was slowly making her way up to the anchorage. The low hills which ran up from the water's edge were all bright green, and Kesa and Marion could still see Mt. Fuji and the Hakones. The boatman sang as he propelled the boat rapidly over the waves.

Up to the great steamer "City of Tokio" they came at last, passing around under her sides to the stairway. With some difficulty they got on the platform and went up the steps.

Kesa had never seen anything like this magnificent vessel before and was almost awed by the size of the ship, its mirrors, carpets, and beautiful furnishings. But there was no time to linger. A peep into Marion's room and she must go.

Mrs. Fielding drew the girl into her arms for a moment and whispered a few words in her ear.

"I think the love of the Americans is deeper than that of the Japanese," said Kesa.

"But the love of the Lord Jesus is deeper than all, my little Kesa," she said, and let her go.

An hour later Kesa stood with Miss Wilton on a high bluff overlooking the sea and watched the departing steamer until it was a mere speck on the distant ocean.

"Dear Kesa, do not cry so," said Miss Wilton. "They who love one another are never separated in heart, and our Father will watch over us all."

Kesa felt better after listening to her teacher's soothing words; but the next day she was listless and indifferent, and at last positively refused to obey some simple command of Miss Wilton.

Miss Wilton was surprised and repeated her order, but still the girl refused to obey.

"'Then, Kesa, take your seat," she said.

Kesa arose, left her class, walked slowly to her seat, and sat down. Then, to the amazement of her teacher and the consternation of the girls, she threw her book across the room.

There was a moment's silence. Never before had such an instance of insubordination been known among the Japanese girls. Insolent disre-

THE MIDNIGHT PRAYER. 339

gard of the commands of a teacher was something unprecedented among them, something that they looked upon with horror, as the breaking of a direct command of their sages and religious teachers.

"Kesa Fujisawa"—the clear voice of the teacher rang through the school—"take your book and go to your room. You are suspended from the regular exercises of the school until you do as I bid you and bring me a sentence written on your slate."

It was quite early in the morning, and all the long summer day Kesa sat in her room alone with the slate and pencil. A girl of her own age, one of her friends, several times went up to her and begged her to obey the command of her teacher. It was touching to see the sorrow of all the Japanese girls, sorrow which even brought tears to their eyes; but Kesa's were dry and her heart was unmoved. She heard the school-bells rung as hour after hour passed away and change after change of class was made. She knew when the noon-hour came. Some one brought her rice and tea, but she pushed them aside and left them untouched. She heard the girls go into the room below for the Chinese writing lesson, and knew when the hour for Bible-reading came, which she usually enjoyed so much. Then she heard the day-scholars go away, and the boarders came up and got ready for their walk and left her alone.

Still by her side lay the empty slate and the unused pencil. Then the sun neared its setting, and when it had almost sunk in the west she heard soft footsteps in the dormitory and felt herself encircled by gentle arms and drawn out to where she could see the sunset.

"Kesa, dear Kesa, the sun is going down."

Then rushed into Kesa's heart the memory of the last Bible-lesson they had before Marion went away and the words that they had read together: "Let not the sun go down upon your wrath; neither give place to the devil." She gave her teacher one look, which lingered long in Miss Wilton's memory, and then rushed for her slate.

In a few moments she brought it to Miss Wilton, and on it was written, "This is a beautiful day, but my heart is dark. God bless me and take away my darkness and give me light." Then sob after sob shook the girl's frame until Miss Wilton was almost alarmed and could do nothing but soothe and comfort.

"Dear, dear child," she said, 'God will give you light."

And something soon came to Kesa which was more of a comfort to her than anything else could have been. The Shepherd sent help to his suffering lamb. When she arrived at home the next day for her Saturday's holiday there seemed an unusual stir and brightness about the house. Listening for an instant, she caught the tones of a well-remembered voice, and in another moment was with Chiye—Chiye come back from Nagoya to be a helper and guide to her younger sister.

Kesa was radiant with happiness when she and Chiye started off to the mission on Sunday morning. How delightedly she anticipated leading Chiye to her teacher! How surprised Miss Wilton would be!

But when they arrived at the school the sad news of Miss Wilton's sudden, serious illness met them, and Chiye had to go home without seeing her. Poor Kesa! Her heart was sad enough. She missed her teacher's sympathy and could not bear to think of her pain.

The evening at the school was very quiet. The girls sat in the dormitory in small groups and talked of the sick teacher. From the chapel came the sound of the students' voices as they read the evening Scripture lesson.

"Kesa, cannot God make the teacher well?" asked little Koko.

"Yes, I suppose so," said Kesa.

"Well, cannot we ask him?"

"Yes, Koko, we will when we say our evening prayer."

The girls went to bed early and the house was very quiet. Kesa could not sleep. She loved her teacher dearly. More than that, she clung to her and feared to be away from her. A terrible thought came into her mind as she lay tossing on her pallet: "What if Miss Wilton should die?" For a moment she felt as though she were sinking in deep waters with no helper near. At last she could bear it no longer. "We must ask God to spare our teacher," she resolved, and going from one pallet to another she roused the sleepers.

"What is it?" asked the astonished girls.

"It is I, Kesa Fujisawa, and we must rise and pray. I fear the *sensei* will die, and we must ask God to spare her life."

The clocks were striking the midnight hour when those Japanese girls arising from their sleep poured out their hearts in prayer for their beloved teacher. With a sweet strong faith they earnestly asked for what they wanted, and then went to their rest again.

"What were you doing in the middle of the night?" asked Miss Wilton of one of the older girls the next morning as, much relieved, she sat propped up in the bed.

"We were having a prayer-meeting. Kesa Fujisawa called us up to pray for you."

"Tell Kesa to come to me."

The girl came quickly, stood for a moment in the doorway, then rushed suddenly to the bedside and nestled in her teacher's arms. "Oh, *sensei*," she said, "I do think I am a Christian now; I never loved God before."

CHAPTER XXVIII.

THE LITTLE VISITOR.

The hearts of Saijiro and his "mother in America" had become closely bound together. The poor minister's wife in Pennsylvania, with her six children to care for, had many a sacrifice to make in order to provide means for Saijiro's education in Japan. But she never regretted the adoption of the boy, and the influence of her loving spirit was very beneficial to her own children. Early they learned to deny themselves many little gratifications, that they might do something for their "brother in Japan," and they watched eagerly for letters from that far-off land which had become such a reality to them.

"What shall we do in order to become more interested in missions?" asked the leader of a "band" one day of a returned missionary.

"Do more work for them," was the reply. And it is a fact that the more we do for them the more interest we shall take in them, the nearer will the heathen nations seem to us.

One summer evening, in the twilight, Clay Rindberg came home from the postoffice with a letter bearing the well-known Japanese stamp.

"A letter from Saijiro, mamma. Do light

the lamp," he cried; and the other children crowded around.

Even "papa" threw down his papers, and all gathered about the table. This is what Mrs. Rindberg read:

"Dear Mother: I know that to hear I have become a Christian and have been baptized will make you very happy. Long time I think I give my heart to God. But my heart very hard, and I think I love not the Lord Jesus.

"I have in mountain a little friend Kojiro. He for long time blind, cannot see anything. One day I go with my kind teacher back to my home at Yamamidzu. I very happy to see my old friends, but I happiest of all to see Ko. The doctor look at Ko's eyes and he say he can make them see. Then we all very glad. Ko's father and mother cry for joy. They think he always be blind, and they very sorry. So the doctor bring Ko to Tokio, and he take the things from his eyes by which he not see. Then first Ko see the setting sun, and he think it the face of God. But the missionary say, 'No, that is not God's face. That is the sun, which is God's work.'

"Then Ko want to know all about God and the Lord Jesus Christ. So I teach him. We beg that he stay here at school, and some of the boys earn money that he may be taught.

Ko soon love God very much. Then he say to me, 'Saijiro, why you not love God?' Ko want to be baptized, but he say, 'No, I wait for Saijiro.' So we read about Jesus curing blind men, and Ko say to me, 'Saijiro, do you not love him because he cure blind men?' But I do not love him.

"Then we read how he hung on the cross to save sinners, and Ko say, 'Saijiro, do you not love him because he save sinners?' Then I think how my father glad when he hear that, and how he believe on Jesus and love him very much. But I still cannot love him because he died on the cross.

"Then my heart sad and Ko's heart sad, and I go to my friend Harukichi and I say, 'Why cannot I love God and be a Christian?' And Harukichi say, 'I do not know.' Then he pray with me and ask God that I might be a Christian. Then all boys pray that I become a Christian; and I pray too, and say, 'Oh, God, make me a Christian.' And still my heart hard.

"Then one day I sit and think of my good mother Kochi, who carried me around when I was a little baby. I think how good my father was and the old *baba* who took care of me when my mother die. I think of Yenoske who was so good, and of the kind missionary teachers, and of my good friend Harukichi, and of my dear mother in America. And I think, 'God give me all these things;' and I say, 'I am wicked boy.'

"Then I cry, and Harukichi say, 'Why you cry?' And I say, 'I am wicked boy, Harukichi.'

"Then Harukichi tell me, 'I am glad you think you wicked boy. Now your heart soft; now you come to God.'

"Then I see, and then my heart soft because I know I am wicked, and because God love me and save me from my sins.

"All Yamamidzu people who are here have receive baptism—Yenoske who was good to me when I little, and Yen his wife, and also Kojiro, who clapped his hands because he so happy for me.

"I send love to my mother, father, sisters, and brothers in America.

"I love you.
                                        "SAIJIRO."

Great joy did this letter from Saijiro give to the little group at the parsonage, and the glad news of the boy's conversion went through the village. Two months afterwards Saijiro and Harukichi read Mrs. Rindberg's answer.

All the while that Chiye had been in Nagoya Harukichi had heard little or nothing of her. But his heart remained unchanged, and great was his joy to see her one day at the service with Kesa, Aka, and Mitsu.

"I must speak with her or in some way make known to her my love," he said in his heart.

The next day he went to his faithful friend and counsellor Mr. West. "Honorable *sensei*, what do you do in America when you purpose to marry a girl and want to tell her of your love?" he asked.

"Sometimes we go to the girl and tell her plainly and in a manly way that we love her, and then, if she returns the love, we speak to the father. Or some speak to the father first. But, as a general thing, the two most interested know first each of the other's love. But will you tell me, Harukichi, of whom you speak and who has now your love?"

"Thanks, honorable *sensei*, yes; it is the officer Fujisawa's daughter Chiye of whom I speak. I was baptized at the same time with her. I saw her face, and felt sure that I should love her more than any one else in the whole world. Then she became ill and went away, but I never let her go out of my heart. Last Sunday I saw her at the mission chapel, and I think she is well, and I want to tell her of my love and ask her to become my wife."

"In this case, Harukichi, I think it best that you should go to the father, tell him of your love, and ask permission to marry his daughter," said the missionary.

So Harukichi went up to the custom-house and asked to be admitted to the presence of the high officer Fujisawa. Fujisawa rather admired the manly-looking youth, with his air of courtesy and good-breeding, and politely inquired what he wanted.

"I have a strong love for your honorable daughter Chiye. For many months I have cherished her memory in my heart. I crave your honorable permission to make her my wife."

"Why did you not employ a go-between?" asked Fujisawa, who had listened patiently enough and without any apparent displeasure.

"Because I do not like the Japanese custom of employing go-betweens," answered Harukichi. "I have come myself to ask for your honorable daughter."

"Tell me of your business and prospects. I hear that your parents are wealthy and are able to give you a fine establishment."

"*Dogu!* in truth, honorable sir, my parents are wealthy, but they have disinherited me," answered Harukichi sorrowfully.

"And why?" asked Fujisawa.

"I have become a Christian and am studying for the Christian ministry, and my parents hate the new doctrines."

Fujisawa's whole manner changed. "You may not say anything to my daughter until you have become reconciled to your parents. These Christians have done great harm in the country by setting one member of the family against the others. What difference does your belief make? The doctrines of the Christians have made trouble and division in my own household, and I will have no more of them."

Then said Harukichi, "Honorable sir, the Japanese families were full of dissension and bitterness before the foreigners came. There is no more disturbance than there was before. And in many a household peace has come where before there was trouble. But it is well. I will not speak now to your daughter." And Harukichi bowed and retired.

"Chiye, come here to me," said Fujisawa, when he returned to his house that evening.

Chiye obeyed in fear and trembling, on account of the sternness of her father's voice.

"What do you mean by encouraging a young man who has not the decency to conform to Japanese customs, who is disinherited by his parents, and is studying to preach the Jesus-doctrines?"

"But, honorable father, I know nothing about it," said Chiye.

Fujisawa would listen to none of her denials. He was unrelentingly angry, and all of Chiye's protestations were in vain.

"I did not know that he loved me, honorable father," she said repeatedly, bewildered and terrified, for the father's angry voice could be heard all over the house.

Mitsu and Kesa had crept into their mother's room.

"*Dogu*," said Mrs. Fujisawa, "this new doctrine makes a great deal of trouble for us, Mitsu. In former times, before you knew anything about it, we were all so much happier. The honorable father never grew so angry."

"*Dogu*, honorable mother, do you not remember how angry the honorable father was when I objected to my marriage?" asked Mitsu.

"What can Chiye have done that he should talk so to her?" wondered the mother, as the father's tones of command and the gentle accents of expostulation came to her ears.

"*Dogu*, I know not, honorable mother," answered Mitsu.

Then Chiye was dismissed, sobbing and trembling, to her own apartment. Fujisawa sought his wife, and the two sisters went to Chiye.

"What is the matter?" asked Mitsu; and Kesa's questioning eyes were filled with tears.

"*Dogu!*" answered Chiye, "the young Haru-kichi, of whom you have heard, and who gave up everything for the sake of preaching the gospel, has asked me in marriage of the honorable father, and he is very angry."

"Do you love him, sister?" asked Kesa.

"I have not thought of it, darling. But I think I might love him. He is good and noble, not like other Japanese young men whom I know."

Chiye said no more, and the subject was not mentioned again. But in her heart a seed of love had been dropped which grew and strengthened. In some way the two young people, without exchanging a word, came to know each of the other's love and patience, and determined to wait with meekness "the Lord's time."

The school year closed, and Kesa was to go to school no more. Fujisawa positively forbade it, and the girls trembled lest they should be forbidden to attend the Sabbath services. Sorrowfully Kesa and her dear teacher took leave of each other. Miss Wilton's heart yearned over Kesa, and she found it hard to leave her with God and to trust him for her.

In the early autumn there came to the Fujisawas a young visitor who did much to restore the happiness of former days, for a time at least. This was no other than Genski, the eldest child of Tama and Mesoburo. He was a straight, manly little fellow of eight, somewhat imperious in his manner, but lovable withal. He brought with him a brightness and freshness which affected pleasantly all the members of the family. It was something new to have a boy. All of the old toys with which Kesa and Rinjiro had played were brought down from their shelf and speedily demolished. Old Meguchi worshipped the lad, and the aunties were only too happy to show him everything which could possibly interest him.

"Do you have acrobats in Hakodate, Genski?" asked Chiye one day.

"Oh, yes; but perhaps not such as you have in Tokio," answered Genski.

"Then we will go over to Asaxa and see the acrobatic performances to-day," said Chiye.

Three in a jinrikisha—Kesa, Chiye, and Genski, with Aka and Mitsu in another cart behind them! They were all happy that bright October morning.

"Hakodate is not like this. It is more quiet. There are only a few pack-horses in the place and a few jinrikishas standing around."

This Genski said as they rode through the crowded city streets.

"Have you ever seen the men fishing for salmon there?" asked Kesa.

"Oh, yes, my honorable father has often taken me out in a boat to see the men fishing. I have also seen the Ainos spearing seal in the waters near Hakodate."

"How does the snow seem when it covers everything up in winter?" asked Chiye of the little northern boy.

"Oh, I like it; we have fun then making snowballs and Daruma Samas, and pelting one another. But it is very cold."

So the young folks chatted until they reached Asaxa, where they were to see the acrobats.

A crowd of people had gathered, and the performers were all ready. They were dressed in bright scarlet, and had feathers in the little caps which they wore on their heads. There were some poles near them, and a platform where a man sat beating a drum and humming a most dolorous tune.

The chief acrobat ascended the platform, and addressing the spectators said, "You are now about to behold a most wonderful performance. Look and wonder, O people."

Then suddenly throwing himself on his back, he raised his feet high in the air, while a small child ran up the sides of the platform like a monkey and perched himself on the man's feet. He stood for a second, bowed to the people, then rolled himself up into a ball and was tossed up in the air and caught on the man's feet, always coming down right side up and always laughing.

When he had finished some boys a little larger came and balanced themselves one on top of another, until the last one, standing on top of all, was a great distance from the ground, and one not accustomed to such things might tremble and wonder how he was going to get down.

But in an instant they were all down on the ground again, and the man, springing up, made a bow, while the people cheered lustily.

Then followed feats of jugglery, knife-swallowing cutting off heads, and other performances. The Fujisawas and their little guest looked, cheered, and threw copper coins until they were tired; and then they went to see wax-figures in the long, low wooden building back of the temple.

The figures were wonderfully human in their

appearance, and Genski was much interested. He knew all the characters represented, and was as familiar with the story of Old Japan as Chiye herself. There in wax was the sacred white horse, the servant of Hachiman; and the changeable goddess Benten was there in a number of forms. Genski recognized Kintaro, the "red boy," Momotaro, Yoritomo, Hideyoshi, and a number of others, all in stalls like so many horses. A man exhibited the figures and told the story of each, pointing with a long stick.

"Don't you go up to worship, Aunt Mitsu?" asked Genski, noticing that none of the party paid any attention to the idols.

"No, Genski, we do not worship idols any more. We have learned of the true God."

"Will you teach me about him?"

"Yes, Genski, we will teach you; and when you go home you can tell your mother."

Fujisawa himself took Genski to see the wrestlers, the "strong men" of Japan. These men give public boxing and wrestling matches in thronged amphitheatres.

On another day the proud grandfather took Genski to see a play. It was one of the old plays of Japan, and Genski in this way learned some of the ancient customs of the country and saw the old armor and court-dresses. There was an execution in the play, when the heads of the actors apparently rolled down on the stage and were carried away in baskets; and the principal actor committed suicide by disembowelling himself in the sight of his retainers.

The play was over by six o'clock in the evening, and Genski was safe at home early. This is a great advantage which Japanese theatres possess over those of this country; everything is done between sunrise and sunset.

Genski's visit did good to all the family. Even the poor mother, whose health had been failing since Hana's death, enjoyed the mirth and pranks of her bright little grandson.

Old Kei came to see him and almost overwhelmed him with caresses; and Aka saw in him something to remind her of her lost Rinjiro.

Greatly to the disappointment of the girls, Fujisawa determined to send him to one of the Government schools. But little Genski, like Chiye and Kesa, had an early, deep-rooted aversion to idols, and dearly loved to hear of the God who made the sun, moon, and stars and the beautiful world.

Kesa studied with Chiye, and found in her a dear companion and friend. And so for the Fujisawas another winter passed away, and Kesa was fifteen years old.

CHAPTER XXIX.

SOME LETTERS AND A WEDDING.

How it rained! Genski had gone merrily off to school in a jinrikisha. The sisters had watched him from the window as long as they could see the top of the cart with its oiled-paper coverings, and when their precious little charge was quite out of sight had turned to their sewing.

As a general thing a Japanese house is a terribly close, gloomy place during a rainstorm. The paper slides, which have to be closed to exclude the rain, do not admit much light, and no one can see out. When the storm is very severe the wooden shutters also have to be closed, and the air becomes very close and oppressive. But Fujisawa had had glass put in the upper room, and the girls could see away down the steep and slippery streets and look up to the heights above them; and although the rain came down heavily and persistently, there was no wind, and the side of the house was open.

The three girls sat on the floor with their sewing. Japanese women have to rip their dresses every time they are washed. The pieces, after being cleansed thoroughly in very hot water, for they have no soap, are spread on boards to dry, and are as smooth when finished as if they had been ironed by the most accomplished laundress. Then the dresses have to be put together again.

The sisters did not usually talk much while thus working. Japanese ladies are generally great gossips, and many are their jealousies, bitternesses, and heart-burnings. But the Fujisawa girls had never been allowed to gossip even in their earlier days, and now that they had become Christians they were still less inclined to it.

The missionary teachers had learned the besetting faults of Japanese women and had faithfully labored to correct these faults. The seeds of truth which they had planted had in many instances sprung up and borne fruit—fruit which had taken the place of the evil weeds of slander, envy, hatred, and malice.

"Chiye, who is that man who comes here so often to see the honorable father?" asked Kesa, who had been quietly sewing her seam.

"*Dogu*, I do not know," answered Chiye, and Mitsu looked grave.

"Sometimes I feel afraid that it is one of those dreadful go-betweens, and that he has come to ask one of us in marriage," said Kesa. "I shall never marry a man whom I do not know because the honorable father wishes it, Chiye; I have made up my mind."

"He will make you do it, darling," said Mitsu, whose suspicions had been aroused by the constant visits of a man, his long talks with her father, and the sighs and averted looks of her mother.

"But, sister, I will not. I will run away. And I am going some time to be baptized. The honorable father seldom looks at me now, and he never speaks kindly, but is always hard and cruel. Sister, I am very unhappy."

Then said Chiye, the comforter, "Dear Kesa, so might I be very unhappy. But you know the teachings of the honorable *senseis* at the school— that God does what is right and that we must trust him."

"You trust him, Chiye, but I do not," said Kesa.

"Who is that coming in the rain?" asked Chiye.

The girls, looking from the window, saw that a jinrikisha had stopped at the entrance. They could not see the occupant, so covered was the cart with oiled paper. And when the person inside got out they could scarcely tell whether it was a Japanese or a foreigner, a man or a woman, so enveloped was the unrecognized guest in waterproof and hood. But soon the girls, to their surprise and joy, recognized Miss Wilton, and hastened to greet her. They removed her dripping outer garments, brightened up the coals in the *hibachi*, brought hot tea, and welcomed her with loving words.

"I am not in the least wet," she said, laughingly submitting to all these attentions. "I have a letter for you, Kesa, from Marion, and as I was not engaged in school this morning something impelled me to come and bring it to you myself. I am hungry for news from Marion myself, so I thought we could all enjoy the letter together. How is the honorable mother?"

"Thanks, the honorable mother is very poorly. Will you go in and see her after we have read the letter?" said Mitsu.

They gathered around the *hibachi*, taking occasional sips of hot tea while Miss Wilton read the letter. Kesa's brightness had come back to her for a time, and she listened with sparkling eyes to the words her young friend had penned.

"DEAR KESA: I have been thinking of you so much to-day that I must sit down and write.

"I am very happy at the school, only lonely now that mamma has left me, and I do want to see you all again. At night when I go to bed and on Sundays I think of Japan, of how the sea is washing its shores, and of how the little children are playing in the water, catching crabs, and of the boats dancing over the waves. I want to see the bay and the river and the little thatched cottages and the mission-houses.

"How are Yenoske and Yen and the funny little baby Cho? I know she must be having a good many falls with her first little clogs.

"I do not see half as many funny things here as I did in Japan.

"How is our garden? Do you take care of the plants now? Oh, I forgot; your papa does not allow you to go to school any more, so of course you cannot take care of the garden. But you can go on Sundays and look after the flowers and see the gold-fish. How many of the fish have died? I am sure some have, because they were always dying.

"Papa and mamma will go back to Japan in October. They have gone away from me. Kesa, I cried until I was almost sick when they went away. It was so hard to let them go, and I wanted to go back to dear, dear Japan too. I love Japan; and, Kesa, I have determined to go back there and be a missionary; and you and I will be together in a school, and we will teach the children God's way.

"I have something else to tell you, Kesa; I am a member of the church. Oh, Kechan, if we could go to the communion together!

"The girls here have a missionary society and I am a member. Next month the subject will be Japan, and I am going to dress in my Japanese costume, and we are to have an exhibition of Japanese curios. Do you remember how much fun we had with my Japanese dress, Kesa? I have had to take out the tuck that Mitsu put in. I have grown so tall that you wouldn't know me.

"I wish you were here at school with me. You will soon see papa and mamma, and they will tell you all about me.

"I am so glad that Chiye is back. Give my love to her and to Aka and Mitsu. Tell them how I want to see them. And oh, kiss a flower or a tree or something in dear Japan for me!

"Please write very soon to your friend,
"MARION FIELDING."

Miss Wilton read the letter in English and then translated it.

Mrs. Fujisawa had come in and listened attentively. She was the first to speak when the teacher ceased her reading.

"*Dogu*, these Christians have a very deep love in their hearts. They never forget. For all your kindness to my daughters we give you thanks; *dogu*, a very great thank-you."

"We love to be kind to all, dear Mrs. Fujisawa. But how is your honorable health?"

"*Dogu*, I am poorly enough these days. I have no strength, and often have fever and sweats at night," answered the mother.

Miss Wilton was not surprised a few days later to hear that Mrs. Fujisawa was prostrated with gastric fever, which for a time seemed to baffle the efforts of all the physicians.

Those were dreary days for Kesa, Mitsu, and Chiye, and in their care and anxiety for the mother the dreaded go-between was forgotten. He did not appear during Mrs. Fujisawa's worst time of sickness and passed out of the girls' minds.

Early in the summer bright little Genski went back to his northern home.

"Good-by, darling," said Chiye as he turned to bid her farewell. "Tell the honorable mother of the true God."

In October Dr. and Mrs. Fielding returned to Japan and hastened to the anxious family, where the mother still lay on her bed of suffering. The doctor's skilful treatment soon effected a change in her condition; and when care and nourishing food were all that she needed a day seldom passed without a call from some one from the mission with some strengthening or appetizing preparation.

One day, as Mrs. Fielding was busily engaged about the invalid, Fujisawa, who was watching them, said, "I have never seen such love as this before. It is wonderful."

Then said the doctor's wife, hoping to make an impression on the man's heart, "It is our religion that impels us to do thus. It is the loving spirit of Jesus."

But Fujisawa's face grew hard and he turned away, and Mrs. Fielding went home sorrowing.

"Chiye, you know how the honorable father let you and Mitsu be baptized and said nothing about it. Do you think, sister, that *I* might receive baptism from the missionary and tell the father nothing?" Kesa said this to Chiye one evening when the two sisters were together in one of the bedrooms.

"You forget, Kesa, that the father has positively forbidden your baptism. He would be very angry if you were to go against his wishes. I hoped that the dear mother's illness and all the kindness of the missionaries would soften his heart, but it seems it has not."

"I hoped, Chiye, that it would, and that I might ask his permission to be baptized."

"Kesa," said Chiye after a little pause, "did you know that that man was here last night again? He brought a large box to the honorable father. I am sure he is a go-between. Oh, Ke-chan, I will never marry any one except Haruki-chi; and if it should be you, darling!"

"Chiye, I will not marry any one in that way. I will run away."

But Kesa's heart was sad and a terrible fear came over her. Something made her feel sure that it was she whom her father was thus bargaining away. She went and sat down by her mother's side. Incapable of understanding her youngest born with all her needs and questionings as that mother was, undemonstrative as she had ever been towards all of her children except Hana, her heart was still the mother-heart to which the child crept in her trouble and hers the sympathy which soothed and comforted.

"*Ka-chan,*" Kesa said, "who is the man that comes here to see the honorable father?"

Mrs. Fujisawa shrank from a direct answer to that question, and Kesa saw the shrinking.

"*Ka-chan*, please tell me. Is he a go-between? and does he want me?"

"Yes, darling," answered the mother. But she was hardly prepared for the cry of anguish which burst from her daughter's lips.

"*Ka-chan, ka-chan!* is the father going to *sell* me? He sold Mitsu, and he will not let Chiye marry good Harukichi, whom she loves and who loves her; and now he would sell me. *Ka-chan*, I hate him!"

"*Dogu, dogu*, Kesa, what can I do? You must obey the commands of the honorable father."

Chiye, hearing the disturbance, went in and spoke gently to Kesa—Chiye, who was so patiently bearing her own cross. "Darling, you are distressing the mother," she said. "Come, and we will do as the teachers at the mission tell us, carry our troubles to God."

So the two girls went to an unoccupied room at the end of the house and knelt there, and the elder sister prayed:

"Dear Lord, this is my sister Kesa and her heart is very sad. She does not know where to turn nor what to do. Lead her through her troubles, soften the father's heart, and bless us all, for Jesus' sake."

"To-morrow I will go and talk to the teacher," said Kesa, rising.

Soon the house was quiet, and Kesa, worn out by her emotions, fell asleep.

The next day Miss Wilton, sitting in her room, heard a gentle knock at the door and was surprised to see Kesa enter in answer to her response.

"What is it, Kesa?" she asked, noting the troubled expression of the girl's face. "Is the mother worse? or is Chiye sick again?"

"No, *sensei;* they are as well as usual. I am troubled and have come to talk with you. *Sensei,* the honorable father is very angry with me. He will scarcely speak to me and does not wish me to come and see you or to be baptized. And, oh, *sensei,* we fear he is going to make me marry a man whom I do not know, and I cannot do it."

Kesa's tears fell fast, and the teacher's heart was sorely pained.

"Dear Kesa, I am sorry to hear all this. I had hoped that the father's heart would be softened and that all would be well with you. It will surely be well, Kesa, if you give yourself to God and trust in him—well with you and with Chiye and Harukichi too, dear child. How would you like to go with me to Shiba this afternoon? I have something to tell you and feel like going under those grand old trees."

The day was warm and bright, although it was already winter; and when the coolies drew the jinrikishas within the temple enclosure Kesa and her teacher could hear the twittering of birds and see bright red camellias blooming among their glossy green leaves.

Miss Wilton directed the coolies to turn away from the temples into the forest which surrounded them. The jinrikishas went on through broad avenues and winding paths until they reached the deepest shade of the trees. Then, ordering the coolies to wait, Miss Wilton led the way to a lovely nook where the golden sunshine poured through the trees, making glorious the mosses and ferns below, while above was a patch of blue sky. It was a lovely, quiet scene, and the two sat for some time without speaking. A peace seemed to steal into Kesa's heart, a deep, sweet peace, as though sent from above.

Miss Wilton's voice broke the silence. "Kesa, I told you I had something to say to you."

"Yes, *sensei*."

"I am going away, Kesa. I am going to be married."

A look almost of terror came into the girl's eyes. She loved and trusted this teacher so thoroughly; she relied so implicitly on her for help in her trouble; she knew that she could flee to her at any moment for protection; and now she had just told her that she was going away, and that, too, in the hour of the girl's greatest need.

"Dear Kesa," said the teacher, drawing her

nearer, "do not look like that. I am not going out of Japan, only down to the southern country. I will come back to Tokio, dear Tokio, some day; and perhaps you will come to see me."

"Is it where old Kei lived, *sensei?*"

"Near there, dear, and perhaps we can find Nantaro, Kei's brother. Kei is talking of coming down to try to find Nantaro and to establish Bible-readings. Dear Kesa, do not sob so, child."

Then with loving tenderness the teacher tried to make this poor weak lamb feel the care of the Shepherd, and at last Kesa grew stronger and calmer.

They separated at the great gate of the temple. Kesa went with her own faithful coolie up to the Kudan, while Miss Wilton went back to the mission-house which she was so soon to leave.

True it was that her work in Tokio was over. The days of patient seed-sowing had not been in vain. Many of the little ignorant Japanese children for whom she had cared had grown to be faithful, intelligent girls and women, rejoicing her heart by their Christian steadfastness. Now a sweet surprise had come into her own life, and with one who loved her, and whom she loved in return, she was to go to one of the cities of the Inland Sea.

Kesa sat by her little table in the evening writing a letter to Marion. Chiye was by her side, now and then helping her to a word.

"Dear Marion:" thus the letter read, "My heart was very sad this afternoon. I have very great trouble in it. My father angry with me. He scarcely speak to me. He will not permit me to go to school any more. He not permit my baptize. I fear he want me to marry some strange man, as my sister Mitsu did so long ago, and she have so much trouble. My heart feel very dark and sad.

"Then Chiye and I go and tell my troubles to God and I feel better. And next day, that is to-day, I go to see Miss Wilton, and she take me to beautiful place in Shiba, and we sit and she say nothing for a long time. But the birds sing in the trees and the wind sound among the leaves and the sun shine down on the grass. And the blue sky is above us all, so beautiful and so peaceful, and I think, 'God is love.' And then Miss Wilton tell me that she go away, and when I cry she say, 'Do not cry, Kesa, for the Lord Jesus is with you.'

"Then I think I will trust him and give him my heart, and I will believe he do right. Now I have peace, and Chiye and Mitsu are very glad. But I not marry the man.

"I see your garden every Sunday. Yenoske take great care. Six gold-fish are dead. And Yen and the baby are well. The baby walk and fall down some time and some time cry. Chiye is better, but she look very white and not strong.

My mother, too, get better every day. Many girls go to church on Sundays. Thanks for your letter. We all send love.

"Your dear friend,
"KESA FUJISAWA."

A few days after this letter was written Miss Wilton was married at the mission. The "girls" were invited to the wedding and saw for the first time in their lives the simple Christian ceremony. Chiye and Kesa were there, dressed in new garments, with bright, beautiful sashes and elegant hair-pins.

"How pretty they all look!" said Mrs. Fielding as she watched the girls partaking of some simple refreshment and noted their gentle manners, their neat dresses and bright faces.

"Dear Mrs. Fielding," said their teacher, "how thankful I am for what you have always tried to impress upon my too doubting heart—that the Shepherd loves these lambs better than I do. But, oh, watch over Kesa for me. My heart bleeds for the child."

CHAPTER XXX.

KESA AND HER FATHER.

No wonder that Fujisawa felt angry with his youngest daughter. He was trying to harden his heart against her, trying to do her a great injury; and we always feel harsh towards one whom we are attempting to injure. Yet after all he was really fond and proud of Kesa. Heretofore he had met with nothing but submission in his children. Mitsu had submitted when he ordered her to marry the man from whom she shrank. Chiye had submitted when he forbade her to marry or to see Harukichi, whom she loved. He had no thought but that Kesa would acquiesce when he commanded her to marry.

It was one morning before he went to the custom-house that he summoned her.

"The honorable father wishes to speak with you, Kesa," said Chiye; and when Kesa went, Chiye prayed that the Lord Jesus would be with her and bless her and give her strength.

Kesa rose when Chiye called her, went quickly, and stood before her father. She did not prostrate herself, but was respectful, and quietly awaited his words.

"Kesa, I have completed the arrangements for

your marriage. You will be the bride of Susumi, the son of the high officer Masanawa."

"Thanks, honorable father, but I cannot marry Susumi Masanawa," answered the girl.

"And whom will you marry? I suppose you are like Chiye, and love some one among those wretched Christians."

"No, honorable father, I care for no one. But I will not marry a man whom I do not know and for whom I do not care. *Dogu*, father, forgive me," she added, seeing the look of anger and hatred on her father's face. "I cannot; oh, I cannot. Oh, honorable father, remember Mitsu and all that she has suffered. Please, please forgive me; but I cannot; oh, I cannot!"

"There is no use in your talking so to me, Kesa. This marriage shall take place, and I command you to prepare for it."

"Honorable father," respectfully began Kesa; but the continued expostulation only angered Fujisawa the more, and he pushed her from him.

"It is the Christian religion that has done all this. I will have no more of it. My youngest child *shall* obey me. Kesa, I forbid your having anything more to do with the foreigners. Neither you, Chiye, nor Mitsu shall with my permission ever go to the Concession again."

In his anger Fujisawa seized some of Kesa's books which were lying near him and threw them into a dark closet.

The poor weak mother, with Chiye, Mitsu, and Aka, sat trembling in another apartment. They dared not go to Kesa lest their interference should still more excite the father.

"I wish not to see you, Kesa, until you have made up your mind to obey me without more ado; for obey you shall. You are already promised to Susumi; the preparations for the wedding will go on."

Fujisawa closed the slides and went away. That there was any danger of his plans being thwarted the father never dreamed.

Poor Kesa! She felt stunned and bewildered. Chiye went and sat down by her side; and after a little time of silent comforting, Kesa said,

"Chiye, I am going to run away. Come quickly and help me; there is no time to lose."

"No, no; don't be in a hurry, little sister. Stop and think," said Chiye gently.

"But, sister, I *have* thought and thought and thought. My mind is all made up."

"But where are you going, Kesa? and how can you go alone?"

"I am going down to Kei's country to find my teacher. Chiye, come and help me. I must be a long way off before the father comes back to-night from the custom-house."

"*Dogu!* where can you go? and how angry the father will be!" said poor benumbed Mrs. Fujisawa.

Mitsu said nothing at first, seemingly lost in her own thoughts. Then suddenly turning to Kesa she asked, "Did you not tell me, darling, that Kei thought of going back to her country?"

"Yes, sister."

"Then I will go quickly and ask her to accompany you."

"Take me quickly to Nippon Boshi," said Mitsu a few moments later, as she got into a jinrikisha.

The coolie was not long in reaching Kei's house. An old man sat on the mat near Kei, and a sickly-looking child lay on the floor. Kei was reading some sweet words of Scripture to them.

"Truly welcome, O Mitsu," she said, as she rose to welcome her guest.

"Kei, can you finish your reading and listen to me?" asked Mitsu.

"Rosuki, you and Tono may go now, and soon I will read you more." But long months passed ere Kei came back to finish her reading.

"Kei, the father insists upon Kesa's marriage, and she is going away to find her teacher in the southern country. We wish you to go with her—and right away," said Mitsu.

"*Dogu, dogu!*" said Kei; and after asking a few questions she made ready, and leaving the house in the charge of a neighbor, went off in the jinrikisha with Mitsu.

"Send word for me to the honorable missionaries," begged Kei; "and, O Mitsu, go and read to my people sometimes."

Mitsu promised to do what she could, remembering sadly that she had been forbidden to have any intercourse with the foreigners. "Aka will do it all," she thought.

Kesa was all ready for her journey when Mitsu and Kei came to the house, and Aka was there. Both Kei and Kesa carried a few necessaries done up in blue 'kerchiefs. Japanese ladies do not need much when they travel.

The servants had prepared rice and made tea, but the family group sitting on the floor by the little table was sorrowful enough. The mother's heart felt like breaking, and Chiye mourned sorely, while Mitsu felt as though the brightness of her life was to be taken away. But there was little time for farewell words or tears.

"*Saionara*, darling, darling!"

"*Saionara*," answered Kesa.

Kei bowed low, and in a moment they were gone—gone from the sheltered home out into the great world. Kesa's childhood was over. She gave one long, lingering look at the house and at the group of dear ones left behind, the coolies lifted the shafts, and they were off.

It was far into the evening before Kesa would let the coolies stop. They went in the moonlight through the fields over which Yetaro, the teacher, had travelled so wearily.

"*Dogu*, darling, we must stop," said Kei as they came into a village late in the evening.

All of the people in the little thatched inn had gone to bed, and the travellers rattled the door and called for some time before any one heard them.

"It is a poor place, Kesa," said Kei when at last they were admitted by a sleepy-looking woman.

"I do not care," said the weary girl; and worn out by her day of suffering and travel, she threw herself down on the poor pallet and fell into a heavy sleep.

CHAPTER XXXI.

A WINTER JOURNEY.

"*Kawaiso!*" It was Kei who spoke the word, and it means sorrowful. She had just risen from her pallet and was looking at Kesa, who was still asleep. The girl looked pale and exhausted, and for a moment Kei thought with dismay of the long journey before them.

"*Dogu*, where is your faith?" she said to herself, and pushed open the slides and went out into the little garden. A glorious morning had broken over Nippon. There was not a cloud to be seen, and the cold air was fresh and bracing.

A servant-girl was washing rice in a little wooden tub. Her long sleeves were strapped across her back and she had a blue handkerchief bound about her head.

"*O hayo*" (good morning), said Kei.

"*O hayo*," responded the girl pleasantly.

"Fine weather," said Kei.

"Truly, very fine," answered the girl.

"Bring me some of your honorable water and get ready some honorable rice. The *jo sama*," young lady, "and I wish to proceed on our journey."

The girl brought Kei some water in a shallow

copper basin, and she washed her face and hands, wiping them on a blue towel which she took out of her sleeve. Then pouring out the water she refilled the basin and left it on the veranda for Kesa.

"*O hayo*," she said when she went in and found Kesa already up.

"*O hayo*," said Kesa.

"The honorable water waits for you, Kesa, and we must set out for the river."

While Kesa was washing the servant went into the room, opened all the slides, rolled up the beds, brushed up the floor with a little paper broom, and then brought in some rice and tea with a few little pieces of *daikon*.

"Truly, a poor breakfast," said the girl as Kei and Kesa took their chopsticks and began to eat.

"We hear that the rice is very scarce this year," said Kei.

"*Dogu*, yes; people are very sad and find it hard work to get enough to eat."

The fresh air, the cold water, and the breakfast made Kesa feel better. "Let us go now," she said.

"*Dogu*, no, not until I have spoken a word of the true doctrine," answered Kei.

There were very few people at the little wayside inn, and only an old man, a woman, and the servant-girl came to listen to Kei.

"*Dogu*, what do you want?" said the old man to Kei.

"To have prayer."

"But already I have worshipped at the shrine of Inari this morning. Where is your god?"

"We cannot see him and we have no image, but we have a book, and I will read it to you."

"Do you not offer anything to him?" asked the woman.

"He tells us to give him our hearts," said Kei.

Then she turned to the Sermon on the Mount and read the Saviour's gracious words to all those who are troubled in their hearts as to food or raiment or shelter; and the old man listened and nodded his head and said it was all very good. Then Kei and Kesa knelt and repeated together the Lord's Prayer.

"What do you call your God?" asked the man.

"Our Father," answered Kei.

"*Dogu*, it has been a long time since I called any one father," said the man.

Kei left them a little book called "The True Way of the Cross," and then she and Kesa said "*Saionara*" and went on their way to the river. Our travellers were well wrapped in padded coats and *dzukins*, and the rapid exercise kept them warm.

There were few people on the road. After

walking about an hour the two passed the inn where Yetaro with Saijiro and Yenoske had spent the night. Kesa enjoyed the keen frosty air and the rapid walking. The color came back to her cheeks and the brightness to her eyes. By the time they came to the river there was a change in the weather. The wind blew sullenly, as though bringing a storm, the sky was overcast, and the water of the river was dark and rough.

"*Hai! hai! hai! Iendo!*" Kei clapped her hands and shouted for the boatman, who was on the other side; but he did not hear.

"Oh, Kei, who is that?" cried Kesa suddenly, and Kei turned quickly and saw a man running swiftly towards them.

To the girl's excited fancy it was a essenger sent after her by her father, and she grew so white and trembled so violently that Kei ran up to her, saying,

"*Dogu*, Kesa, don't be so frightened; it is only a postman running with the mail."

The man was all out of breath when at last he reached the river and threw the mail-bag on the sand.

Another man, with two horses, had come up, and they all stood on the bank and gave one prolonged "*Hai-i!*" which brought the ferryman over.

The boat was large and flat-bottomed, and there was room for the horses too. So they all got in, and the ferryman worked the boat rapidly through the water.

"There are not many travellers on the road," said the postman to the ferryman.

"No; I get very little money from the ferry now, and rice is scarce and high. In the summer the boat is constantly going to and fro, and it is always filled with people," said the ferryman.

"Do you ever carry any of the honorable foreigners?" asked Kei.

"Oh, yes; some of them drink a great deal of *sake*."

"But those are not the Jesus-teachers."

"No; I can always tell the Jesus-teachers. One of them gave me a book once, but I cannot read well enough to understand it."

"The doctrine is very good. Try to get some one to read it for you," said Kei.

Kesa and Kei had their noon rice at a miserable little inn, and Kesa felt wearied and homesick. It began to drizzle. Dogs and chickens huddled under the eaves of the house, and some half-naked beggars, covered with loathsome sores, came up and asked alms. Kesa put some copper coins in their hands, and turned away disgusted.

The jinrikisha ride that afternoon was dreary enough. The two travellers wrapped themselves up in the blankets and had the top of the cart covered with oiled paper, so that the only outlook

A WINTER JOURNEY. 381

they had was from the front. Occasionally from one of the houses they would hear the "twang, twang" of a *samisen* mingling with the sound of the rain pouring from the eaves. Once or twice a jinrikisha passed them, and several times they passed a traveller on foot, closely muffled and carrying an umbrella.

"Kei," said Kesa, "I wonder what the mother and Chiye and Mitsu are doing, and whether the honorable father knows I have gone. O Kei, do you think he will be very angry and make the others very unhappy? I heard him say that they should go no more to the church; and how sad that will make them; and I have brought all this on them!"

"Ah, Kesa, they would rather endure the father's anger than have you marry that man. Be of good courage and all will be right. The honorable teacher will advise you what to do. Let us be patient, and all will be well."

"But, Kei, I thought when the honorable *sensei* was sick that I had learned to love God; and now my heart is dark. Mitsu, Chiye, and Harukichi have sorer trouble than I have, but they are happy, for they love and trust God. But I am not. What can I do, Kei? I do not like the Japanese way, but I am not a Christian. I can't believe anything, and I don't love any one, and my heart is cold and hard and full of anger."

"*Dogu*, Kesa, we will read the Book, and you

can talk with the honorable *sensei*, and all will yet be well."

Kei longed to have Kesa talk with the teacher. She felt utterly unable to guide the poor wanderer herself. But the Shepherd was looking after his sheep all the time, and Kei felt his comforting presence, although Kesa did not.

In the late afternoon, while the cold rain still came pouring down, they reached the great city Odawara. The hotel servants came out to greet them, and the weary, wet travellers were taken up to the best room, where they warmed themselves over *hibachis* filled with glowing coals, and had hot soup and tea.

"This is very good," said Kesa, holding the soup-bowl close to her mouth and tossing in the soup with chopsticks.

"What is it made of?" asked Kei of the girl who sat near them, ready to pour more tea or to fill their rice-bowls.

"It is made of *tai*-fish, and has eggs and *tofu* in it," said the girl.

"Very good *tofu*," said Kei.

Tofu is a very light sort of omelet which the Japanese like very much.

It grew dark, and the girl brought in candles.

"Have any of the Jesus-teachers been here?" asked Kei. Her heart was ever in her work.

"Yes; they stop here very often, and sing hymns about Jesus and a happy country and talk

A JAPANESE SANDAL-MAKER.

to us. They have left us some of their books," answered the girl.

"Are there any believers here?" asked Kei.

"*Dogu*, no; but there is an old woman here who wants to learn. You might go to her."

After dinner, in the pouring rain and through the dimly lighted streets, Kei and Kesa followed a man with a lantern to a house back of the hotel. They could hear through the storm the sound of the waves beating on the shore.

"Ah, much snow has fallen. It will be rough for the *jo sama*."

"The *jo sama* is strong and not afraid of the storm. But can you tell me where to buy some high *getas*, that our feet may be kept out of the wet?"

"Yes," said the man; "here is a shoe-store now."

Down went the shoe-seller on his forehead when he saw his customers. "You have well come, honorable strangers," he said.

Kei and Kesa bowed.

"It is truly bad weather."

"Truly, bad weather."

"The *jo sama* will like some fine *getas* ?"

"Thanks, the *jo sama* is travelling and wishes some high shoes to keep her feet from being wet."

Then the man brought down from the shelves some common wooden *getas* with very high underpieces, and Kei and Kesa each selected a pair.

"*Dogu*, Kei, I never wore such high shoes," said Kesa.

"Nor such rough ones; but you will need them," answered Kei.

They paid two *boos* each for the shoes. The man thanked them over and over, and they said good-by and went to find large rain umbrellas.

"Now let us go to the woman who wishes to learn the Jesus-doctrine," said Kei.

The house was not much larger than Kei's own and was all dark. But when they called, "*O tano moshimasu*," they heard a rustling within, and soon the slides were pushed open by a middle-aged woman.

"Ah, Kato," said the woman, "is that you?"

"Yes, honorable mistress. I have brought some strangers from Tokio. They are learned in the honorable doctrines of the honorable foreigners."

"They are welcome, truly welcome. Condescend to enter my humble abode."

"Truly, thanks," answered Kei and Kesa, and they all went in.

"Honorable husband has just retired, but he will rise when he hears of the honorable guests from the great city."

The woman lighted a tallow candle which was stuck in the end of a high wooden candlestick, fanned the coals of a *hibachi*, and put on them a kettle of water for tea.

It was Kei's own precious book, the Gospel according to Mark, that the woman had; and soon they were deep in the story of the Saviour's life upon earth. And so absorbed were Kei and the woman and the man that they could not stop until they had gone through most of the volume.

Poor Kesa, weary with the journey, fell asleep, and it was nearly midnight when Kei roused her to go back to the hotel. But Kei was radiant.

"You are very happy, Kei," said Kesa, wondering.

"Yes," answered Kei; "teaching the Jesus-doctrine is very happy work."

Kei might have sung,

> "I love to tell the story,
> It did so much for me;
> And that is just the reason
> I tell it now to thee."

The next morning they stood at the hotel door all ready for a climb, looking up at the mountain. The rain was over and the sun shining brightly, but the roads were muddy, and up on the mountain they could see the snow lying in great drifts.

"I have seen the Hakone Mountains all my life," said Kesa, "but I have never been so near before."

Kago men pressed about them, eager to carry the old lady and the *jo sama* up the mountain, but Kei refused to engage them. She and Kesa were strong and carried trusty mountain-staves, and why should they not walk? So said Kesa; and they went out of the city in the early winter morning and began the ascent of the mountain.

"It is over this mountain that Yenoske has gone so often, and he has often told Marion *san* of how he used to gather lilies for Saijiro," said Kesa.

They stopped for their noon rice at the little tea-house at the turn of the road which led down to Yamamidzu. Inari and Jizo stood up in the snow as pleasant and smiling as ever. They might have told Kei and Kesa how often Saijiro and Yenoske had stopped there to worship, but they were speechless, and neither Kei nor Kesa knew how near they were to Yamamidzu, of which they had heard so much.

In the afternoon they fell in with a party of travellers going, like themselves, to Hakone, and a merry time they all had in the snow. It was Kesa's first experience, and many a tumble she had on the high *getas*, and many a shout of laughter was heard on the mountain that afternoon.

It was bitterly cold when they got into Hakone. Snow lay on the ground, and the wind howled dismally. The lake was rough, but looked very beautiful with its setting of white and pure snowy mountains encircling it.

"The missionaries come here every summer and hold meetings, and many people on the mountain read the Jesus-books, and some believe," said the landlady, in answer to Kei's question as to whether they had listened to the Jesus-teaching.

The woman was the same one who was so kind to Saijiro when he passed over the mountain with Yenoske. She listened to the Scripture-reading and heard Kesa sing, and she and all the people who gathered in the hotel that evening said the doctrine was "very good."

And so for several days did Kei and Kesa travel, going down the highway to Nagoya. They found the weather warmer on the other side of the mountain as they journeyed south.

They came at last to Nagoya, and found Kesa's aunt. Her house was the very perfection of neatness—not a spot on the white mats, not a speck on the dark, polished wood-work. Beautiful camellias were blooming in the garden, and splendid gold-fish, the finest Kesa had ever seen, were swimming in the pond.

The aunt herself was one of the strictest of Buddhist women, and had her head shaved as a sort of priestess; she wore no ornaments, went three times daily to the temple, fasted often, and repeated the name of Shaka Sama a thousand times a day.

"I am Kesa Fujisawa, the sister of Chiye," said Kesa, when she was ushered into the presence of this grave personage.

"*Dogu, dogu!*" said the aunt, at first somewhat surprised out of her usual calm dignity. "And what are you doing here, child? Did the honorable father send you to me?"

"No, honorable aunt. I have run away from my father, because he wanted me to marry; and I am on my way to the southern country."

"That is what comes of letting children go to foreign schools and learn foreign religions," said the aunt. "I warned your honorable father against it and told him no good would come of it. Chiye was always reading her Christian books, and never went to the temple nor repeated Shaka Sama's holy name nor counted her beads. *Dogu, dogu!* what is to become of Nippon?"

Nevertheless she invited Kei and Kesa to make their home with her while they remained in Nagoya. Unfortunately the next day was Sunday and they had to remain two nights, and Kesa and her aunt grew more and more antagonistic all the while.

"Your eyes are too large and your cheeks are too red and you have no manners," she would say to Kesa; and Kesa would return these compliments by thoroughly disliking her and wondering how Chiye endured her so long. It was a relief to all when Monday morning came at last and the travellers could proceed on their journey.

"I hate her!" exclaimed Kesa as soon as they were well away from the house; "I hate her shaven head and her nun's dress!"

"Kesa, that is one reason why you cannot love God and become a Christian. Your heart is so quickly filled with anger. You are hard and unforgiving to your father; you are half inclined to despise your gentle mother; you hate this person and that person without much reason; and when you do love any one you cling to that person instead of to God."

"*Dogu*, Kei!" protested Kesa. But her eyes were filled with tears.

Kei looked sorrowful and wished that Kesa had not met her aunt, and wondered how she could ever follow the loving Shepherd with so much hatred in her heart.

Still they went on, patiently treading the great highway, hoping to reach Kioto before the next Sabbath.

"Kei, do you think you will find Nantaro?" asked Kesa one day.

"I am asking God every day to lead me to him," Kei answered; and that evening she asked Kesa to read to her the story of Joseph. They wept over the beautiful history, and Kei said, "If God so led Joseph's brethren to him, he can lead me to Nantaro."

As they approached the great spiritual capital, Osaka, they passed many temples and pagodas and noticed the great number of priests on the road. "They must worship a great deal down here," said Kesa; and Kei sighed.

But when they entered the hill-surrounded city with all its grand temples and images, Kei's heart was delighted by the number of those who were listening to the words she loved so well. There she found schools and colleges and missionary houses and churches. And they told her that in all the mountain solitudes, even at the holiest shrines, the doctrines of the cross were presented and that there were many believers, as well as in the city itself.

"Let us go to the temple where I lived with the woman and where I studied with the priest," she said to Kesa one day.

They went through a long, crowded street and came to the same little house that Kei remembered. She stood and called, "*O tano moshimasu*," and a woman of about her own age came out. It was the friend of years ago, and she had become a Christian, and there was great rejoicing.

But the priest was dead, and Kei sorrowed much because she could not tell him the glad story of the cross. She showed Kesa the pavement where she had walked until her feet were sore, and the money-box into which she threw the beans, and the bell which she rang to call the attention of the god.

"*Dogu, dogu, dogu!*" said Kei.

Then Kesa begged to climb the pagoda; and they went up the rickety old stairs, which shook so that Kei was afraid and clung to the side of the building. But when they reached the top of the pagoda they had a glorious view of all Osaka, with its canals and splendid bridges, its castle and Government buildings.

"Truly a great city, and truly to God a great thank-you," said Kei.

From Osaka they went by train to Kobé, and spent a pleasant Sabbath in that little city by the sea. They saw the school on the hill where so many girls have been trained for service in the Master's cause. There was a meeting of the Christians from Kioto, Osaka, the hill country, and the islands round about, and Kei heard an address from a man who came from her own native region; she clasped her hands in thankfulness when she knew that the "Word" was preached there also.

But Kei was anxious to continue the journey, so they took passage for Onomichi, and one morning when the sun rose they were sailing among the countless islands of the Inland Sea.

"It is very beautiful, Kei," said Kesa as they stood on the deck of the steamer.

From all the little islands fishing-boats were coming, darting out of hidden nooks and dancing in the glory of the sunshine. The steamer was winding in and out among islands of fantastic shapes. Now before them stood a huge elephant, now a monstrous sugar-loaf, now a castle with domes and towers, and now a humped camel.

In the evening they came to Onomichi and went ashore.

It was not until the next morning that they could go to the fishing hamlet.

"Here is the place where honorable mother fell by the wayside," Kei said.

To a woman whom they met Kesa said,

"This is Kei, who used to live here, and we have come to get news of her brother Nantaro."

"Only a few days ago," said the woman, "we had news of Nantaro."

"Do you know where he is?"

"*Dogu, kawaiso!*" said the woman; "he is in prison for a great robbery."

"In what prison?" asked Kesa.

"In Hiroshima."

Kei heard this sad news, and yet she rejoiced; not because he was in prison, but because she knew where to find him, and could go to him and tell him of peace and pardon through Jesus.

The two travellers remained in the hamlet all night, and Kei talked with her old friends and promised to return and tell them more.

The next day they went back to Onomichi and took another little steamer for Hiroshima.

The next morning they came to the little island Ujina, clambered down the side of the steamer into a small boat, and were rowed to the shore.

CHAPTER XXXII.

THE HOME AND THE PRISON.

On landing, Kesa and Kei climbed up on a high bank, on one side of which were fields, with mountains in the distance, and on the other a river, whose clear waters, rippling over the sandy bottom, seemed in the sunshine to flow over golden sands. Coarse grass, reeds, and rushes grew on the water's edge, and the wind murmured gently through them. The tide was full, and fishing-boats were going out to sea.

"Ah," said Kei, pointing out an island higher and bluer than the rest, "that is Itsukushima, or Miajima, the Beautiful."

"It is one of the seven places in Japan noted for beauty. I have read about it and have seen pictures of it," said Kesa.

Some of the hills about Hiroshima were but dimly visible through the mist; others stood out clear and distinct; the islands rising out of the sea looked themselves like mountains. The views were wondrously fair, and Kesa thought of Chiye, and wished that she too could enjoy that bright morning view.

"Look at these beautiful fishes," said Kesa.

Some men were passing, carrying large baskets filled with fish of most exquisite colors. Some were all silver, some silver tinged with beautiful pinks and blues, and some a golden red. In the fields to the left grew egg-plants and sugar-potatoes; and pumpkin-vines with bright yellow flowers trailed along the ground.

But as they gazed on all these beauties they saw a gang of prisoners in flesh-colored garments coming across the field, and Kei turned aside her head.

"How shall we find the *sensei?*" asked Kesa.

"*Dogu*, there are few foreigners in Hiroshima; we can inquire."

A laborer was coming towards them, carrying a large rope and a basket.

"*O hayo*," said Kei, accosting him.

"*O hayo*," returned the man. "Where are you going?"

"Thanks, we are looking for the honorable foreigners' home," answered Kei.

"Ah," said the man, pointing to the roof of a quaint old Japanese house just ahead of them, "you will find the honorable strangers in that house."

"Thanks, truly," said Kei, and she and Kesa walked rapidly on.

A flight of stone steps led from the bank down to the gateway. Entering the gates, they passed on towards the house. But before they reached the door Kesa heard a familiar voice in the garden on the other side of the enclosure. "*Sensei! sensei!*" she cried, and in a moment stood beside her beloved teacher.

When the first excitement of meeting was over, the travellers were taken into the house and a warm breakfast was given them. Kesa told of her refusal to marry Susumi and of her running away from her father; and Kei told how she had heard that her brother was in prison in Hiroshima, and that she could not rest until she had seen him.

Then said Mr. Levering, the missionary, "I will go with Kei to the authorities and see if we can gain admittance to the prison."

So they went off, and Kesa and the teacher were glad to be left together.

"I must show you my house and garden first, Kesa," said Mrs. Levering. "It reminds me somewhat of your father's house and garden in Tokio, only it is not kept so nicely."

It was a strange, rambling old house, built for a noble of the olden time, and containing many rooms which were never used.

"This is my bedroom; you will think it a perfect labyrinth."

Mrs. Levering pushed open the slides and they entered a narrow place that suddenly widened into a square, eight feet each way, which formed the main part of the room. The windows were of paper, and for protection against thieves there were bamboo bars, which looked very frail indeed. The third division of the room was a closet, with a board floor nicely polished, and an inner closet with sliding doors. Then there was a dressing and bath room.

"*Dogu*, I should think you would not find this very comfortable," said Kesa.

"Oh, it is comfortable enough. I rather like the slides. There are no doors slamming and swinging on their hinges. The only door in the house on hinges is this one," pointing to the bath-room door, "and this is where I saw the ghost."

"*Sensei!*"

"True, Kesa. One morning I hung a sheet over this door and forgot it. When I came back in the evening I saw this tall white thing moving silently to and fro, and it was a moment or two before I fully comprehended that it was the sheet hanging on the door. I thought it a veritable Japanese ghost, like the one Hono saw."

Kesa laughed merrily.

"Oh, *sensei!*" she suddenly cried. There before her on the washstand was an enormous spider, and creeping over the walls were two or three lizards.

"Well, I have found that these things are harmless," said Mrs. Levering. "At first I was terribly afraid of them, but now I watch the rats playing on the rafters above my head and see these spiders running around without fear, and can touch one of those cold, slimy lizards in the dark without screaming. But the worst things are the little worms which eat our bamboo chairs, and in the summer the mosquitoes are terrible, I am told."

"How the furniture sinks into the mats, *sen-sei*."

"Yes, Kesa; beds, tables, and chairs are sadly out of place in a Japanese house, but we cannot do without them."

"This is our cellar," said the teacher, taking Kesa into a dark apartment in which were hanging-shelves. On the shelves were covered stone jars, the lids of which were held down by bricks, flat-irons, and every available heavy thing.

"You see we have to protect ourselves against rats," said Mrs. Levering.

"*Dogu!*" said Kesa.

Then they went into the kitchen, which contained a range and an oven for baking bread, and from there into the dining-room, furnished with table and chairs.

The sitting-room had a little stove in it and some glass slides, and opened on a long veranda, very much like that of the Fujisawa mansion in Tokio. There was a cabinet-organ in one corner, and there were book-shelves, tables, chairs, pictures, and other things which gave the room quite a home-like appearance in the eyes of the missionaries in this far-away land.

"We will go out into the garden before we have our talk up stairs," said the teacher; and she and Kesa went and stood by the side of the lotus pond.

The wind was swaying the immense leaves gently, and they were bowing like so many Japanese. A little arched bridge crossed the lotus pond, and Kesa and her teacher went over it to a bamboo grove. The place was charming. The sunshine crept in and out between the leaves, which, like those of the lotus, moved in the slightest breeze. Azalea bushes with pretty, delicate flowers made the garden attractive; and there were artificial hillocks, with stones scattered here and there over them. Under the bamboos down by the pond, hidden by the coarse grass and leaves, twining over the bushes and clinging to the trees, grew vines of many varieties, and in the low, damp places were ferns and ivy.

"I like the garden," said Kesa simply as they turned and went into the house.

Mrs. Levering led Kesa to the one room in the upper story and drew aside the slides. The view was magnificent. Everywhere the plain was bounded by mountains or mountainous islands, and Kesa could catch a glimpse of the river and watch the clouds in their ceaseless changes and the lights and shadows on the hillside.

Kesa and her teacher sat quietly for a while. At last Kesa raised her eyes to Mrs. Levering's face, and in answer to their mute pleading the teacher said,

"Now, dear child, tell me all about it."

"Oh, *sensei*, I could not marry the man, and so I came away."

"But, Kesa, your father can find you and compel you to return."

"Yes, *sensei*, but I hoped he would think about it and not insist on it."

"Did Chiye advise you to come?"

"No, *sensei*; but she and the mother and Mitsu helped me to get ready."

"How is it with your own heart, Kesa?"

"*Dogu*, *sensei*, I cannot feel happy. I have been angry with my father and I hated my aunt. Why cannot I be like Chiye?"

"Dear Kesa, I hope there are better things in store for you. Will you put yourself under my guidance and do what I ask?"

"Yes, *sensei*, if I can."

"Then sit down and write a letter to your father and tell him where you are and why you went away; and try to put anger and hatred out of your heart while you write. Will you do this?"

"Yes, *sensei*."

Kesa was supplied with materials and began her writing; Mrs. Levering took up her needlework, and the room was quiet again.

"I have finished, *sensei*," said Kesa at length, and proceeded to read her letter.

"HONORABLE FATHER: Compliments, compliments.

"I beg your honorable forgiveness for running away from my home. I could not marry that man. Oh, honorable father, please do not make me. And do not think it is because I am a Christian that I ran away. My heart is hard and heavy and I am not a Christian. Mitsu is a Christian and she does what you tell her to do. Chiye is a Christian and she submits quietly to your honorable will. But pity your poor Kesa and do not make her marry that man. Please, compliments, compliments.

"KESA FUJISAWA.

"AT HIROSHIMA."

"That will do nicely, Kesa, and now I have something for you. Did you think I was not expecting you?"

Mrs. Levering put a letter in Kesa's hands.

"It is from Chiye," she said as she took it, and burst into tears.

It was written in English and was the first word she had had from home. Thus it read:

"DEAR SISTER: You will want to know how we all are at home. The father not know you have gone for two days. Then he ask, 'Where is Kesa?' and I tell him that you have gone away. He say nothing, but his face grow very black and he go away. For three days now he say nothing at all, but is always quiet, and we do not know what to think. But he not try to find you.

"The mother is very sad, but she never say she sorry you go away; and sometimes I read the Bible to her.

"Dear sister, we miss you. Mitsu and I want our dearest sister. We talk often how you comfort us when you come and sit beside us when we feel sick or sad. And every day we pray, 'Lord Jesus, bless Kesa and bring her back; but oh, soften her heart and make her a Christian!' And we know God will hear our prayer.

"We send much love to you.
"Your loving sisters,
"MITSU AND CHIYE FUJISAWA."

Mrs. Levering said nothing as she listened to Kesa's passionate sobs after reading this letter. She let her weep on, and prayed God to comfort her. Her own letter from Chiye had touched her very soul, with its strong faith in the midst of this hour of trouble and its fulness of love and pity. "Surely Chiye Fujisawa is a Christian if ever one lived on this earth," she thought.

"Seal your letter now, and we will take it to the postoffice," said Mrs. Levering gently and firmly to Kesa after a time.

The letter was sealed and directed, and as they walked to the postoffice they talked on indifferent subjects and discussed the beauties of the landscape.

When they returned to the house they found Kei. She had been weeping, indeed, but joy shone in her eyes. Sick and in prison, after a life of desperate crime, she had found Nantaro, and although he turned away from her at first, he had at last talked with her and seemed softened.

"He must serve his time out, and at the end receive that dreadful flogging," said Kei, and she shuddered. "But then I shall have him, and I will teach him of the Lord Jesus, and of how his blood can cleanse us from all sin."

CHAPTER XXXIII.

JINRIKISHA RIDES.

"WHILE you are waiting for an answer to your letter we will take some peeps at this beautiful country," said Mrs. Levering to Kesa the next morning.

So in the afternoon Tom, the horse, was brought to the gate all saddled and bridled, ready for the missionary to ride, and jinrikishas were called for the ladies, while all the children in the neighborhood assembled to see the "honorable foreigners" start out.

"Have there never been any foreigners down in this part of the country before, *sensei?*" asked Kesa, as she noted the eager, expectant look on the dirty little faces.

"Very few, Kesa. An English gentleman was here with his family for a while, but the people are not much accustomed to foreigners."

The shafts were lifted, and Tom was all ready for a start; and then began a race between the coolies, the horse, and the children, the latter being at last outstripped.

They looked like little savages. Some had very scanty clothing, and others none at all. One boy seemed like a very imp of mischief, and Kesa watched him with some interest as he stood now on his head and now on his feet; then, gathering up his dress, he would start off on a run, and at last Kesa, thinking he was left far behind, turned to see him breathless and grinning at a turn of the road.

The friends were going to Nigitsu, the finest temple in the city. They passed through some of the most crowded streets, and then crossed a long bridge and came to a part less densely populated. To the left was a canal, with great cedar-trees on its banks. Above was the blue, cloudless sky, and all around were hills upon hills and islands upon islands. Oh, the beauty of these southern winter days! with sunshine warm enough to give heat to the old people, who sit out of doors in preference to shivering over charcoal braziers in the house.

The entrance to Nigitsu was beautiful. From the soft turf rose great cedar-trees, and at intervals under them were placed huge stone lanterns. The gateway was ornamented with the usual gilding and carving; it was very old; its builders had long been sleeping in the Buddhist graveyard.

"What a magnificent pavement!" said Mrs. Levering, as they went up to the old unsightly temple, the walls of which were crumbling away.

"Why is it that these people, with so much building material around them, do not build better houses?" asked the missionary, as they looked at the blocks of granite and the decaying mud.

Having seen Nigitsu, the party took horse and jinrikishas again for Iwahana. Out of the town, past rows of tumble-down cottages in the outskirts, into a pleasant road with hills on one side and a clear stream on the other, rolled the jinrikishas until the coolies dropped the shafts at a little tea-house opposite Iwahana.

"Do you know what Iwahana means, *sensei?*" inquired Kesa.

"Yes; rock-flower, Kesa; and very pretty it is too."

On the hill were rocks lying scattered about, and from these the hill derived its name. There were other flowers beside the "rock-flowers" there, and the whole party climbed the steep ascent, and came down with hands filled with bright blossoms and leaves of red sumach.

"How beautiful it all is," said Mrs. Levering as they started off again.

They turned into a lane skirted with hedges, and passed pretty little farmhouses almost hidden in the foliage. Then they went far out into the fields, where men, women, and children were at work.

"What long distances your people walk. They could not do that in America, where it is so far from one town to another, with no tea-houses scattered between."

A mist filled the valley as they went home, but it seemed to make everything even more beautiful as it lifted to disclose now a mountain and now a gleam of shining water.

"*Dogu!*" said Kei, out of breath.

Two or three days had passed, and the friends were climbing some steps cut in a steep hillside, going up to a temple.

"What are those little sticks with papers for?" asked Mrs. Levering.

"There are prayers written on the papers," said Kei; and Mrs. Levering noted the Chinese characters on every one.

The temple, which they gained after some hard climbing, was on a ledge just about large enough to hold it. From three sides they could look down a precipice.

Climbing still higher up the steep hillside, they at last gained a point from which the islands burst upon their view.

"There is Miajima," said Kesa.

"Yes; we can always tell it by its blueness and its three curves," said the teacher.

"Did you ever walk on such hollow ground before?" asked Mr. Levering.

It did indeed seem almost as though it might give way beneath their feet.

"How do you account for it, Lynn?" Mrs. Levering inquired.

"Only by supposing that there are lava-beds

under us. You can see the effects of ancient fires over there."

The descent was very difficult, but at last, after sliding and slipping several times, they reached the jinrikishas and Tom, and were off again.

"Towards the sunrising," called the missionary to the coolies, and away they went to the castle, across a bridge, and by the side of the river. Then turning to the east, they came to a broad road and rolled along under grand cedars. Another turn, and they saw before them an oddly shaped hill. And so the jinrikishas went winding in and out among the hills until they reached the rice-fields. Here the road was so rough that the ladies all preferred walking to enduring the jolting of the springless jinrikishas. Next came a bamboo grove, the sunlight glancing through the leaves.

Some people came out of their houses to see the foreign lady walking through the fields.

"The people down here are afraid of us, Kesa," said Mrs. Levering; "they think we will bewitch them;" and Kesa smiled to see a woman pulling her husband into the house.

In the afternoon they came to a temple. Kesa counted a hundred steps as they toiled up to it.

"I wonder why the Japanese put their temples in such high places," said the missionary.

"Do they think there is any merit in climbing up to them, Kei?" asked Mrs. Levering.

"*Dogu*, yes, honorable *sensei*," answered Kei. "They can climb up and down a certain number of times, and thus do penance."

"The view is certainly grand," said the missionary, as they stood on the edge of a precipice and looked over the country. Rivers, hills, islands, plains were spread out in one grand panorama before them.

For the next few days there was a storm of wind and rain which kept them all in the house.

Kesa felt the time pass a little heavily, so she was glad to awake one morning and find the sun shining brightly, with only a few soft white clouds floating lazily in the sky.

"Now for our trip to Hijiyama," said Mrs. Levering at the noon meal.

So the jinrikishas were called, and they were soon making their way over the bridges and across the fields to Hiji hill.

The hill was very steep, and at its foot the coolies let down the shafts. The ascent had to be made on foot. It was hard climbing, but the road was exceedingly beautiful. On one side of the narrow footpath there was an abrupt descent, and on the other the hill towered above them. Trees, shrubs, and grasses were of the richest green, and occasional rocks gave variety to the coloring. At the feet of the climbers and on all the hillside bloomed quantities of wild flowers.

"Let us stop and see this little cemetery,"

called Mr. Levering, who was acting as guide, to the climbers behind him; and they all went in to wander for a time among the graves. The tombstones were of handsome granite, and not crowded together as the stones in the Buddhist cemeteries usually are.

On one granite stone Kei read, "To my eldest son." The eldest son is the most important member of a Japanese family. He is "*ni san*," honorable brother, to the younger children, and his father's hope and heir.

On other graves hung straw sandals, and on children's graves toys were placed. The Japanese fill the children's coffins with their playthings; and in former times the young *samurai* took with him into the grave his little sword.

"Ah," said Mrs. Levering suddenly, "here is something homelike;" and she pointed to a stone on which was written in English, "Fell asleep in Jesus."

It marked the grave of a little English child, whose mother had to go far away when the father's engagement at the Government school in Hiroshima terminated.

"His mother in England must often think of her baby lying here," said Mrs. Levering; and they lingered a while near the baby's grave and laid some flowers upon it.

The view which greeted their eyes from the top of the hill fully repaid them for all their toil.

It was more beautiful than anything they had seen before, and they stood for a long time gazing on the entrancing scene.

The place where they tarried was a soldiers' cemetery. One stone was cut into a beautiful urn, while others were cubes and others still were small shafts; in all were hollow places for holding water, and in many of them were fresh flowers.

"The Japanese bring flowers to the graves of their loved ones as we do," said Mrs. Levering.

"It reminds me of an extract I found the other day," said her husband; "I will read it while we are resting:

"'Do not keep the alabaster boxes of your love and tenderness sealed until your friends are dead. Fill their lives with sweetness. Speak approving, cheering words while their ears can hear them and while their hearts can be thrilled by them. The thing you mean to say when they are gone, say before they go. The flowers you mean to send to their coffins, send to brighten and sweeten their homes before they leave them. I would rather have a coffin without a flower, and a funeral without a eulogy, than a life without the sweetness of love and sympathy.'"

But the darkness drove them home. The hillside was all quiet as they went down; no sound of human voices reached their ears.

CHAPTER XXXIV.

A SABBATH IN HIROSHIMA.

THE Sabbath is not entirely disregarded through the Japanese Empire. It is a holiday. Few indeed among the people of Hiroshima understood its sacredness, but it was an advantage to the missionary to have it observed to the extent of being an official and school holiday. It gave the officers and pupils leisure for study of the Scriptures, and the old *daimio's* house became the resort of those who wished to study the Jesus-way.

One summer evening, when the rain had been pouring down all day, and the missionary had given up all thought of any more guests and had shut up the house for the night, he heard the familiar call at the door, and opened it to admit a grave-looking man of pleasing appearance. He had come up in the rain from the village. His parents were Buddhists, bitterly opposed to the teachings of the foreigners, but he had heard of the new religion and had come to learn for himself. Since then, during the fall and winter evenings, after the lamps were lighted and when the fire was crackling in the stove, a little company of learners had gathered around the table in the sitting-room to study about Jesus. The stranger who came in the summer rain attended faithfully himself, and sometimes brought others. Then Bible-classes for Sabbath mornings were started and a preaching service was asked for. Thus was the way opened for proclaiming the gospel in Hiroshima.

All this Mr. and Mrs. Levering told to Kei and Kesa the Sunday after they reached Hiroshima.

Several men from the village, with Owada, Masuda, Imai, and Noda, young men from the Government school, came in to the Bible-lesson, and the morning passed pleasantly.

They were just beginning the study of Genesis, and Iwada read in Japanese,

"In the beginning God created the heaven and the earth."

"Ah, Mr. Iwada," said the missionary, "the almighty God, the everlasting Father, created the world. Is this any harder to accept than your old belief that 'Isanagi' made it?"

"No, *sensei*. There are many ridiculous stories connected with Isanagi that Japanese who are not Christians do not believe," answered Iwada.

They read on how God made the light and the expanse of heaven, the dry land and the seas, the grass and trees, the lights of heaven, fish and reptiles and birds, the beasts, and last of all man, and made them all "very good."

"Is there anything unworthy of our belief in all this, Mr. Owada?"

"No," answered the young student.

"I wish more of our people would come and learn these truths," said one of the men from the town.

"What does this mean, *sensei?*" asked Noda, and he read, "And God created man in his own image."

"It refers," said the missionary, "to the spirit of man, which God made to bear a likeness to himself in its power to know and think and will and love, but especially in the holiness of its thinking and willing and loving. Made thus in the image of God, man at first knew and loved and obeyed God. How he lost this holy likeness to God by disobedience we shall see in another lesson. When we learn that man was made to know and delight in God we cannot wonder that now he is restless and dissatisfied until he finds Him."

"No, *sensei;* many of the Japanese feel so," said Noda.

The young men were much interested in the lesson and promised to think of it all at home.

In the afternoon Kesa and Mrs. Levering sat for a while on the upper veranda. For miles and miles around them in every direction, in the valleys and on the islands of the Inland Sea, were the heathen people bowing to their false gods and worshipping their graven images.

"Are you not lonely sometimes, *sensei?*" asked Kesa.

"Yes, Kesa, sometimes. No one can be thus far away from home and friends and not feel lonely. Sometimes I even long for the storms and cold of northern climates and dream of ice and snow. But how is it with you, Kesa?"

"Oh, *sensei*, I do long sometimes so much for my home. I hope that I shall soon get a letter from my father and that he will tell me that I can come."

"I hope so, dear. But I have been thinking to-day, sadly, I fear, of Sabbaths at home, of our grand churches and solemn music, and of how the multitudes go up to worship."

"Would you rather be there than here, *sensei?*"

"No, dear child," was the hearty reply.

Mr. Levering, who had joined them while his wife was speaking, said, "And I too have been thinking of the difference between Christian life here and at home, and I rather like this phase better than that. True, we cannot go up to the house of God with the multitude, have our souls uplifted by the music of the organ, join in the singing, or bow in prayer with the great congregation; but we can as certainly have the presence of God, and our religion *must* be real heart-worship, without hypocrisy; there's no room for that here. When I look at the people in our plain churches, sitting on mats or on rude benches, and drinking in so eagerly the simple word of life, I cannot wish for more luxury, more elaborate display, more learned preaching."

"Ah," said Mrs. Levering as her husband stopped speaking, "there are the boys coming to sing. Let us go down to the organ."

Soon over the fields floated the old tunes, "Antioch" and "Coronation," as both Americans and Japanese joined in the singing.

CHAPTER XXXV.

A BEAUTIFUL ISLE OF THE SEA.

"Do you think we can venture, Lynn?"

Mrs. Levering was standing at the gateway looking anxiously up at the clouds. Four jinrikishas were waiting, and the missionaries, with Kesa and Kei, were all ready for a trip to Miajima, the beautiful island down the coast.

"What do *you* think about it, Julius Cæsar?" asked the missionary.

"Julius Cæsar" was a coolie who bore a curious resemblance to the pictures of the hero of that name in old Roman history. He now looked wisely at the clouds, scratched his ear, and answered, "*Dogu*, honorable master, the honorable rain comes not down to-day."

The friends had relied on Julius Cæsar's favorable prophecy the day previous, when the clouds looked equally threatening, and had no occasion to regret their trust; so they had confidence in him again and started off.

After crossing several long bridges and riding over some pretty fields they reached the little town Kusatsu. Here a few drops fell, followed shortly by a few more, and at last the rain came down in torrents. The road over which they were travelling was the most romantic they had yet seen. Even in the pouring rain and the partially obscuring mist it was charming. On one side the sea, dark and stormy, dashed up against the shore; on the other towered a mountain half concealed by the fog.

The roadway itself was very bad, being sandy and full of holes. It seemed as though it would all be washed away at no very distant day. At length the island rose before them like an immense sugar-loaf, with small cedar-trees growing on its steep sides in strange positions and at nearly regular intervals.

"It is trying to lose so much of the beauty around us," said Mrs. Levering, as they went on in the view-obscuring storm, through green fields, and with the "everlasting hills" about them.

The weather was forlorn enough when they reached the place where they were to take a boat for Miajima, and they went immediately to the landing.

"How much for a boat to Miajima?" asked Mr. Levering.

"Seventy-five cents," said the boatman.

"I will give you thirty cents," said Mr. Levering.

"Fifty cents," said the boatman.

But the charge was too high, and the whole party went to the hotel, dried their clothes as best they could, and ordered dinner. They had rice and fish brought them, and while they were eating the expected message came; the sailors would go for thirty cents.

It was almost dark when the party reached the landing to cross to the island, and the gray, rough water did not look inviting. The boat was tolerably large, but it had the usual low cabin, into which they crowded, and in which they could not stand upright. A single lantern swung from the cabin roof.

After a time the moon came out and shone dimly through watery clouds, and as the rain had ceased, the party crept out of the cabin and stood on the deck, watching the scarcely visible shore and the dark water. It was a strange scene. The coolies, as they worked their oars, were rapidly chanting a peculiar strain and rocking their almost naked bodies backward and forward, while ahead loomed Miajima, growing more and more distinct, until at last the boat struck the shore. A rope was thrown out, a plank was laid down, and the travellers crossed over and were in Miajima.

As they turned to go up the hill a deer crossed their path and Kesa stopped to pet it.

"How tame it is, *sensei*," she said.

The landlord of the hotel to which they were going went out to meet them, politely ushered them into the best room, and brought tea and cold water.

While supper was being prepared the travellers sat on the veranda and viewed the place as well as they could in the darkness.

At supper they talked with the landlord and landlady about Miajima and the deer.

They passed a comfortable night on mattresses stuffed with cotton and placed on the floor, but all night long the rain poured in torrents on the roof and ran in streams from the eaves.

In the morning the prospect was no brighter. "I do not fancy being shut up in a Japanese hotel all day," said Mrs. Levering; but the words were scarcely uttered when there came a cheering burst of sunshine, and the clouds all rolled away.

"Go to Momiji first," the landlord advised.

This was a grove of maples, and as they went towards it beautiful views greeted their eyes in all directions. They came first to a place where a rapid mountain-stream rushed over immense rocks, making tiny cascades and whirlpools. A bridge crossed the stream, and the friends went over the bridge and clambered down on the rocks to a little tea-house built in the middle of the stream. There were chairs in the tea-house, but they all preferred sitting in Japanese fashion on the floor, so as to be near the water as it came hurrying and tumbling over the rocks. At the entrance of the beautiful grove Momiji was an old man selling toothpicks.

"Please buy, honorable foreigners," he said

as the missionaries passed; and they bought some, the old man assuring them that they were medicated and that one using them would never have toothache.

The next visit was to an old temple, on the walls of which hung some curious pictures, and among them was one evidently given by the Dutch. It was a queer old picture, and they all looked at it with a great deal of interest. A king and queen were standing by the seashore with courtiers and maids of honor behind them, and a ship under full sail was just coming into port. The picture was painted in brilliant colors.

"That shows that we are in the country of the Dutchmen," said Mr. Levering, referring to the long residence of the Dutch in that part of the country.

Then they clambered down some stone steps and made their way to the seashore, to see the famous *torii*, or bird-rest, which is found in front of the temple gates. This is about the largest *torii* in Japan. When the tide is full it is in deep water, but at this time it stood high and dry.

"It will not do not-to stand under it," said Kesa; so off came her wooden clogs and short stockings, and she waded out in the shallow water, stood under the *torii*, looked up at the massive timbers, and smiled at the friends on the shore.

The temple to which this *torii* was the entrance

was the most curious one they had ever seen. At high tide it also is in the water. It consists entirely of long open galleries with pictures on both sides. Some of these pictures were of wood, and carvings of animals and flowers attracted the attention of the travellers.

"Oh, *sensei*, here is another Dutch painting," called Kesa; and there, indeed, hung another one on the wall beside the antiquities of Japan.

At the end of the last gallery was a bright-eyed little boy, who accosted them politely and asked them to buy some of his beans to feed the deer. Kesa bought some for a few *cash* and let the pretty creatures come up and eat out of her hand.

But the day's bright hours were hurrying away, and the party wished to reach home by nightfall. So, returning to the pretty hotel, they called for a boat. Strange to say, although the day was perfectly clear, the sailors had a superstition that on the next day there would be a great storm, and all the boats were put away in anticipation of the hurricane.

It was some time before the men could be persuaded to bring out a boat, and the ladies spent the intervening time in exploring the hotel garden. At last a boat was obtained, and bidding farewell to the kind people of the inn, the travellers started homeward. The boat-ride was more pleasant than the dark voyage of the night before, and they all sat on top of the cabin and watched the magnificent sunset.

"I wait for these sunsets every day, wondering what new beauties will be disclosed," said Mrs. Levering, as they watched the grand display.

Nearing the shore, they discovered Julius Cæsar and his friends waiting for them, bowing and smiling on the breakwater.

"Truly, fine weather," said the coolies.

"Truly, fine weather," responded the travellers, as they took their places in the jinrikishas.

It was late when the friends reached the house by the river.

"An honorable guest has arrived," said one of the servants as they entered the gates.

Wondering who it could be, they went into the house, and Kesa stood face to face with her father.

CHAPTER XXXVI.

HOME AGAIN.

"HONORABLE father!"

"My daughter!"

Nothing more was said, and the low bows were very formal, but Kesa, looking into her father's eyes, felt that all was right.

"It is in answer to Mitsu's and Chiye's prayers," she said afterwards; and she wept as she thought of the love and patience of her sisters, the real affection of her parents, and her own waywardness and ingratitude.

"God is good to me, *sensei*, God is good," she repeated over and over; and Mrs. Levering in her heart thanked the Good Shepherd for thus following his sheep.

"How is the honorable mother? And the honorable sisters, are they well?" asked Kesa of her father when the first salutations were over.

"The honorable mother and the honorable sisters are well, my daughter, and wait for your return," answered Fujisawa.

Then the missionary and his wife came in and welcomed the guest, and all sat down to a cheerful dinner, served partly in Japanese and partly in American style.

The few days that Fujisawa spent in Hiroshima were occupied chiefly in going about the town, in which he was much interested. He and the others went to see the workmen fashioning umbrellas and immense Chinese lanterns. They looked at the castle, and went again to visit Nigitsu, Iwahana, and beautiful Hijiyama. Mr. Levering told Fujisawa of the busy work in the cotton-fields during the previous summer, when all the people were gathering cotton and the whole town was white with the snowy balls.

The day before Kesa and her father went away was sad for them all. Kei's brother, Nantaro, was released from prison, and had to receive his stripes. From the house, though all the doors and windows were closed, they could hear distinctly the sound of the lash and the cries of the victim. Poor Kei shut herself in her room, and rocked to and fro and moaned, as the sound of her brother's agony reached her ears.

"*Dogu*," said the indignant Fujisawa, "such punishments are abolished by law."

"I thought so," said Mr. Levering, "but it seems that the law is not enforced down here."

Then Fujisawa told them of the great reform in the prison system throughout Japan, and gave some details of the horrors of Japanese prisons and punishments in former days.

"The prisoners were crowded together in filthy places where they could not get a breath of fresh air," said he; "and heads were cut off by the dozen, the victims kneeling in rows, with hands tied behind them, each awaiting his turn. Heads were placed in the public thoroughfares, where all could see them."

At last the terrible sounds in the prison-yard were over. The gentlemen went with Kei and took charge of her brother. A bed had been prepared, and in less than an hour Kei sat by the sufferer's side, happy in once again being allowed to minister to the wants of her beloved Nantaro.

The leave-takings were cheerful this time; Kesa felt glad to go home, and her teacher was thankful and hopeful for her. As the boat bore them away from the shore Kesa's eyes rested for a moment on the glory of the mountain-tops. "It would remind Marion of the 'City of God,'" she said to herself. Then she called her father's attention to some fishermen who were standing in the water casting their nets. They passed the little island Ujina. The water was bright and sparkling; all the hills were sunlit; they had a pleasant ride over a placid sea, and in due time reached the steamer, clambered up the side, and were soon going rapidly in the direction of Kobé. They saw the pretty city Tomo in the morning, stopped at a town on the great island of Shikoku, spent a whole day again among the little islands, and landed in Kobé at midnight. Then a sea-trip to Yokohama, a railroad journey of an hour to Tokio, a rattle through the streets of the city in a jinrikisha, and Kesa was at home again with her dear mother and sisters.

"We prayed for you all the time, Kesa," said Chiye.

And Kesa answered, "I knew it."

Saturday afternoon had come, and Saijiro and Harukichi were in the little room that they had occupied together for so long.

Saijiro was now almost nineteen years old. He was taller than the Japanese ordinarily are and very studious. He had nearly completed the course of studies in the school and was a young man of whom the "mother in America" might well be proud.

Harukichi had just laid down the sermon he had been studying. On the next day he was to preach for the first time as a regularly ordained minister in his own church in Tokio. By teaching and working during his entire theological course he had managed to support himself.

"I wonder, Harukichi, how you have waited and have had patience all these years," said Saijiro. "I could not have done it."

"You do not know, Saijiro. God gives us strength. But I cannot tell you how often I have felt my patience giving way. I long for my parents, and I long for the time to come when I can have my beloved one to myself and when she and I can work together in this great harvest-field."

But later on this Saturday afternoon, when Saijiro had gone off on some expedition with the other boys, Harukichi sat by the window in the twilight when two jinrikishas appeared, coming slowly along the road. At first he watched them mechanically; but as they drew nearer the figures in them seemed strangely familiar. Could it be possible? Yes, surely! Nearer and nearer they came, and Harukichi's heart gave a wild throb and he hastened down to greet his father and mother.

The old lady literally lifted up her voice and wept. "My son, my son," she said, "we can live without you no longer and have come to see for ourselves."

Oh, the happiness in the mission family that evening! The news was carried from one to another, "Harukichi's father and mother have come. The Lord has answered his prayers."

Among those who heard Harukichi's first sermon to his beloved flock the next day were his "honorable parents" and his heart's love, Chiye.

CHAPTER XXXVII.

SOME HAPPY DAYS.

AND now there came some bright, pleasant times for our friends. The Fujisawa mansion was all thrown open again and filled with children, who ran and laughed and shouted through the house and played in the garden; for Tama and Mesoburo came down from the north and brought Genski and his sisters—two dainty little ladies—and his baby brother.

Almost the first thing Genski did after the salutations were over was to go to his aunt Chiye and whisper in her ear, "Honorable auntie, we all go to the mission-school and the honorable father and mother attend the mission chapel." And Chiye thanked God in her heart.

Tama had not been in Tokio very long before she made a discovery. "Who is that young man who looks so often at Mitsu? and why does he hang around the house and follow her to the church?" she asked.

Then Kesa laughed and said, "Oh, that is Toichi, and we all make fun of him, he is so tall and awkward."

But Mitsu said nothing.

And it happened that one day two young men

called on Fujisawa at the custom-house, one being the aforesaid Toichi and the other Harukichi.

Toichi, being the elder, spoke first, and said, "Honorable sir, I know and esteem your daughter, the honorable Mitsu. I am not wealthy and am engaged in Christian work, but I will love and protect her."

And what answer did the high officer Fujisawa make? He knew something of Toichi, and he said, "My friend, if you will consent to come into my family, adopt my name and have your children bear it, and be to me as a son, you may have my daughter Mitsu." For the husband of long ago was dead and Mitsu was free.

Then Harukichi made his request and said, "Honorable high officer, some years ago you refused me your daughter Chiye on the ground of my parents' disinheritance of me. I have the pleasure to tell you that they have received me again as their son. I am now a Christian minister settled over a church in Tokio. I am able to make your daughter comfortable and happy. Your honorable permission I crave."

Then Fujisawa gave to Harukichi the beloved Chiye to be his wife.

Not long after that day there was a double wedding in the Fujisawa mansion in the Kudan. Toichi and Mitsu and Harukichi and Chiye stood up before the venerable Makichi and promised in the name of the Lord to be faithful husbands and wives.

Kesa was happy as a princess; and when Makichi in his earnest prayer thanked the Lord who had given such grace and patience to these dear young people, tears rose to her eyes—not rebellious tears, but tears of love and peace. She slipped her hand into Mrs. Fielding's, saying, "I wish Marion were here."

Then came a pleasant year for Kesa at school, and both she and Marion finished their course of studies the next June.

One happy day Kesa accompanied Marion's mother to Yokohama, and went out to the great American steamer in a *sampan* to meet and welcome her young friend.

"Dear Kesa," said Marion when they had an opportunity to talk together, "are you not yet a Christian?"

And Kesa said, "I cannot be like Chiye, Maichan; Chiye is always the same, but my heart is often dark; but I do love the Lord who died for me, and I do think I am a Christian. I was waiting for you to come and now I will be baptized."

So one August Sunday Kesa was baptized. Then, by Marion's side, she ate of the broken bread and drank of the poured-out wine, while the presence of the Lord filled both their hearts with peace.

CHAPTER XXXVIII.

CHRISTIAN HOMES AND CHRISTIAN WORK.

One cold winter morning Fujisawa was indulging in a romp with his little grandson, the child of Mitsu and Toichi. The old home still looked bright and pleasant; Mitsu was well and happy, and Toichi seemed very proud of her and the baby.

"It is the time for the morning worship," called Toichi at last.

"Will you not remain, honorable father?" asked Mitsu.

But Fujisawa shook his head and went off, although not at all angered.

Then came the servants and the gentle mother, who, although still worshipping her idols in secret, would always listen to Mitsu when she read the Scriptures to her, and attended family prayers and went occasionally to the meetings. Kesa followed her mother and some of the neighbors came in. Toichi read and explained a few verses of Matthew's Gospel and prayed, and then Kesa led in singing a Christian hymn.

"Where are you going to-day, Kesa?" asked Mitsu, when the simple service was ended.

"Thanks, honorable sister, I am going to see

Chiye, and then to the girls' missionary meeting at the school," said Kesa.

Chiye's house was near Shiba. Money in plenty was at Harukichi's command, but only so much as was sufficient to maintain his family in comfort did he retain. The rest was given freely to the work of spreading the gospel among the Japanese.

When Kesa arrived at the pretty little house she called, "Excuse me," and then pushed open the slides and went through to the back room, where Chiye sat near a *hibachi*.

Harukichi stood beside his wife, and in one corner a merry little girl was playing with some toys. The baby looked up and smiled when Kesa entered, and Harukichi and Chiye welcomed her with loving words and looks.

"Where are you going to-day, honorable brother?" asked Kesa.

"Thanks, young Saijiro and I go to the outskirts of the city towards the west, to hold meetings, and shall be away all day. Good-by, dear wife; good-by, honorable sister; good-by, little one."

"It always seems so quiet and peaceful here, Chiye," said Kesa when Harukichi had gone.

Then Chiye pointed to a long scroll on which was beautifully written in Chinese characters, "Peace be unto this house;" and Kesa understood.

Then came a cry at the door, and the servant

soon after entered with a letter lying on a beautiful lacquered tray. She stooped low to the floor and handed the tray to Chiye.

Her pale cheeks flushed and there was a glad look in her bright eyes. "It is from Kei, Kesa," she cried; and the sisters read the letter together.

"BELOVED, beloved, greetings in the Lord. I rejoice to tell you how blessed I am in my work. God has kept me in peace and in health, although I have travelled much over mountains and through valleys and in boats on the sea. The people listen gladly, and the work is blessed. Nantaro, my brother, goes with me and will not leave my side. I think he will soon believe. Pray for him. Please, your honorable prayers I crave. Compliments, compliments to the honorable mother and sisters and to the honorable husbands. Compliments, compliments."

Great was the rejoicing over this letter, and Chiye and Kesa read it over and over, while the baby Michi played in her corner.

Early in the afternoon the two sisters took a jinrikisha for the mission-school, where Marion met them, and the three went together to a room consecrated by work and prayer for many a long year. Bright girls and pleasant-faced young women gathered here, and after some opening exercises took out their work. Some were embroidering, some were dressing dolls, and others had plainer sewing. All the articles were to be sold for the benefit of some poor church or Sunday-school, and the workers talked together pleasantly of what they had heard concerning the progress of the cause that they loved.

"Old Momo died trusting in Jesus," said one.

"Momoki believes," said another.

A third had a sad tale to tell of one who had gone back to heathenism, and they all grieved, and prayed that the girl's faith might be restored.

The subject for the day was their neighboring country, Corea.

"Good news has come to us," said Kesa; "work among the girls has begun in Corea. Some are already studying with the honorable foreign teachers, and some are learning to be nurses in the hospitals." Then Kesa, taking an English magazine, fluently read and translated an account of the good work begun among the women of Corea.

A girl was then asked to thank God, and she said, "Dear Lord, we thank thee that thou hast been so good to the women of Corea, and we thank thee for the new schools in Osaka, Kioto, and Kanazawa, and we pray thee to bless the schools in Yokohama and in Tokio and all over the land. Bless the Bible-women and all the Christian workers all over the land. This we ask for the dear Saviour's sake."

"I am never happy except when I am working hard," said Kesa to Chiye as they rode home together in the jinrikisha. "I could never be quiet and suffer pain like you, and be happy."

Then said Chiye, "I hope you will have some hard work given to you, Kesa."

"You and Mitsu do so much in speaking to the women and children and living such beautiful lives."

True it was that Chiye and Mitsu found constant opportunities of usefulness in a quiet way, and many wandering ones were directed by them into the safe and happy path. Aka too was useful; she had long ago joined a class for married women, and what she learned she imparted to other women in her neighborhood. She was contented and cheerful, very different from the sad weeper of days gone by. Fusa, Chiye's friend, was in a training-school for nurses; and slow Haru had found that medicine was her forte, and was studying to be a doctor.

Connected with the various schools were kindergartens, and there were normal classes for the girls who wished to learn the system. Some of the older pupils taught the little ones; and there were Bible-readings, prayer-meetings, and schools for poor children—work in plenty for all.

Look at Tokio on a Sunday morning not long ago. Kesa, Mitsu, Aka, and other Christian women and girls are starting out to gather poor and outcast children for the Sunday-schools. To the fishermen's children, to the *jinrikiyas'* children, to poor, blind, halt, and withered, they go; and by nine a large number are gathered together to hear the Christian teaching. Later come the great congregations to the churches; to the Foreign Concession, to the Kudan, to the Tori, to many a place in the suburbs, they flock, and all Tokio resounds with Christian hymns and the melody of organs and the voices of the under-shepherds as they tell of the love of the chief Shepherd for his sheep.

And not only in Tokio, but in many other cities of Japan—in Yokohama, in Hakodate, in Kioto, Osaka, and Kobé, and even in far western Kanazawa, the gospel is preached. On the Hakones, on the islands of the Inland Sea, everywhere the good news is being carried, and hearts rejoice.

Besides all this, many a little seed is dropped in private and many a heart in secret goes up to God in prayer.

CHAPTER XXXIX.

SAIJIRO'S RESOLVE.

THE story of the Good Shepherd searching for and leading home his lost sheep cannot be told too often, especially in this present age, when so many are looking for a better way than that marked out in the Word of God and a better leader than the Lord Jesus Christ. There are even those born in Christian lands who are trying to persuade men that Buddhism is a better religion than Christianity. But what has Buddhism done for the world in comparison with the blessings of which Christianity is the source? What is its art compared with Christian art? its music compared with Christian music? its science compared with Christian science? its literature compared with Christian literature? its morality compared with Christian morality? its charity compared with Christian charity? What sins has it washed away, what fears has it banished, what tears has it dried, and what soul has it led safely through this world to that of which the gospel tells us?

You have seen the great changes which have taken place since the spring day when Kesa came into the world and when Saijiro cried for his mother on the mountain. But do not think that all the work is done. It is true there are schools, colleges, theological seminaries, normal classes, training-schools, mothers' classes, Bible-readings, prayer-meetings, and churches scattered through the land. The Bible has been translated into Japanese and some Christian literature has been given to the people. There are thousands of educated young men and women, and scores of preachers and teachers; but the cry ever is for more laborers, and the motto on the Christian banner is still, "FORWARD!" For the Japanese are numbered by millions and the native Christians only by thousands. The number of idol-worshippers is appalling; and infidelity, as soul-destroying as superstition, is abroad in the land.

One evening Harukichi and Saijiro stopped to rest after a day of labor at one of the temples in the suburbs of Tokio. The mountain child whom we first knew was now a strong, vigorous young man, just completing his course of studies in the theological seminary and ready to go to work.

Harukichi had listened with joy and thankfulness to his earnest talk that day to the crowds who had gathered to listen. "God bless you, my brother," he had said as they left the preaching-place.

But Saijiro was quiet and thoughtful and did not speak until the two were resting on the grassy slope in the temple enclosure; then suddenly he said, "Oh, my friend, I have thought over the proposal made me to take charge of one of these city churches. It would be pleasant to work with you and have you ever by my side, but my heart is in the mountain with my people, and to them I must go."

Then Harukichi, although grieved to lose his young friend, stretched out his hand to him and said, "It is well, Saijiro; you have decided well; and the blessing of God be with you."

But Saijiro had something more to say. "Oh, Harukichi," and he spoke with kindling eyes, "my heart goes out to the youngest daughter of the high officer Fujisawa, your beloved wife's sister. *Dogu*, I have nothing but poverty and hard work to offer her. Do you think that I might ask her to be my wife?"

Then Harukichi smiled wisely and said, "Ask her, Saijiro; and God be with you."

A week or two later there had been a gathering of Christians in the grand temple enclosure Uyeno. The church members had held a solemn convocation. Hundreds had met to pray and talk and sing, and three hundred Christian women had come together and told of what the Lord had done for them. And now the crowds were dispersing and the people were going back to their homes.

In one corner of the temple grounds a little group had gathered, all friends whom we well know. There were Mitsu and Toichi, with Saikichi, their queer, bright little boy, between them, and Chiye and Harukichi, with little Michi. Aka was near talking with Kojiro, still under instruction in one of the missions, and not far away were Dr. and Mrs. Fielding and Marion; while Yenoske and Yen were arranging some baskets, and Cho was trying hard to help her mother. The sun was setting, and long beams of glory streamed through the trees.

"It is time to go home," said Chiye at last; "but where is Kesa?"

Harukichi smiled and pointed down the walk, saying, "See, dear wife."

And, truly, there came Kesa and Saijiro hand in hand. When they reached the little group Saijiro said, "Rejoice with me, my friends, for Kesa has promised to be my wife and go with me to the mountain."

Then the others crowded about the newly-betrothed pair, and there was abundance of joy and well-wishing.

Chiye came and stood by Kesa's side, and when the others had ceased speaking she said,

"You will have your longed-for hard work, dear sister. May the Good Shepherd be with you for ever!"

And all the others responded, "Amen."

GLOSSARY.

AINO, singular and plural. The aborigines of Japan.
AITCHU. The burden of a coolie's cry or song.
AMA. A Buddhist nun.
AMIDA. A title of Buddha.
BABA. Grandmother, or nurse.
BAKEMONO. A ghost.
BENI. A pink coloring matter.
BENTEN. The name of a goddess.
BENTO. A little wooden box.
BON. A Japanese priest.
BON-SAMA. A respectful title for a priest.
CASH. A petty coin; 10 make a cent.
CHAN. A term of familiarity, added to the first syllable of a child's name or title. Thus "Kechan" means "Dear Kesa."
DAI. Great, noble, exalted.
DAI BUTSU. A chief idol of Japan.
DAIKOKU. A Japanese idol.
DAIKON. A large radish.
DAIMIO. A territorial noble of former days.
DAI NIPPON. "Great Japan."
DOGU! Alas! a common exclamation of surprise or sorrow.
DZUKIN. A winter hood for females.
FURUSHIKI. A kerchief or scarf.
FUTON. A stuffed mattress.

GETA. A wooden shoe.
HAI! Yes, or Look out!
HIAKUNINISHIU. "One hundred poems," a collection very popular in Japan.
HIBACHI. A brazier or fire-box.
HOTOKE. A saint.
JINRIKISHA. A two-wheeled carriage drawn by men.
JINRIKIYA, singular and plural. Men who draw jinrikishas.
KAGO. A sedan-chair.
MIKADO. The title of the emperor.
MOCHI. Hard cakes made of rice.
MUSHI. The hot and wet season in Japan.
NIPPON. Japan.
ONI. Evil spirit.
SAIONARA! Farewell! If it must be so!
SAKÉ. An intoxicating drink made from rice.
SAMA. A title of respect to men, women, or idols.
SAMISEN. The Japanese guitar.
SAMPAN. A small boat.
SAMURAI. The military class.
SAN. A respectful title.
SENSEI. Teacher.
SHAKA. A title of Buddha.
SHOGUN. A military commander-in-chief.
TAI-FU. A "great wind," or typhoon.
TAI-KUN. "Great ruler."
TAYKOSAMA. "The great lord," the name of a famous prince of old Japan.
TORIYE, or TORII. A bird-rest before a temple.
YASHIKI. A gentleman's dwelling and outbuildings inclosed.
YEBISU. A Japanese idol.
ZORI. A sandal.

www.ingramcontent.com/pod-product-compliance
Lightning Source LLC
Chambersburg PA
CBHW051859300426
44117CB00006B/457